Praise for *From Sage to Artisan*

"Not an extreme or a fad, but a balanced diet for developing a holistic leader. I found it a common sense approach for leadership development."

> J. Michael Bowman
> Vice President and General Manager
> DuPont Advanced Material Systems

"*From Sage to Artisan* has caused me to reflect upon my strengths and weaknesses and to better balance my team's mix of the nine roles. This is a book that I will constantly be reviewing and learning from."

> Steve Bottcher
> Vice President
> Selling and Delivery
> Pepsi Cola Co.

"A powerful book combining management theory with leadership techniques. Hard to put it down. Interesting and innovative approach to understanding management and leadership principles."

> Peter M. Joachim
> Former Director of Quality
> Applied Materials

"A quantum leap forward at representing the essential qualities of leadership needed to succeed in a global business arena."

> Barie McCurry
> Organizational Renewal
> Amoco Energy International

From Sage to Artisan

From Sage to Artisan

The Nine Roles of the *Value-Driven Leader*

Stuart Wells

DAVIES-BLACK PUBLISHING
Palo Alto, California

Published by Davies-Black Publishing, an imprint of Consulting Psychologists Press, Inc., 3803 East Bayshore Road, Palo Alto, CA 94303; 1-800-624-1765.

Special discounts on bulk quantities of Davies-Black books are available to corporations, professional associations, and other organizations. For details, contact the Director of Book Sales at Davies-Black Publishing, an imprint of Consulting Psychologists Press, Inc., 3803 East Bayshore Road, Palo Alto, CA 94303; 415-691-9123; Fax 415-988-0673.

00 99 98 97   10 9 8 7 6 5 4 3 2 1

Printed in the United States of America

Library of Congress Cataloging-in-Publication Data
Wells, Stuart
      From sage to artisan : the nine roles of the value-driven leader / Stuart Wells
        p. cm.
      Includes bibliographical references and index.
      ISBN 0-89106-093-6
      1. Leadership. 2. Executives. 3. Title.
    HD57.7.W454   1997
    858.4'092—dc20

                                        96-43657
                                            CIP

FIRST EDITION
First printing 1997

Contents

Preface

Every day you face a variety of situations that place different demands upon your skills. You notice that some of these situations are more easily handled than others. The degree of difficulty may reflect different preferences or capabilities you currently possess for these skills. Your choice in reading this book and others like it reveals that you recognize that new learning is always possible and desirable.

Therefore, for something to be *practical* for your own managing or leadership experience, it must have insightful and challenging ideas that you can translate into action. You do not need idealistic concepts that do not seem to fit into the realities you face. Yet you also recognize that with appropriate management you can transform these realities to higher states or greater effectiveness. You do not need preaching about what you *should* do; you can set your own level of motivation. But you do want guidance in building the capability to put good ideas into practice. On the other hand, if you are looking for some step-by-step guidance such as "the ten steps to more motivated employees," you will be disappointed. Good managing and effective leadership are not about memorized techniques; they are about the kind of capability that begins to feel like a natural part of your being. Any book that promises instantaneous excellence in managing and leading simply from the techniques it contains will be a bigger disappointment. If this book proves valuable to you, it will open the door to different ideas and aid your ongoing development of capability. There will be plenty of guidance herein to building the necessary skills to make the capability natural, but you *must* put in effort beyond the book. You *must* practice in situations of increasingly higher risk.

You would never dream of learning a new physical skill simply by reading a book. Here is a simple analogy: Golf is one of the most studied sports, with no end to the number of instructional books and video tapes available. Most of these contain good ideas, but there is no known case of a good golfer whose only effort has been mastering the books and tapes. Such a person may know a lot *about* golf, but it is not part of that person's being. Practice in low-risk situations—the driving range; higher risk situations—on the course; and even higher risk situations—playing with the boss—all this is necessary. In each learning phase, the golfer's mind is filled with many thoughts and routines in an effort to pay attention to a wide variety of body movements. The process does not come naturally. Good golfing only happens when the mind is relatively free and the body moves, almost by itself, in a graceful cohesion of intricate, subtle moves.

Effective managing and leading is even more challenging. The manager's mind must always be engaged. Thought precedes action. That is why this book has various forms of clear, practical guidance to develop useful skills of thinking and acting for real-life situations. I recognize that as you read a book it often feels disruptive to stop for an exercise. If that's the case, read first. Make a note of the ones that seem interesting, and return to them when you are ready to move your learning to the next phase. You may want to use the guidelines as a starting point, modifying them to suit your own needs.

The *tool* in this book is a set of nine leading-edge roles with a common foundation in core values. Too frequently, books on managing or leadership contain a short list of items for effectiveness. The lists need to be short as long lists are difficult to remember, but often it is hard to discern why the particular list is being used. Also, logical or systematic connections among the items may be somewhat obscure; it is natural in reading these approaches to wonder if something is missing. Detailed questionnaires to people about what they experience as good managing or effective leadership commonly form the basis for such lists. I have asked these types of questions of hundreds of people and have found great consistency in their responses: They focus heavily on skills related to managing people, personality attributes, communication, organizing work, and vision.

These skills are important, but they do not represent all the things a manager or leader must do to keep an organization competitively effective in changing and challenging circumstances or to keep any part of the organization making a valued contribution to the success of the whole. This book gives a full view of the range of distinctive managing or leadership roles needed for the varying situations of a dynamic organization. The nine leading-edge manager roles are easy to remember even though comprehensiveness demands some degree of complexity. They clearly and logically depict the reality people encounter in organizations. At the same time, they provide a strong basis for ongoing individual development and for altering that reality to ever higher standards. You will find that the roles work for you.

Please remember that the leading-edge roles are a model—a representation of reality. Although I have had great success in using this representation with more than five hundred people, it is not the ultimate truth. I would rather have you read this book and reject these roles than see them as the ultimate truth; they are only one portrayal of truth. I certainly hope you value my approach and continue to use it, but you should feel free to modify or change it to better suit your own style. There is no doubt, however, that you will find a well-designed, coordinated set of roles (mine or yours) far more valuable over the long term than some simple list.

Significant organizational improvement is impossible without the continuing leadership development of individual managers. Individual capability is and always has been the key to sustaining organizational effectiveness, maintaining competitiveness, and operating successfully in a complex and changing environment—there is no other way. A string of hot products will generate money and cover many errors, but it will not be sufficient for the long haul. Cutting costs, getting lean, and eliminating redundancies may be necessary short-term measures, but when the dust settles, it will still be *people* who make the crucial contribution to long-term viability.

Applying leading-edge management at all levels of the organization inspires individuals to contribute their best, act cohesively to get product out the door, move in a strategic direction, and bring about necessary improvements. The chief aim of this book is to accelerate the development of such leadership and management competencies by giving you a better perspective on your own unique strengths, clear ideas for self-guided leadership development, and the means to better understand others.

To that end this book is focused on several major objectives:

- Assessing your strengths and weaknesses
- Guiding your chosen focus on further learning
- Gaining greater effectiveness in a wider range of circumstances
- Developing an appropriate career path
- Understanding and appreciating the strengths of others
- Evaluating the effectiveness of a work group
- Balancing capabilities within a work group

To support these objectives, there are two questionnaires for assessing your relative strengths or preferences for the nine roles of a value-driven leader. Appendix B contains a self-scoring version that will give you immediate results. Appendix C contains a mail-in version (we will give you free scoring when you use the form at the back of this book) that is considerably more accurate. The differences between these two versions of the Leading-Edge Portrait are described in the appropriate appendices.

This model of nine roles reflects management thought, from a wide variety of sources, my own work experience, and considerable testing with managers. The chief aim of leadership development reflects my own career path.

For most of the twenty-four years since completing my MBA and Ph.D. degrees at Stanford's Graduate School of Business, I have maintained an active teaching career to MBA students and a consulting career. My teaching to these students has always been guided by a desire to make sure they are learning concepts and skills that will have a practical impact on their careers. I hope that spirit emerges in this book. Consulting to governments and public agencies throughout the world, Fortune 500 companies, and numerous start-ups has reinforced my insight into the widespread need to provide methods for leadership development that are effective and reflect differences among people.

Acknowledgments

This model has been developed over the past few years as I worked with managers and students on their leadership development. There are too many people to name, but I am extremely grateful to all of them. I believe readers of this book will benefit greatly from their efforts and insight. I am grateful to Melinda Merino, Lee Langhammer Law, Laura Simonds, John Walker, and Sharon Sforza of Davies-Black Publishing who have helped tremendously to shape this manuscript. In particular, Melinda symbolizes all their strengths through her combination of remarkable enthusiasm and intelligence in taking my original manuscript and encouraging me with thought-provoking questions. Finally, I am in the deepest state of appreciation to my wife Daphne, for the gift of our long-lasting relationship, her absolute mastering of the mentor and ally roles, and her unrelenting support and insight.

CHAPTER ONE

The Nine Roles

A View of the Terrain

Managing versus Leading—
Ain't Gonna Study This War No More

It seems to me that we are searching for something we feel is missing from managers: that something we call *leadership*. Why do we continue to find this topic of leadership so compelling? We want it in our business and political lives. We seek it in prominent people. What is it that causes us to continue to search for that quality? We must feel managing is not enough; it will not lead us into the future.

Leadership is about three key things:

- Creating order
- Inspiring action
- Improving performance

In a world that seems to be growing more complex, where things seem to be less predictable, where so many possibilities seem open, where the hazards seem greater, where the problems seem larger and more intractable, we want someone to bring some semblance of order, to shine a light on the chaos around us and say, "Here is a way. Here is something that brings us together. Here is the choice we need to make."

I think if you ask anybody about what they want to do in life, you will get a common thread regardless of the specific desire:

People want to be committed to something worthwhile. They want to know that what they do matters. People without fear crave the future. They want to be moved to act. So a leader must inspire action.

It is very common for people to say, Is there more? Can't things be better? Haven't we learned enough to make some change and reach new heights? So a leader needs to improve performance.

When we talk about leaders, we spend a lot of time talking about some great person beyond all of us. But we know what we are really seeking is not just that leader out there but also our own leadership skills that we can bring to our jobs, no matter how large or small. Those qualities that we so admire in leaders are qualities that we can exhibit in ourselves. In fact we have almost come to the point of thinking that leadership is "good" and management is "bad." But this book is not about wasting time complaining about managers, praising leaders, and thinking there is a great difference between them. If you are going to manage, you must demonstrate leadership.

On the other hand, there is no leadership if there is no focused effort. There must be content. A leader can create order for us, inspire us to act, or improve performance, but when we are following, we constantly ask, For what? In other words, we are saying, What is this order? How are we going to make it happen? What is this action that you are inspiring me to do? What specifically do I need to do? What results can I expect? What are the problems we are experiencing now? Don't spend time describing the problems, tell me about the improvement. What specifically is it? How will that make things better?

These are real questions. Leadership is a process for any manager to provide answers to those questions. If you want to say leadership is about character and managing is about content, fine. But what good is working on content without character? What good is having character if you do not have content for which you are responsible? Leadership needs content. It is not an empty vessel floating on the ocean. It is about form and function, style and substance. We respect you as a messenger if you have those leadership qualities, but what is the point of the message? Ultimately we judge good leadership by the *content* of the message. We do not want people in an organization to simply *deliver* messages: We want them to take the responsibility to implement and act upon them. Leadership is not about giving commands with everyone falling in step; it is about being in the trenches with the troops, being part of that implementation process, part of the changes, in the midst of the fray.

Searching for that one leader is like searching for the Holy Grail: It doesn't exist. It's just a symbol, a story meant to illuminate a point. We cannot believe in personal responsibility and crave a magical leader at the same time. As long as we have this image of a leader on a white horse charging in to make things better, we will never get the leadership we want and need, because we will never value those qualities in every manager in our organization.

We need to seek leadership in every person who claims to have managing responsibility. We need people to demonstrate leadership when they are working in peer groups in which there is no official authority. It is not a question of the person with the loudest voice or strongest will taking charge of the group but of people within the group ensuring that all leadership processes are present. Anyone who has management responsibility must show leadership. Of course, we want it at the top of the organization and at the top of our government, but is that really enough? Can we depend upon one person providing leadership for all the other people in the organization? Do we want leadership and management embodied in different individuals? Do we believe that an organization can be competitively effective if the responsible people are either managing or leading, but not both? No.

I am not going to separate managing from leading. I do not want to waste effort on a difference that simply does not and should not exist. Perhaps we continue to separate managing from leading because we all want something to which we can aspire. Every manager, I think, aspires to be a leader, and that is admirable. But it is not concrete enough. So I want to inspire you to choose those roles in which you desire mastery and to become an effective leader and manager. The nine leading-edge roles in this book are not about being a leader versus manager. Each one is the intersection of a leadership process (creating order, inspiring action, or improving performance) and a focused content of management (systems, people, or work).

What questions should people ask of leaders in organizations? Simple. What is the strategy (sage role)? What future do you see for all of us (visionary role)? What large-scale change is necessary to make us the kind of organization we want to be (magician role)? How are we bringing people together in some type of culture that is cohesive (globalist role)? Is there a way for me to develop my skills and make a greater contribution (mentor role)? How do we keep increasing the effectiveness of people working together in this organization, because no one person can work alone (ally role)? Who is empowered to make decisions and how are they responsible (sovereign role)? How are we meeting the goals (guide role)? How do we keep raising the standards of everything we do, of every product we make, of every service we offer (artisan role)? Every time you act on an answer to one of these questions, you have shown leadership.

There are two other things we want from leaders: We want them to have integrity and we want them to have credibility. That means they must have clear values consistently acted upon, which is the foundation for everything they do, for everything the organization does, and for any attempt to become effective at managing and leading. Therefore, each of the nine leading-edge roles must have a foundation in core values. Leadership must be value-driven.

Managing on the Leading Edge

The Nine Roles

The grid on the following page provides a clear picture of the nine leading-edge roles as intersections of a leadership process and focus of managing effort with the foundation in core values. Each role has a name, such as *sage,* to create imagery for the wide range of qualities, skills, and thoughts of a person in that role. These names, usually nonbusiness terms, serve as symbols that allow fuller appreciation of the role's significance and avoid some unnecessary restrictions that the language of business could impose on our thinking. To balance this broader perspective, each role has a key content with a clearer business perspective, such as *designs strategy,* that captures the organizational essence of that role as described in Table 1. I have found that people quite quickly use the role names to work on leadership and communicate with each other. The key content helps trigger focus on the organizational value of the role. It is easy, it is descriptive, and it is memorable.

Sages develop wisdom through expanding their knowledge about wide-ranging subjects. In the organization, they *design*

Leading-Edge Manager Roles			
	Principal Leadership Process		
Principal Focus of Managing Effort	**Creating Order**	**Inspiring Action**	**Improving Performance**
Systems	**Sage** Designs Strategy	**Visionary** Innovates the Future	**Magician** Orchestrates Change
People	**Globalist** Bridges Cultural Differences	**Mentor** Motivates Development	**Ally** Builds Partnerships
Work	**Sovereign** Empowers Decisions	**Guide** Achieves Goals	**Artisan** Pursues Excellence
FOUNDATION OF ALL ROLES **CORE VALUES**			

strategy by being cognizant of the past, present, and possible future of the organization and the various forces, people, and organizations in the environment. They are curious, always learning, open to different ideas and ways of thinking, and energized to strive for understanding of ambiguous, complex situations.

Visionaries dream the seemingly impossible dream and turn it into a real possibility. In the organization, they *innovate the future* by articulating, in simple terms, a powerful idea about the future that inspires the whole organization to act. They are creative, undeterred by obstacles, and optimistic.

Magicians make things change form without wasting effort. In the organization, they *orchestrate change* by keeping a balance among the organization's structures, systems, and processes as the old state dissolves and the new state forms. They are restless with the status quo, able to let go of the present without a guarantee of the future, and calm despite the transition's turbulence.

Globalists are world travelers in body, mind, and spirit. In the organization, they *bridge cultural differences* by demonstrating

Table 1 Organizational Value of the Leading-Edge Roles: A Quick Overview

A Quick Overview

Sage	Pulls together diverse information and designs a coherent strategy
Visionary	Thinks about the future to specify a vision that inspires others to act
Magician	Maintains flexibility to bring about large-scale change when necessary
Globalist	Operates across cultures and consolidates different perspectives
Mentor	Motivates others and assists their professional development
Ally	Forms highly effective and productive teams and alliances
Sovereign	Accepts responsibility for consequences of decisions
Guide	Sets clear and challenging goals and organizes work to achieve them
Artisan	Sets and meets increasingly higher standards of quality and excellence

interest, understanding, and appreciation of different cultures and finding the common ground among cultures so that productive work can occur. They are comfortable in different cultures, excited by differences, willing to question their own cultural beliefs, and adaptable to cultural ideas they view as preferable to their own.

Mentors are committed to ongoing personal and professional development. In the organization, they *motivate development* by helping people advance their careers through a variety of learning opportunities, honoring the development desires of each individual they mentor. They are completely concerned with the interests of others, unburdened by personal motives, and devoted to the uniqueness of the individual.

Allies are with you in the best of times and the worst of times. They do not abandon a relationship for their own needs. In the organization, they *build partnerships* by seeking ever higher standards of effective, mutually beneficial collaboration in any work group, team, task force, or interaction, formal or informal, with any people inside or outside the organization. They are concerned with and aware of people's state of being (mentally, emotionally, and physically), expansive in their willingness to trust, patient in working with others, and as willing to support as take center stage.

Sovereigns are thoughtful users of power. In the organization, they *empower decisions* by taking responsibility for decisions made by them (whether individually or with a group) and giving significant decision authority to others. They are willing to take risk, able to face uncertainty, aware of and responsible for all the consequences of their decisions, direct in what they say and do, and completely reliable in honoring their commitments.

Guides are flexible organizers keeping people and things in directed motion by making the journey as worthwhile as the destination. In the organization, they *achieve goals* by using clearly stated principles, based upon core values, to guide action on tasks. They direct these tasks toward goals important to the whole of the organization. They are as happy to do the work as to support the efforts of others. They are action oriented, tireless, enthusiastic, excited by the challenge of keeping things moving forward regardless of anticipated or unexpected restraints, relaxed but focused, and stimulated by reaching for accomplishments with others.

Artisans devote their lives to mastery of a craft. In the organization, they *pursue excellence* by questioning the quality standards of the product and the production process. They are concerned with the aesthetic as well as the practical, finding ways to maximize the value to customers and ensuring simplicity, effectiveness, and efficiency in processes. They are unattached to past efforts, open to criticism, attentive to detail, impatient with indifference, always seizing opportunities to raise standards, and always pushing the limits of their own expertise.

Role Preferences and Individual Capability

Roles are much more comprehensive than a simple list of desirable traits. To play any role, we need a range of qualities, skills, and thoughts. We customarily play different roles in life, such as parent, spouse, friend, student, employee, or community member. In each of these roles, we alter our thinking and behavior. Your children do not need the behavior you bring to work, and your co-workers do not need the behavior you bring to your children. It is not a lack of sincerity that drives how we change; each circumstance demands something different from us.

In an organization, there are many ways of looking at different roles. For example, some people play marketing roles, production roles, or financial roles. Each of these roles has its own attitudes, particular perspectives on the organization, and methods of accomplishing tasks. It is often quite a challenge to move from one role to another; most people spend a significant portion of their career within one type of function.

We are drawn to play different roles. Our preferences vary, as does our relative capability for roles. Perhaps we develop more capability where we have stronger preferences and also have increased preference for roles where we have higher capability. Consider the analogy of learning a language to understand the relationship between preference and capability: The capability to learn any language in the world exists in all infants. All sounds are possible. Ongoing exposure to one or two languages begins to alter the preference for some sounds as opposed to those not part of the language. Gradually the capability for fluency in these languages dramatically increases, and the capability to perfectly mimic some sounds disappears. An adult with a strong preference to learn and use a new language may never have equal capability for perfect pronunciation in that language.

This practical tool of nine leading-edge roles also reflects different preferences (or capabilities). What makes each of us unique on this framework is that we each exhibit different preference patterns for these roles. This is not a model to typecast you in one role for life; that would be as limiting to you as it is to actors. A preference pattern means that you may have higher preference for a few of the roles, moderate preference for some, and lower preference for the remaining roles.

Although individual preference patterns may remain relatively stable, it is possible for each person to alter capability for any of the nine roles. It is likely that your capabilities and preferences are closely linked, and you may find it valuable to build more capability in those areas where you have lower preferences. However, this model does *not* imply that mastery of all nine roles is necessary for successful managing or leading—that would be an impossible standard for all of us. It is no contradiction to place a high value on continued learning and building of capability while at the same time acknowledging that high degrees of effectiveness are possible without full mastery of all roles.

This learning of new capability in roles with lower preferences is crucial. We can get caught by our own strengths. We instinctively rely on them, especially in challenging situations. The purpose of development is to enable deliberate choice of the appropriate role for the situation even if it is one in which we have a lower preference or capability. This tendency can easily be seen in what is probably a genetic predisposition to favor one side over the other. It has taken me a long time and some injuries—a broken right ankle and a badly cut right hand—to notice that when I fall I am significantly more comfortable falling on my right side. This is not a big problem until you are skiing and lose your balance in a turn to the left; the instinctive choice causes the body to twist toward its favorite side. There is no doubt in my mind that this is the reason for many ski injuries. We instinctively use our strengths in a crisis situation, even if it is inappropriate and could create severe problems. Therefore we need to consciously choose a different approach to fit the situation.

By looking back at the grid on page 5, we can now see how an individual manager moves among different roles. The three roles in each column have a leadership process in common, and the three roles in each row have a managing focus in common. Each of the nine roles has its own unique combination of one focus of managing effort and one leadership process. For example, the sage role is the most effective choice when a manager faces circumstances requiring the creation of order (leadership process) for systems (focus of managing effort); a strategic design is the order needed for systems. As the circumstances change, the demands are different, and that same manager will need to be in a different role to maximize effectiveness.

Instinctive use of a role preference pattern by a particular manager could lead to a different role choice regardless of the situational demands. We often tend to see the world through the filter of our higher preferences or stronger capabilities and define situations based upon our personal perspective rather than a true reflection of the situations requirements. Two managers with different preference patterns facing the same situation could easily see a need for different roles. This is an all too common situation. The framework gives us a deliberate method to analyze a situation and choose an appropriate role rather than allowing our personal preference patterns to make an instinctive choice for us.

You may never master all the roles, and you will always have a preference pattern favoring some roles over others. You do, however, need to have the ability to move among the roles to increase your effectiveness in a variety of situations. Use the grid and summaries to determine your own preference pattern or capabilities. It is quite easy to say that your response depends upon the situation. Therefore, think about a wide range of circumstances that you face in your work. What you are trying to do is get a first look at the situations that strongly attract you or in which you are more effective because they correspond with your higher preferences or capabilities.

One of the great problems of most organizations is the unspoken tendency to value only one style of managing or leading (one preference pattern or set of capabilities); anyone who receives management training faces the same process or course. People may feel that there is insufficient value for their particular capabilities or that someone else is deciding how to improve them. In this environment, they will not be motivated to learn or to fully use their strengths. I hope this book leads to greater appreciation of different ways of being an effective leader and that future training will recognize this diversity. Table 2 summarizes the key points to remember about these roles.

Roles in the Organization's Hierarchy

Inevitably people wonder if roles reflect position in the hierarchy of the organization. It is reasonable to expect that top management has more concern with strategy, vision, and change (the systems level). It would be a mistake, however, to exclude these subjects and the corresponding roles for other levels of management. Do we truly believe that middle managers can support and appropriately implement strategy, vision, and change by simply receiving marching orders from the top? In fact, middle managers need to periodically engage in varying roles to tune their own work group into the flow of the overall organization. They will use strategic thinking and design, innovation of the future, and change management for their part of the organization. Their challenge is to use these system level leadership processes for their

Table 2   Key Points for the Leading-Edge Manager Roles

Each role is a unique combination of a leadership process and focus of managing effort symbolizing useful strengths.

Mastery of all roles is unlikely in any one person.

No individual is type cast in a single role.

Any individual will possess strength in more than one role.

Individuals are unique in that their preference patterns for the leading-edge roles differ.

It is important to determine one's own role strengths and use these as basic ways to lead and manage.

It is also important to recognize the problems created when one's own strengths overwhelm one's own weaker capabilities.

We each have a tendency to work from our strengths and avoid our weaknesses. When we are attentive to these choices, we are likely to improve our effectiveness in a wider variety of situations.

There is no hierarchy of importance inherent among the roles. Different strengths, however, are more appropriate to different situations faced by managers.

There are distinctive aspects to each of these roles. There is also some degree of overlap and interdependencies among them. Full mastery of any role often requires some degree of competence in the other roles.

Full mastery of any role requires a high level of attention to the foundation in core values.

area of responsibility and coordinate efforts with the whole organization as well as with the parts led by other middle managers.

Principal Focus of Managing Effort

I do not wish to take you on a whole history of management. I have, however, built upon the past in choosing the three issues for focus of managing effort. Two of the more enduring approaches to management styles have been Blake and Mouton's Managerial Grid® and Theory x versus Theory y. Both of these approaches contrast qualities of management that essentially focus either upon work or upon people. But whenever we contrast two things, our minds seem to naturally create a "good" versus "bad" scenario. Therefore, I prefer to emphasize the positive benefits of alternative styles of management.

Also, neither the Managerial Grid nor the Theory x versus Theory y approach addresses the needed focus of managing effort on systems. People are often asked, What constitutes effective leadership? Inevitably their responses focus on characteristics of managing people and work but leave out the focus on systems. Recently, it has become more important to emphasize vision and leadership. Our bookstores are filled with advice on raising the competitiveness of whole organizations. These books address system-level topics but typically deal with ideas about the organization rather than developing the leadership or managerial skills to innovate and implement these ideas. I prefer to marry the two streams of thought: the standard approach to managing, with its primary focus on people and work, and the necessary focus for competitive effectiveness on the system level.

Systems, people, and work are three distinctive levels to focus managing effort. It is reasonable, to say, for example, that a systems focus is primarily conceptual; a focus on people is primarily personal, interpersonal, and interactive; and a focus on work is primarily action oriented. Each level is important, and there is a mutual dependency among them. Yet only one is in the forefront of attention at any one time, and the other two are in the background. Whatever is in the forefront will absorb most of the effort of the manager, who will concentrate thoughts, emotions, and observable actions and behavior upon this level.

Managing Systems

This is the level of the big picture: connections among different activities and among parts of the organization, demands of customers (external as well as internal), projections about the future, and changes for the whole system or organization. This level involves understanding *why* specific things are important to the organization. The hazards of being excessively focused on systems compared with people or work are as follows:

- Failure to successfully address existing needs of people within the group and organization
- Neglect of the day-to-day management and work needs

Managing People

This level actualizes thoughts of "valuing people" or "people come first." Attention is paid to individuals (motivation, development, promotions, etc.) and teams or groups (collaborative work processes, conflict resolution, etc.). Issues of cultural diversity, individual differences, and a unifying corporate culture are also important. The manager directs energy toward those efforts that make the workplace rewarding and interesting to people and in turn enable them to contribute their best efforts to the success of the organization. This focus is about understanding *who* is affected by the operations of the organization. The hazards of being more focused on people than systems or work are as follows:

- Loss of connection to the larger organization and the long term by failing to blend the needs of people in the group with the needs of the organization
- Avoidance of any change that is seen as causing too much stress for the people involved
- Lags in work accomplishments because of a focus on personal and interpersonal issues

Managing Work

This level represents the daily managerial effort of getting the work done. In this mode, all the interactions with people in the work group relate to the work that is currently demanding everyone's time. Goals, schedules, and deadlines create significant time pressures. Frequently these pressures lead many managers to spend most of their time managing work, directing energy at the decisions and tasks that the team or group must fulfill for its particular responsibilities in the organization. This mode involves understanding *how* actions need to take place for efficient and effective operations.

Time pressures of deadlines and work schedules lead to a higher likelihood that a manager will be more focused on work than on people or systems. When this excessive emphasis occurs, the following hazards can be encountered:

- People begin to feel that they are interchangeable with machinery.
- People feel that all decisions will be based on the work with little or no concern for their welfare.
- Work becomes stressful and employee dissatisfaction and turnover increases.
- Little or no attention is given to development of individuals.
- Insufficient thought is aimed at long-term strategic planning.
- Work becomes increasingly habitual as there is insufficient emphasis on maintaining flexibility to meet changing needs of customers or changing capability of competitors.
- Movement of the organization guided by core values toward a vision is lost.

Principal Leadership Processes

Understanding the three leadership processes is a little different from the three issues for focus of managing effort. Sometimes our dualistic approach to contrasting things does help. Therefore, if we ask, What are the most stifling and detrimental things a manager can do in an organization? we get the following kinds of answers:

- Get sufficient rules and procedures in place to keep things under control and minimize exposure to any differences that could divert thinking or action.
- Be sure people know only as much as they need to get their job done.
- Maintain the status quo, so "if it ain't broke, don't fix it."

I hope that these statements seem both negative and positive to you. There is some merit in each of them, but operating an organization in this manner is the surest route to ultimate failure in a dynamic, competitive environment.

I call the management behavior embodied in the first statement *premature ordering* or *regimented chaos*. The manager appears highly organized but fails to keep fully engaged with reality. The order needed to effectively run a business does not come through control and avoiding complexity or divergent thought but by fully engaging in ambiguity, facing challenging choice, and deliberately emerging from that apparent chaos with full awareness of the different possibilities, opportunities, and hazards.

The second statement will ensure that people know *what* to do but not *why* they are doing it. I call the management behavior embodied in this statement *entropy champion*. People are on track and doing what they should, but their energy is being whittled away. Unless enthusiasm, commitment, desire to make a difference, and achievement are irrelevant to work, this is a sure road to eventual disaster.

The third statement seems quite prudent, especially if the organization has been successful. I call the management behavior embodied in this statement *living in past glory*. It seems quite reasonable to hold on to a position that has been difficult to achieve, especially when expertise has been developed and significant investments have been made: "sunk costs" in the jargon of economics. You cannot recover or change what you have already done. But you have to prove yourself tomorrow. Reputation helps, but only if the organization continually reinvents itself. Managers must know how to continually raise standards, because others will be trying to do the same thing.

The three principal leadership processes form a complete cycle of leadership whether it is at the systems, people, or work level of management effort. If you ask yourself or any one else, What is effective leadership? You would get widely different answers. With these three processes, we are picking up the essential aspects of leadership while at the same time being fairly comprehensive. I think you will find that most of the behaviors, characteristics, or qualities of effective leadership will support these three major processes.

Creating Order

The leader is able to create order in highly complex and seemingly chaotic environments using specific qualities such as the following:

- High tolerance for ambiguity and complexity
- Processing of large amounts of often conflicting information
- Engaging multiple perspective to see points of convergence as well as divergence
- Discrimination between what is relevant and what is peripheral to the issue at hand

The importance of this leadership process for each focus of managing effort should be clear. At the systems level, the manager designs a successful strategy. At the people level, the manager bridges the variety of cultural differences encountered internationally, in alliances with other organizations, within the organization among different people, and even within the organization among different departments. At the work level, the manager faces the continuing stream of challenging decisions met in daily work and empowers others to do the same.

Inspiring Action

The leader is able to access individual and organizational potential and inspire actions toward the accomplishment of worthwhile objectives using qualities such as the following:

- Clarity about the future
- Motivation and support for people to move toward that future
- Articulation of measurable and qualitative goals
- Balance between directive and shared leadership
- Openness to alternative means to achieve the ends
- Use of value-based principles to guide the means or processes toward the desired ends or objectives

The importance of this leadership process for each focus of managing effort should be clear. At the systems level, the manager innovates the future by identifying a vision that is truly worth pursuing. At the people level, the manager works with individuals to elevate the level of motivation and enable continued development. At the work level, the manager guides tasks to achieve the goals most important to the success of the whole organization.

Improving Performance

The leader is always wondering if there is a better way to operate and finding ways to move toward that higher level of functioning using qualities such as the following:

- Creativity
- Flexibility
- Willingness to challenge as well as be challenged
- Willingness to embrace change as a regular part of life
- Drive to achieve ever higher standards in the way people are working and the results of their work
- Lack of attachment to existing methods
- Belief that "if it ain't broke, don't fix it" is a prescription for failure

The importance of this leadership process for each focus of managing effort should be clear. At the systems level, the manager enables whole organizations to move through the difficult transitions met in any necessary change process. At the people level, the manager helps people meet continually higher standards for any form of collaborative work within the organization and with relevant groups outside the organization. At the work level, the manager dedicates effort to relevant improvements in quality standards in products and services.

Going Forward

The assumption behind this approach is that every activity of a person managing or leading in the organization takes place within one of these nine leading-edge roles. The role names and key business contents symbolize a wide range of skills and capabilities. You can anticipate some of the content of the role chapters with these questions:

- What interests, motivates, energizes, challenges, and inspires a person in this role?
- What kinds of things would this person think about?

- How would a person in this role relate to others in the organization?

- What are the most likely actions or behaviors of a person in this role?

The chapters on roles contain practical guidance for developing improved effectiveness in each of these roles by responding to these questions. The practical guidance makes this a challenging "how-to" book. You will get some good ideas from reading about these roles, but your own development ultimately depends upon the effort you expend when you close the book and apply the ideas to your work.

The purpose in these chapters is to see the distinctiveness of each role. It is natural when looking at one role to sense an overlap with the other roles; although the roles are unique, they are not totally independent. Effectiveness in a situation may require a combination of talents. But I want to maintain a separation among these roles so that each can be seen for its own contribution and so that you can easily determine your development needs. Learning requires us to understand how things integrate while at the same time breaking them apart to refine competency. There are only nine roles, and the world is very complex. Each role contains many different avenues for learning. A separation among roles is necessary so that you can choose a role skill—a way of thinking or acting—that is most appropriate for your work situation and your learning.

One other caution as you think about the nine roles: Trying to be all things to all people or equally effective in every situation by seeking mastery of all roles is a worthy but impractical goal because it diffuses learning by dividing effort in too many directions. Focus your efforts. Perhaps these learning objectives will serve you:

- Seek mastery in a few roles where your preferences are strongest.

- Seek increased competency in those roles most critical to your organization or your own career path.

- Seek sufficient competency in your weakest roles or lowest preferences so you will be able to recognize the relevant managerial response in any situation.

Learning Role Skills

Testing the Leading-Edge Manager Roles

- Test the nine leading-edge roles for meaning with your own experience of different managers you have known and what you consider to be your own strengths or preferences.

- Determine how successful you and each of these managers are in balancing efforts across the three levels of managing systems, people, and work. Identify where you or they have difficulties balancing efforts and the causes of those problems.

- Determine how you and other managers use each of the specific leadership processes—creating order, inspiring action, and improving performance.

- Determine how you and other managers use the leading-edge roles.

- Determine how you and other managers have used the foundation of core values to affect performance in each of the roles.

- Contrast the impacts on people in your work group in situations when the nine roles were in balance with those when they were out of balance.

- From your own experience of the roles, add thoughts to the descriptions that will aid you in thinking about the roles and developing more capability for them.

Improving Team Performance

- Have each member of the team share the results of his or her own assessment of personal strengths or preferences for the nine roles.

- Given these assessments, draw conclusions about the likely strengths and weaknesses of the whole of the team.

- Use the assessments to form reasonable expectations for each member of the team and the team as a whole.

- Determine how the team can function to perform its work responsibilities and aid the development of each individual in the leading-edge roles.

Principal Focus of Managing Effort	Principal Leadership Process		
	Creating Order	Inspiring Action	Improving Performance
Systems	**Sage** Designs Strategy	**Visionary** Innovates the Future	**Magician** Orchestrates Change
People	**Globalist** Bridges Cultural Differences	**Mentor** Motivates Development	**Ally** Builds Partnerships
Work	**Sovereign** Empowers Decisions	**Guide** Achieves Goals	**Artisan** Pursues Excellence

FOUNDATION OF ALL ROLES
CORE VALUES

CHAPTER TWO

The Foundation of Core Values

Integrity, Meaning, and Results

Why Core Values Are Important

Being a value-driven leader means absolute integrity with core values for each leading-edge role. High effectiveness requires awareness of the values guiding behavior in any situation. If they are not core values, the behavior must be changed. Value-driven leaders will seem relentless in finding ways to keep core values present. If pressure intensifies to take the easy way out, capitulate, or sacrifice the core values for the expediency of the situation, the manager will persevere. If a situation creates a conflict of values, the manager will not opt for an easy compromise.

Inevitably we all know that whichever role we are playing, we are bound to encounter extremely challenging situations. Regardless of how strong our preferences for a role and how much capability we have, we need this solid foundation in values to guide us through ambiguous, challenging circumstances, to provide us with the integrity that makes our behavior credible.

Managers improve effectiveness in the nine leading-edge roles when values are the source of behavior. Often it is unnecessary to continually think about values, but there are many occasions in which conscious attention is appropriate. Referring to the foundation may be helpful in situations in which there are serious con-

Table 3   How to Be a Value-Driven Leader

- Honor the basic values of individuals.

- Help to connect those values to those of the organization.

- Try to resolve any conflicts among values.

- Remain cognizant of the foundational importance of core values for successful managing in the nine leading-edge roles.

- Create an organizational identity with specific core values that provide an enduring foundation for all of its endeavors.

- Choose core values that reflect the organization's needs in serving its customers.

- Ensure that actions are consistent with core values and restrain or eliminate those that are not.

- Encourage people to express personal core values and confront inconsistencies of actions with personal or organizational core values.

flicting demands, contradictions between values, ambiguities, or difficult challenges.

We do not casually arrive at our core values. Although we do not want to abandon them, we are all subject to the influences of challenging situations that may overwhelm our capability to keep core values present in our thoughts and actions in the leading-edge roles. Table 3 summarizes the ways to use core values.

Basic Premise

VALUES drive BEHAVIOR
BEHAVIOR leads to RESULTS.

This basic premise is critical to understanding the importance of core values. Any behavior, no matter how trivial, will have some value that drives it; everything we do has a value at its base. This idea seems rather obvious, yet it is mostly behavior and results that capture our attention: If we do not like the results, we try to change *behavior*. An effective manager, however, causes behavior to change by working with *values*.

This chapter contains much discussion about core values, but behavior and results in people and organizations often stem from values that have displaced the core values. These are the *operating values*. Other people observe our behavior or experience the results we create and deduce the values that are driving our choice. They often correctly surmise that our operating values differ from our desired core values.

To test this notion, accept a simple challenge: Think over the last week, and identify instances when you feel your behavior did not match the core values you chose to hold, when some other value displaced your core value. This includes that piece of chocolate cake you ate while you were trying to watch your diet. If you can think of no instances, congratulations on your sainthood; you can skip the rest of this chapter! For the rest of us, it is quite easy to identify several instances, some trivial and some more significant, when we would like to change the behavior or obtain different results. Such examples illustrate the need to constantly remember core values during any behavior. It becomes more evident when we are using the leading-edge roles and confronting the normal deadlines and stress of work, which can cause us to forget how we really want to be.

If behavior or results are unacceptable, we need to identify the *actual* values—those that have displaced core values and currently guide behavior. Our integrity requires upholding core values by shifting behavior to become consistent with them. We cannot change the past, but we can use it to learn how to alter the present and affect the future. Sometimes our core values cannot lead to the desired results; then it may be time to face the rather challenging process of changing core values.

Core values do not make life easier. They challenge us to minimize compromise, avoid expediency, and live by what we consider truly important. Every situation is not easily amenable to living by core values. There are innumerable times in organizational life, regardless of which leading-edge role we are using, that our values compel us to make choices that may set us apart from our colleagues. They may think we are "throwing a wrench in the works" or "rocking the boat." We achieve true mastery of a role when our core values remain intact despite the hardships we face. I warn you that there will be many instances in your organizational life when defense of stated core values will cause turmoil and criticism.

An individual must depend upon his or her own set of core values. In an organization, however, effectiveness in any of the leading-edge roles also requires that organizational core values form the foundation. Thus both personal and organizational values are important to any manager. Building integrity through self-awareness is necessary so that deliberate action can be taken to keep core values alive in challenging situations. We must also face the inevitable conflicts among values that will occur in the complex circumstances one often encounters in business.

Identifying Core Values

Personal Core Values

When we begin to consciously deal with values, we are moving from answering "what do we need to do" questions to "why do we need to do it" questions. If we are serious when we answer a "why" question, we are able to see the answer's true importance: its meaning, significance, and uniqueness. There are several ways to answer a "why" question because there are several levels at which we experience values. For example, usually the first answer to, Why am I doing this task? only skims the surface, as in, I am doing this task because I am paid to work and I value money.

This initial response is not a core value. A useful approach is to work with a whole series of responses and "why" questions—a response, followed by a "why" question, followed by another response, followed by another "why" question, and so on. Each answer to the "why" question reveals some level of values that is relevant to us. For example, take the first response above and ask, Why am I paid to work? One possible answer is, I am paid to work because I have talents or skills that I want to use. Another possible answer is, I seek pay for work because I want to provide a secure standard of living for my family.

We could continue the series of "why" questions and responses until we arrive at a level of values that reveals some fundamental personal truth. These would be our *personal core values*. Others may not hold these values, or they may have similar values but not consider them to be of fundamental importance. Fundamental truth does not mean lasting philosophical significance throughout the centuries; it is our own truth. It is also reasonable to expect that there are some values that bring all of us together regardless of our different backgrounds and life experiences.

Alternatively, it is quite simple to restate the question. The new question needs to be challenging and thought provoking. For example, the initial question was, Why am I doing this task? The question can be restated as, Why among all possible tasks have I chosen this one at this stage in my life? The second question is more difficult to answer than the first.

Core values may represent our natural inclination or uniqueness. We also learn values from our background: Families, religions, education, and culture teach us values. But direct teaching is not the only method for learning values from one's background: We often learn values by observing the behavior in our surroundings. Sometimes we are only seeing operating values, but if we observe long enough, we will see behavioral patterns that give us a better insight into values. This experience is similar to joining a new organization and trying to discern the values from the way people behave rather than by what they say.

Although these values from our background are enduring, they are not immutable. There are times when we find that the values no longer work and undergo what is often a difficult period of change to transform ourselves to behave according to a new set of values. Often when we face a significant crossroads, we have trouble choosing. This usually implies that all alternatives have very compelling aspects, very difficult aspects, or both. Our difficulty in deciding can be a result of the very different values reflected in the different alternatives. Resolving that conflict is a matter for a later section of this chapter. At this point, I simply suggest that we use these decision challenges as a vehicle to reveal our values.

Sometimes we identify very broad core values for ourselves, such as, Be honest. If we think about it, however, people often want more specific things from us. The advantage to us is that it is easier to live by a core value that is more specific. As I talk to different people in a variety of organizations, I hear many common themes. One desire that people have is for others—managers, peers, or subordinates—to *make commitments and stand by them.* This is a powerful core value that gives us definite guidance regardless of which leading-edge role we are using. Another frequently stated desire is for others to *seek out and understand different perspectives,* which is also a clear core value that affects all the leading-edge roles.

Organizational Core Values

Think about your own work environment and your regular co-workers. Consider the expectations you have of them and the expectations you believe they have of you. Do any of these thoughts lead to clearly defined core values? If you have a discussion with others about this level of expectations, you will be well on your way to uncovering core values for the organization. As it turns out, organizational core values only have meaning if they reflect people's true desires for their workplace.

You want values that provide the best foundation for the company's efforts to sustain a competitively viable identity in its markets and an effective internal work environment. Annual reports often contain an organization's value statements. Values may also appear implicitly or explicitly in its advertisements. Sometimes organizations communicate values to employees but not to the public because they see their values as a source of competitive advantage.

Internal values have meaning because people have talked about them. Thus problems with inconsistent behavior within the organization are solvable. But values open to the public must be self-explanatory; there is usually no opportunity for discussion. Inconsistent behavior could undermine the credibility of the organization.

Several different questions can help identify appropriate core values: What is the public image we want to have? What are the one or two most important things about this organization? When people think about this organization, what do we want them to see? What is most important to people in the organization? What values will be important to the organization for the next year, five years, twenty years?

The organization must have a small set of core values that will motivate each person and serve as a foundation for each of the nine leading-edge manager roles. Values are usually stated in very few words, so the words become symbols. Thus if you read the values of an unfamiliar organization in its annual report, they may seem vague or general, but the words have symbolic value if that organization has worked to give them very rich and full meanings. If there are long explanations of the values to make them more explicit, it may be useful for people outside the organization but may also mean that there is no experience of depth of meaning within the organization. Breadth of explanation often means that people in the organization do not fully understand or follow the values—nobody internalizes long statements.

It is not enough to identify and beautifully reproduce values on charts posted around the organization, nor will giving people a policy manual or pointing them at one of the charts create the same meaning for the values. Rather it is important to understand expectations for shifts in behavior caused by the values. If you think about different situations that the organization will face and that you will face in your responsibilities, you can identify the challenges to the values. Plan ways to keep values alive when there is pressure to ignore them for the expediency of the situation. Self-awareness is one such method.

Building Integrity Through Self-Awareness

All people occasionally experience situations in which they lack clarity about values. We get caught up in the pressure of the moment and tend to focus on what we are doing. We want to do tasks well, so we focus attention on requirements and methods of task performance, perhaps failing to maintain a conscious connection to underlying values for the task. Thus actions, behaviors, and use of the leading-edge roles can become inconsistent with values. We may experience a number of things when we become disconnected from values: We do not create what we really want, we lose a sense of meaningfulness or significance, we find insufficient fulfillment in work relationships with others. Work may feel lifeless; we go through the motions, sometimes putting much time and effort into the job but seeing real life occurring solely outside the workplace.

Integrity is crucial in those situations that challenge values. People with integrity are predictable in the sense of being consistent, reliable, thoughtful, and steadfast in the face of adversity. Integrity comes from some degree of self-awareness. Self-awareness is quite simply being conscious of the perspective you use when working with people and tasks in the world around you. Without self-awareness, it is difficult to ensure that values are present. To manage others, one must first be able to manage oneself. As the saying goes, "Know thyself."

We often think poorly of ourselves or others when core values are subverted. It would be much healthier for all of us if we got past the notion of seeing this as a sign of bad intentions and began to think of it as an opportunity to develop increased capability in self-awareness—knowing thyself.

Integrity and self-awareness are keys to effectiveness in all leading-edge roles. Traditional university education and most management training sponsored by organizations do not address the development of self-awareness. These learning processes often treat management and leadership as technique—if a person can learn the right steps in the right sequence, then there is a chance of becoming more effective. But technique is ultimately meaningless if it is disconnected from the core values the manager follows.

We seem to value those managers more highly whom we feel to be authentic, who work from a strong sense of themselves. We know when this managerial quality is there because we have experiences in which the manager seemed really genuine and others where he or she seemed to be merely following a technique.

Contrast two experiences you have of being managed, one positive and one negative. Think about the impacts on you, the actions of the manager, and your beliefs about what the manager was thinking and valuing. Draw conclusions about the qualities of effective management and the role of self-awareness and integrity. Overall, your responses to the positive experience probably focused on qualities such as, trust, respect, confidence, ease of interaction, concern, ability to listen, interest, enthusiasm, or openness. You may have said that the manager felt present, not distracted, completely focused on the people, the work situation, and the broader context. You may have said that the manager did not seem to be ego driven. Your impression may have been that the manager was strongly self-aware, in addition to having the management techniques to stay on top of the situation and make a decision. His or her behavior probably seemed entirely natural: Sometimes we would call this quality charisma. Therefore we often conclude that it is not possible to learn, or, if it is possible, we search for some steps or guidelines to follow so we can approximate that behavior. But managers are not being authentic when they try to follow some prescribed steps; authenticity requires work on the dynamics of self-awareness so that others experience our core values. When we act from self-awareness, we put thought before action. The purpose is not to delay the action and get caught in contemplation; it is to ensure that the actions we take are consistent with our values.

If you want to develop further self-awareness, use this simple model, which has been around for centuries, to remember the four different ways we all experience the world:

Spirit—The degree to which we find things truly interesting, energizing, inspiring, or significant

Thought—The ideas that we bring to a situation

Emotion—Probably a taboo subject in business but a very real part of everybody's daily experience: being excited, frustrated, compassionate, angry, challenged, fearful, etc.

Action—Our behavior, willingness to act, and responsibility for the consequences of our actions

It is clear we can go through much of the day being quite effective without paying any conscious attention to our values. Self-awareness is a path back to values. Those four categories are a very useful checklist to look at our own experience of a situation and the effects we believe we are having on others in order to determine if appropriate values are present. Identifying core values is an essentially introspective process; you can sit down quietly some place and do it. Self-awareness is an in-the-moment phenomenon; you need to carry out your responsibility and simultaneously pay attention to observing yourself and your impact on those around you. This is a challenging process but the only one that will ever keep you on track in difficult circumstances when it is easy to get side-tracked and lose sight of core values.

Managing Value Conflicts

Conflicts in Personal Values

Life is intriguing and harsh because so many situations occur
where values are in conflict. Conflicts occur because different values lead to alternative courses of action. Every time you look in the
window of a bakery, you could be facing a conflict between your
value for pleasure and your value for health or weight control.
Every time a charity makes a request for a donation, you could be
facing a conflict between your value for the work of that charity
and your value for the personal benefit of spending your own
money. The way most people deal with these simple value conflicts
is to plan their allocation between indulgence and diet or charity
and personal needs.

Similar value conflicts happen to managers. For example, a person is responsible for a team that completes a project with cost
overruns and delay. At the end of the project, there is much ill will
among members of the team. Perhaps this manager was lacking in
some skills of the ally and did not know how to build a truly productive partnership. Maybe the manager wanted participation (the
core value) but acted from a need to control (the operating value)
and lacked the self-awareness to notice the problem. Alternatively,
it is possible that the manager was unable to resolve a conflict of
core values and chose between them. The original project esti-
mates may have been too low and the manager acted from a value
for meeting obligations to the organization's customers (a possible
core value) over the health of that team (another possible core
value).

With recurring events, we can always adopt a decision rule that
we will do something one time and something else another time.
We can feel fairly comfortable that our values are relatively intact in
these situations. The more interesting situations occur when the
stakes are higher and the events are not recurring. A choice to follow a core value over a more transient value may mean that we
choose challenge and possible defeat over expediency. King Henry
VIII separated the Church of England from Rome because he
wanted a divorce. Even though the English clergy recognized the
king's authority, Sir Thomas More chose death because he valued

the supremacy of the Church of Rome. If you do not share his value, it is very difficult to understand his action. It is a challenging question to ask oneself, What am I willing to sacrifice to uphold a value that I feel is important?

Stakes are usually not that high for managers, but there are times when upholding a value puts a person at risk of losing a job or missing a promotion. There are numerous possibilities for value conflicts between work and family. Work may demand long hours, travel, job relocation. Family health may require stability and presence. Choices such as these are practically a daily occurrence for many people.

Working in any organization offers numerous possibilities to challenge your core values. Is there ever a time to become a whistle blower within your organization? What are the issues that will compel you to take a stand? To what issues do you close your eyes? We often face difficult choices, and it is not my place to tell you what you should do. It is in these challenging situations that you can learn the most about your attention to core values.

Increasing the frequency of acting from a core value is an important development issue for all nine leading-edge manager roles. Self-awareness is one approach. There are a few other steps you could follow in situations where you experience value conflicts (among core values or between a core value and an operating or more expedient value). These are discussed in the Learning Core Value Skills at the end of the chapter.

Conflicts Between Personal Values and Organizational Values

If there is a substantial difference between the core values of an organization and those of an individual, the relationship is not sustainable. The way an organization conducts its business and its products and services all reflect its values. Vegetarians do not seek employment on cattle ranches; religious fundamentalists do not work for Planned Parenthood; Newt Gingrich is not a spokesman for the American Civil Liberties Union; Joan Baez is not on the board of the National Rifle Association. Similarly, if you really do not believe in its values, products, services, or ways of conducting business, it will be difficult to put your full energy in the organization. Your spirit will be drained; your thoughts and emotions will be diverted. You must have the stamina to seek change or an unusual willingness to forego your own values if you do remain in an organization diametrically opposed to your own views.

Regardless of the source of conflict between an individual and an organization, serious symptoms can occur. People rationalize that it is just a job, even though it occupies half of their lives. Spirit and emotions remain outside the organization and directed toward other activities. Only the mind and body show up at work. Work becomes more mechanical, and the organization loses its competitive edge. The climate in the organization may diminish people's physical and psychological health. Excessive stress, high absentee and turnover rates, and burnout may occur. This type of conflict is usually not resolvable. If it happens to you, you may need to separate from the organization. If there is a serious conflict between your values and those of the organization, you will have trouble developing a solid foundation for effectiveness in the leading-edge roles in that organization. This is not a situation of inadequate management skills but of poor fit between person and organization.

Conflicts Within Organizational Values

There are many possibilities for conflict among different values held by the organization, so it would not be unusual to find behavior inconsistent with at least some core values. Inconsistent behavior (that is, behavior derived from some other values) may include the following:

- Pressure for conformity, compliance, and control
- Internal competitiveness
- Bias against not-invented-here
- Energy expended to protect oneself from failure
- Hesitation to voice one's thoughts or ideas
- Lack of understanding and respect among different cultural groups

If you look at these problems, you can probably identify a variety of different values that could displace core values and lead to these disruptive behaviors. There is so much uncertainty in the world, so much complexity, so much ambiguity, that we begin to place higher value on clinging to the status quo, pursuing stability, and keeping things under tight control. However, such behavior cannot possibly help to sustain a long-term competitive stance. It is also in sharp contrast to the essence of the core values and is a blatant signal to a manager that it is important to bring core values back into discussion. It may be necessary for you to take a stand and endure criticism for discussing core values while you have responsibility for fulfilling the obligations of one or more of the leading-edge roles.

As another example of conflicting values within an organization, consider the number of organizations that state a "value for people." The economy turns down, competition has intensified, and business has decreased. The value for survival now becomes more prominent. Survival, of course, is not one of the stated core values of the organization beautifully emblazoned on its walls. It is now necessary to reduce the size of the organization. If the organization is lucky, it can achieve workforce reduction through attractive early retirement proposals; this approach can still give credence to the value for people even though survival is driving the action. But suppose the only realistic alternative is to fire people. Is this inconsistent with the value for people? It depends. The degree of importance attached to the value for people influences the process used in layoffs. If the value is weak, the process will lead to anger in the people being dismissed (a response that is difficult to avoid) and fear in those remaining. However, organizations that take the value for people seriously face a challenge. Some give people significant amounts of advance warning or long periods of termination pay to help with the transition; others provide significant assistance for retraining; still others help people relocate to another job within the organization or find employment elsewhere.

All of these measures are costly. When values conflict, there are no easy choices. A value that is truly worthwhile is never cheap. Many situations will occur where it would be more expedient to let the value slip away. On the other hand, an organization can hold a core value for people and terminate employment for those unable to meet performance standards.

Businesses face many situations where the value for profits and survival conflict with other values. Do you bribe officials in foreign countries? Do you do business in countries with poor human rights records? Do you fight environmental legislation to increase your profits? Do you move a plant location because you can reduce costs and remain more competitive? There are no simple right answers to these complex questions. The significance for developing increased competency in the nine leading-edge roles is that any value conflict potentially undermines the foundation and your ultimate effectiveness.

Learning Core Value Skills

Identifying Personal Core Values

You can experiment with one or more of the following:

- Choose some personally relevant situations, work or otherwise, and get to core values by using a series of "why" questions and responses.
- With the same or similar situations, get to core values by asking yourself a challenging question about each situation's meaning to you.
- Reflect on your background, independent of any current situation, and identify those values that were taught to you and that you still hold in high regard.
- Think of a difficult decision you face now or have faced in the past. Try to discern the values you were holding that may have caused this difficulty. Decide which of these values you would call "core values."
- Think about your work environment and your co-workers. Consider the expectations you have of them and the expectations you believe they have of you. Do any of these thoughts lead to some clearly defined core values?

Working With Self-Awareness

This approach starts from a management situation and works back through the dynamics of self-awareness to core values.

- Look at some specific situations involving others where you have management responsibility. Use the following ideas to get a sense of the self-awareness that you now bring to that situation:
  - Meaning you have for it
  - Significance it holds for you and others
  - Standards of conduct that guide you in it
  - Guidance for your assessment of what is right or wrong
  - Feelings you typically experience
  - Feelings that others typically seem to have
  - Thoughts that keep recurring to you

- Thought processes you typically use, for example, the way you solve problems, analyze things, use intuition, see opportunities, or make judgments
- Effect of that situation on the physical well-being of yourself and others
- Responsibility you take for the various physical or material objects
- Consequences of your actions

- Describe the impact of your current patterns on others and on the situation.

- Identify how others would describe the values that are motivating the way you behave in the situation.

- Consider any changes you experienced in the level of your self-awareness, for example, new thoughts or feelings, a different sense of spirit, as you thought about the ideas in the first question. Identify any internal contradictions—core values that are not being fully expressed or lived out.

- Assess the level of your integrity in that situation. Consider how you think others would assess it.

Resolving Personal Value Conflicts

Step One—Start Playfully

Take some smaller-level recurring events and treat them as one-time events.

Some examples:

Before you eat a meal, see how different values affect your food choice.

When you have free time, see how different values affect your activity.

When you have some extra money, see how different values affect your spending.

Step Two—Laying the Groundwork

Choose a more important situation.

Be clear about the possible choices of action.

Associate values with those actions.

Determine if other actions are possible with these values.

See if there is any action that avoids the conflict.

Step Three—Making the Choice

Describe a worst-case scenario of what you will risk if you stay with each value.

Describe a likely scenario for what you will risk.

Create questions for yourself from the model on self-awareness that help you better understand you own position.

Determine all consequences of your choice: benefits or costs imposed upon others, impact on the organization.

Step Four—Living With the Choice and Learning From It

If you chose a core value, use self-awareness to see how you deal with sacrifices and the consequences of your choice.

If you chose an operating or more expedient value, do not berate yourself.

Determine what you need to do the next time if you want to use your own core values.

Principal Focus of Managing Effort	Principal Leadership Process		
	Creating Order	**Inspiring Action**	**Improving Performance**
Systems	**Sage** Designs Strategy	**Visionary** Innovates the Future	**Magician** Orchestrates Change
People	**Globalist** Bridges Cultural Differences	**Mentor** Motivates Development	**Ally** Builds Partnerships
Work	**Sovereign** Empowers Decisions	**Guide** Achieves Goals	**Artisan** Pursues Excellence

FOUNDATION OF ALL ROLES
CORE VALUES

CHAPTER THREE

Designing Strategy

Learning the Role of the Sage

Profile of a Sage

Sage is the role name chosen to represent people with wisdom. This wisdom comes through an expanding knowledge of the world around them, an ability to understand and interpret this knowledge base, and the reasoning necessary to draw appropriate conclusions.

A sage is a jigsaw-puzzle player on a large scale, who likes to discover new pieces, fit them in with already known pieces, and thus change the whole picture. Drawing from broad-ranging interests, a sage can gain insight into organizations by creating analogies with novels, history, anthropology, physics, music, painting, sculpture, or sports.

Sages will always be asking questions and seeking new understandings. They prefer complexity because they are able to see order and patterns where others only see chaos. They get to the essence of issues by a willingness to tolerate ambiguity and contradictions rather than making assumptions to eliminate information and avoiding the mental challenge. Beyond merely tolerating ambiguity, sages experience this challenge as energizing, as this is the milieu in which they are most effective.

Wells' Field Guide—How to Spot a Sage

Habitat

The sage can be found everywhere surrounded by ideas. Dwelling will be inundated with more questions than answers. Usually can be seen soaring like an eagle to get a broad view of as much terrain as possible.

Habits

Develops broad-ranging knowledge of complex issues.

Uses multiple approaches and perspectives to understand ambiguous situations.

Encourages an open flow of ideas and information among people.

Learns from experience.

Is relentlessly inquisitive.

Often has broad interests beyond work and can apply essential ideas from these interests to work-related needs.

Develops insight leading to wise, practical judgments and the discovery of opportunities unseen by others.

Sees order emerging where others only see chaos.

Is comfortable operating at a more abstract and conceptual level of thought, knowing that it is never possible to fully understand everything.

Through this ability to grasp and connect divergent information, they are able to uncover opportunities. Obstacles that emerge drive them to further understanding, insights, and ideas. They are adept at identifying possible courses for action where the amount of information overwhelms other people, leading them to ignore what they are unable to comprehend.

Sages enjoy expanding their own understanding through the perspectives, insights, knowledge, or information of others. They maintain an open flow of information and ideas with people both inside and outside the organization. This is not the same as a focus on people nor is it cold and impersonal; a sage's interaction with others is in the world of ideas.

This role is the most conceptual of all the roles and the least active. As organizational life is often quite rushed with little time for reflection, this role tends to be the least emphasized. It is also the role for which the fewest people score high preferences in the assessment, yet, as with the other system roles, it is critical for the long-term viability of any organization. Do not be surprised if you find it to be a more difficult role to comprehend than the other roles.

The challenge in developing sage skills is to avoid premature limits on thinking. Sage thinking techniques impose complexity because they expose areas that are ambiguous, uncertain, or beyond our individual current knowledge. The complete willingness, even desire, to confront ambiguity helps avoid a rush to quick conclusions when things are unsettled or difficult to understand. As you go through the rest of this chapter, be aware of your own desire to try to move things too quickly toward what you judge to be a practical level. Often personal capability drives this judgment rather than the more appropriate practicality standard used by a sage: to expose oneself to the true reality that exists in order to continually advance the long-run interests of the organization.

How the Sage Helps the Organization

This role reflects the combination of the leadership process of creating order and the systems focus of managing effort. Why is there a need to create order at the systems level? What is the nature of disorder or chaos?

At the systems level, we are looking beyond the confines of a particular work assignment, work group, or division, and often beyond the confines of the organization. Whatever you do, whatever boundaries define your realm of responsibility, there is always something beyond. Effectively managing any responsibility means dealing with the different people, groups, institutions, and broader forces (economic, political, technological, and social) that surround your work. As we extend our thinking further outward, we see increasingly complex connections among things. We also have greater uncertainty about the dynamics of these connections as we move into the future.

Yet it is the responsibility of a manager in this role to be able to see through that chaos and come to some conclusions. It is necessary to plot some course of movement into the future even though the future remains complex, ambiguous, uncertain, and subject to unexpected change. Order emerges through understanding this context of complex, divergent, and often contradictory information and ultimately identifying opportunities for the organization within it. Success occurs by outthinking one's competitors and *designing a strategy* that moves the organization forward.

Sages construct strategic possibilities for the organization based upon various techniques for innovative and fluid thinking. A manager in the sage role needs to understand complex, interrelated systems. This approach helps match capability within the firm with the dynamics of its environment. It broadens one's time perspective to balance the necessary but often too dominant focus on short-term results with thinking and direction for long-term competitive staying power in an industry. The sage sees opportunities and discerns the best way to position an organization in that overall dynamic context.

As with the other system roles, it is very easy to see its necessity at top levels of the organization. With my own writing, I have probably added to the common view of the sage role—that it is the private reserve of the CEO or a small group of top executives. But that view is erroneous. This restriction of the role was useful when times were relatively stable, but the increasing rapidity of change, the challenging dynamics of global competition, and the higher demands of customers mean that such ability must flow through the organization. Flexibility and adaptability of managers, other employees, and therefore the whole organization require that many individuals have the practical wisdom of the sage. Without widespread capability, the organization's response to change will be seriously hampered, and the survival of the organization may be in jeopardy.

Managers throughout the organization need to implement the strategy of the whole organization. If there is no ability anywhere in the organization except at the top levels to be effective in this role, then there will be no ability to fully understand the strategy and make the necessary adaptations as the unfolding future challenges the validity of the original strategy. It is relevant to have managers support the necessary endeavors of other groups within the organization as they manage their work groups to implement the overall strategy of the organization. It is relevant to have people throughout the organization thinking about how their work affects the organization's customers, about the influences to the demands of customers, and about what competitors are doing to meet those demands. The sage role is not really about a particular strategy: It is the use of systemic and strategic thinking in the process of designing strategy.

We have very little education in this type of thinking and ways of understanding complex subjects. We are usually under pressure to simplify things, and therefore we lose the significant broader perspective of what is really happening. We spend much of our lives learning how to analyze, divide, separate, and segment. Narrow thinking also occurs when we try to completely protect ourselves or our jobs from any outside influences; when we focus only on our own immediate responsibilities and not on the effects of our actions on others; when we have educational processes, such as those in high schools and universities, that segment knowledge into discrete subjects and insufficiently emphasize connections among different fields of knowledge. With this training and experience, it is sometimes a challenge to use systems thinking—understanding our environment as complex, vibrant, and interwoven whole systems.

How a Sage Is Value-Driven

Given what we have said about the sage, how can core values improve effectiveness in this role? One important way is through understanding the core values of others. The sage designs strategy by understanding the choices that others will make—customers, competitors, suppliers, people in the organization, etc. Core values influence our choices as well as our behavior. Thus, for the sage, core values will influence the perspective with which he or she views the world and makes choices. There is no such thing as a fully objective view of the world. Even sages see the world through the filter of their experience and core values.

Core values play a central role in helping a sage choose and interpret information about that environment. A sage, however, unlike the rest of us, will expend greater effort in ensuring that this foundation does not obscure phenomena from their understanding. If your religion teaches that the world is flat or the earth is the center of the universe and you have high core values for following your faith, it is going to be very difficult to perceive strategy that requires a willingness to see the world differently. Sages need core values that guide their behavior but do not restrain them from thinking about and considering different possibilities.

Finally, the sage is able to see the organization's core values from a strategic perspective. It is always reasonable in an organization to consider the strategic significance and competitive advantage of relentless adherence to well-founded core values. Think of it from your perspective as a customer: If a firm has people consistently operating in conformance with core values, does it alter your willingness to do business with them?

Building Sage Skills

The three major sage skills developed in this chapter are the following:

- *Looking at the World Through Sage-Colored Glasses*—the mental attitude and capability to face ambiguity and complexity and to use multiple perspectives to look at issues
- *Perceiving the Possibilities*—building a web of associations among aspects of the organization's environment, seeing patterns in seemingly disparate information about the environment, and projecting distinctive, alternative environment scenarios
- *Gaining Competitive Advantage*—viewing things in the way they add value, altering belief systems or paradigms about an industry, and identifying those elements most important to the success of an organization

Warning Signs of Excess

You know you have overdone the sage role if you

Lack attention to specific details or day-to-day issues

See so many possibilities and interrelationships that you cannot make a decision

Cannot stick to one vision

Cannot complete a change because new possibilities keep arising

Think that individual needs do not matter

Have little patience working with other people who seem to lack understanding

Always want to study something further and avoid any action

Seeing the World Through Sage-Colored Glasses

How I Learned to Stop Worrying and Love Ambiguity and Complexity

Each of the sage techniques described here adds to sage wisdom. They also increase the complexity with which a sage views the world. This can be quite overwhelming to any manager. Travel down the road of any of these techniques and you will meet things that are difficult to understand. You may feel that being in the sage role opens areas that will take you away from your main responsibilities, the pressure you feel to get things done. To you, sage thinking may be intriguing but you feel it is peripheral to the needs of the moment. The unsettling effect of complexity and the rush to come to some quick conclusions can unduly restrain sage thinking.

There is no doubt that sage thinking leads to increased complexity of ideas. It is a disaster, however, if it leads to increased complexity of action. It may seem as if the sage is saying, How can I make things more complex? In reality, the proper sage question is, How can I understand the true, complex nature of things to reach more effective simplicity?

A sage embraces ambiguity by having patience to let knowledge accumulation continue with faith that appropriate conclusions will emerge. There is always risk that a conclusion will not emerge or that the pursuit of knowledge continues beyond a useful point, but the pressures that exist in most organizations minimize these risks. In fact, there is usually more likelihood of insufficient use of the sage role than excessive use.

Bureaucratic organizations—businesses and government—that have multiple layers of approval or endlessly form committees to study problems are *distorted* examples of sage qualities. We all lose patience working in these environments; nothing ever seems to happen. Such experiences make us highly suspicious of the sage's desire for knowledge. But the quality of an effective sage is not patience for taking a long time to understand things: It is patience for ambiguity in the pursuit of knowledge. A strong sage is just as happy as anyone else to avoid ineffective committees or other mechanisms that stretch the time to gain insight. However, sages are significantly more willing to stay with issues where insight is difficult to achieve.

For example, once a sage has moved into multiple perspectives, he or she has moved into the terrain of ambiguity. Each perspective can give a different meaning to the same data or event. Intolerance for ambiguity is usually part of the belief that there is only one truth. Yet often truth is only what a person sees from his or her own perspective. The sage seeks the "truth" that is illuminated from different perspectives.

Walking a Mile in Everybody's Shoes

A key sage wisdom is drawing conclusions from disparate data, and the sage's source for that wisdom is observable facts. Different perspectives are a tool to aid the sage's understanding of the facts.

The sage is clever enough to know that there are two kinds of facts: objective and subjective. Objective facts are frequently quantified—information exists in the form of demographics of communities, market shares, and costs. Qualitative objective facts include descriptions of new technologies, partnerships formed by other organizations in the industry, and new products from competitors. Opportunities emerge from these facts.

Subjective facts are the meanings, interpretations, and opinions of observers with different perspectives. Subjective facts also lead to identification of opportunities. Therefore, the sage strives to increase understanding of both types of facts. The sage's interest is in knowledge, not in conflict resolution among different perspectives. The sage is seeking anything that will lead to more effective strategy design. Therefore, in the four applications in the Learning Sage Role Skills section, do not think about resolving problems among different perspectives but rather using the perspectives to gain new insights.

Perceiving the Possibilities

Expansive Systems Mapping

Ancient wisdom says that everything is connected. We experience unexpected repercussions or unanticipated chains of causes and effects because we do not understand these connections. Chaos theory carries this phenomenon to the extreme by using the analogy of the "butterfly effect"—the fluttering wings of a butterfly in Vermont causing a typhoon in Asia some time in the future.

Sages create these seemingly impossible connections by starting with a focal point and tracking the growing number of connections to that focus. For example, looking at any object, you could ask the question, What happened so that this object is now in front on me? As you answer that question, you begin to see something akin to a growing spider web or the representation of dendrite connections in the brain. Such a process maps the terrain of possible "unexpected repercussions" or "unanticipated causes and effects" and quickly has serious overtones when the complexity increases.

For example, I am looking at a photograph of a group of people. The most obvious starting point for expansive systems mapping is the camera and film. When I think of the camera, I think of glass, plastic, metal, and electronics and the production and delivery of each component to the camera manufacturer. When I think of the film, my first thought is of silver—I wonder if fluctuating silver prices affect the cost of film. Of course, there are many different types of films, produced with different qualities, used for different conditions, and sold for different prices. I think of the retailers who carry this selection in competing brands and wonder how well they are able to help the customer choose the best film. If I start to think about the content of the photograph—who the people are, where they are, why they are there—I enter another realm of thinking and a whole other series of connections. I could go into detail in any or all the things mentioned. I could find other things I had not thought about. I would find areas where I had reasonable knowledge and areas of significant gaps. The chain of events to get one photograph on my desk is overwhelming.

What is the point of this exercise? It is a low-risk opportunity to expand your thinking, to get a feel for the complexity that is possible. When the stakes are high—when you are doing something that matters to your organization—your tendency may be to limit thinking and miss some important things.

Why search for all this complexity? It is useful to any of the businesses mentioned in the example of the photo. From a business perspective, I would probably want an even more expansive and detailed mapping of relationships. I would want to think about why someone wants a photograph and how they intend to use it, how the other businesses work and what their needs are for their own competitive effectiveness, what I could do better, how I could improve the success of the other businesses, and how I could improve the value of photographs to the customer.

Pattern Recognition

This method is similar to detective work. A piece of information here, another one there, and soon it is possible to draw some conclusions. The test of the conclusion's validity is that the seemingly disparate facts have a logical connection to it. A conclusion brings order to the chaos of information. One challenge for a sage is to try to place some limits on the information search—gathering information is time consuming and costly. Unfortunately we only know the value of any single piece of information when we recognize a pattern.

The more mundane work of intelligence agencies is pattern recognition: They track vast amounts of environmental information and draw conclusions about the relevance to their own countries. Businesses abound that sell information to other businesses. Success in this field depends upon the sage qualities of the personnel—the more they are able to group information with logical conclusions, the more valuable the information becomes. The data itself, without the pattern recognition conclusions, may only add to information overload.

For example, when I talk to my insurance agent, who owns a small four-person office, and ask him about his business, our conversation touches on many subjects, including the economy, the quality of vehicles, changing demographics, and home renovations and construction. He keeps his mind connected to a wide variety of facts to understand problems and opportunities that may affect his business. Naturally conversation is a way for him to build his business with clients. It also provides him with crucial information and pattern insights.

Identifying patterns observable in the environment is challenging; there is no simple method. It requires knowledge of data and a bit of an intuitive leap to the conclusion. Data must be explicit and observable:

- About your business and industry
- In newspapers, magazines, and television news
- In technological changes in other industries
- In the concerns people in your community have about different issues

Now you have many little pieces of information floating around in your head. One trick used by a sage to tap into intuition is to formulate a question in order to focus thinking and perhaps crystallize an answer. For example, what do the data tell you about the best place to make personal financial investments? Is it a good time to buy a house? Which regions of the country will experience growth? Which will experience stagnation? What are the major problems on the horizon for your organizations? What are the possible opportunities? Pattern recognition is an important technique to make sense of the wide range of information evoked by the expansive systems mapping. Once you identify patterns through this questioning method, you can position yourself or your organization to take advantage of any opportunities or minimize any hazards that could occur through these patterns.

Scenario Planning

A scenario is a narrative about the future describing a coherent, plausible, and challenging picture of the confluence of different environmental forces and participants. Scenario planning provides value by creating a few distinctive pictures of the future that are likely to have substantively different effects on your strategic decisions. Although it is not useful to describe a best case, worst case, and most likely case, it may be useful to take an optimistic view and a pessimistic view by looking at some key events or possibilities in the environment and working with different outcomes.

Scenario planning begins by identifying a key question, decision, or issue that is strategically important to your organization. This creates a practical and relevant context for your thinking about scenarios. The amount of information that exists in the environment is so broad, diverse, and complex that you need something to focus your attention. This step is similar to the questioning process used to see patterns in the environmental information. A scenario, however, is more comprehensive than pattern recognition in that the desire is to get a complete, integrated view of an environmental future.

The next phase is to think about different key aspects of the environment that will significantly influence the success (positive response) or failure (negative response) of your decision (or question). Key aspects of the environment include economics, technology, market demand, and competitor capability. In viewing the environment in this manner, you should be able to differentiate between what is central and what is peripheral to your strategic thinking.

Greater understanding of a future scenario occurs by identifying probable states for each key aspect and the "causal factors" for those states. For example, economic issues such as interest rates, income levels, and inflation rates may be key aspects related to your original question. You would simply identify different possible interest rates (or any other environmental aspect) that could exist in the future. You would then identify the different factors that could cause changes in interest rates.

This approach to scenario planning will probably lead to a great proliferation of data. If you started with only three or four key aspects, each of which had a few different states, and each state had a few different causal factors, you would have a huge number of possible combinations. A scenario is nothing more than a unique combination of causal factors and states. This is a challenging leap of thinking as you must look at the range of possibilities and make a choice. Think about choosing those combinations that are distinctive from each other with each choice giving you an alternative view of the future that is both possible and challenging to your strategic thinking about your organization. Each scenario creates strategic possibilities and hazards related to your initial key question, decision, or issue.

Gaining Competitive Advantage

Systems Dynamics

There is a sharp contrast between thinking about something as an *object* versus as a *system*. As an object, we usually describe what something is. As a system, we usually describe how and why something operates. Object thinking is inevitably static—a picture at a point in time. Seeing things as systems automatically leads to a notion of dynamics—things in motion through time. This is the way a sage can use knowledge to find strategic opportunities.

For example, if you think of the heart as an object, you would identify different parts of the heart. With something alive such as the heart, however, there is a strong tendency to see it as a system—its role in the circulatory system, its interaction with other body systems, and its value to the whole body.

When we are dealing with something inanimate such as a job, there is a greater temptation to see things as segmented objects rather than as connected systems. Treating the job as an object, we describe responsibilities, authority, and task procedures. We know we are part of the organization but see the job as a separate entity with clear divisions between what this job is and what it is not. We seek a definite description of work responsibilities and treat the work as territory needing protection. With objects, we use analytical thinking—breaking things into parts and examining the inner workings of each part. Systems dynamics is a different depiction of reality that brings things together or synthesizes the actions of many systems so we can see the wide-ranging consequences from the action of any one part.

In the example of the heart, the heart is seen as a subsystem within an individual that contributes to the overall health of the individual. It is connected to several other subsystems that interact with each other. Once we begin to think in systems terms, we can always see one system as a necessary component, a subsystem, of some larger system. The heart, as any other system, is in ongoing, dynamic, interdependent relationships with other systems in its environment. Each system receives inputs from various sources, engages in some basic process to transform the inputs (for example, creating enriched blood), and delivers outputs (the transformed inputs) to some other system, which in turn conducts another transformation. If we trace these system connections far enough, we will have a complex, interwoven pattern of systems that cycle energy and matter through a variety of changes.

Similarly, perspective broadens when you think of your job as a system rather than an object. You get a greater sense of movement or see a broader range of responsibilities; you notice a larger number of things upon which your job depends; you perceive the consequences of the quality of work you do. Most importantly, you may become aware of new possibilities for improving the effectiveness of your job. Thinking about a job as a system is exactly analogous to the approach used by sages, who view the organization in the context of other systems or organizations—competitors, suppliers, customers.

The key idea from systems dynamics is to find ways to alter the established patterns of system relationships so that your organization can enhance its ability to add value to its customers. It is quite simple: The customer pays you to deliver value to them. Once you understand the dynamic interrelationships of the various systems in your industry (the expansive systems mapping is a key starting point for this technique), you increase your ability to see new strategic possibilities and gain competitive advantage.

Paradigm Shifting

Paradigms are views of the world that we hold to be true, sets of assumptions, fundamental beliefs, or theoretical frameworks that we use to explain how things work and to guide us in our engagement with people and all facets of our lives. We often act as if our own paradigm is the fundamental truth about reality, as though reality were an absolute. We avoid the age-old philosophical question, What is reality? The answer, It depends upon your paradigm, is not very satisfying.

Regardless of how open-minded we try to be, we need some basic way to make connections among things, and we need some conceptual structure to deal with the world. A paradigm provides all this; it puts boundaries into our thinking. We become so accustomed to the paradigms of our own culture, upbringing, or experience that we ignore the possibility of other, equally valid, depictions of reality. We forget that the same paradigm that aids our understanding also creates subconscious barriers to other views of reality. These barriers prevent us from seeing new opportunities. Your whole industry is embedded in paradigms that have that dual nature of usefully describing reality and seriously inhibiting creative thinking.

The sage's strength is the willingness to question his or her own paradigm and test other paradigms to elevate the level of insight into reality. For example, think of how you would teach children if you held the belief that they have short attention spans. If you believed that children have a curiosity and desire to learn, would you alter teaching behavior?

The paradigm underlying this book is that learning and development occur throughout life. A learner is willing to take risks and be less capable in some situations. If you hold the paradigm of continuing to demonstrate a high level of expertise as a sign of strength, you will choose not to learn.

Your current management style and most operations of your organization derive from often unspoken paradigms. "Not-invented-here" is a paradigm that inhibits people from learning from others. General Electric's "best practices" is a contrasting paradigm that has its employees studying many different organizations to find superior ways of operating and learning from the experience and expertise of others. A belief that people are generally reluctant to work and will only be motivated by rewards and punishments surrounding pay, promotion, and firing leads to a particular management style, whereas a belief that people want to do something worthwhile and contribute to an organization leads to an entirely different management style.

By *mentally* shifting paradigms, the sage is saying, If I alter sets of beliefs, how would I view the world? What would I understand? How would I behave? What new possibilities would I see?

Observation of behavioral patterns will enable you to determine existing paradigms and see opportunities for changing those paradigms. For example, behavioral patterns of different environment participants include the following:

- The way competitors have responded to changing market conditions and the way they have shown initiative in providing market leadership

- The way customers have responded to different products and marketing techniques and the kind of expectations they have held

- The approaches used by suppliers, distributors, and producers of complementary products in running their businesses

The prevailing industry paradigms are statements of belief or assumptions that consistently explain this past behavior and predict future behavior. You can then determine how you see prevailing paradigms facilitating actions and decisions for different organizations in the industry. People hold paradigms because it enables them to do something. You can also determine the possible actions or decisions the paradigms would constrain. People hold paradigms that eventually prevent them from seeing possibilities. By defining contrasting paradigms, you can identify strategic possibilities and hazards these alternative paradigms would pose for your organization and for your competitors.

Critical Success Factors

Critical success factors provide a third major prospective for gaining competitive advantage. They are the items most essential for the organization to manage in order to enhance its competitive effectiveness and most likely to determine who will prevail on the competitive field. It is necessary to realize the strategic nature of critical success factors; in some cases, they represent the minimum requirements for being a player in the industry. For example, if every organization is creating quality products, it is not possible to gain competitive advantage by emphasizing quality; in such a situation, quality is necessary merely to survive within the industry. If you follow the evolution of any industry, you will quickly see that new critical success factors that give certain organizations competitive advantage gradually become the necessary entry qualifications. Industries continue to evolve in this way.

There are several ways to identify the different types of critical success factors:

- The current minimum standards necessary to remain within the industry (which may at one time have given one firm a competitive advantage but which other firms eventually copied to sustain their position)
- The industry's prevailing wisdom about the factors that determine competitive advantage
- The factors that seem to matter the most to customers in their purchase and use of the product
- The factors that firms use to aid or influence purchase and use

Some of these critical success factors will become minimum standards as the industry evolves, and new critical success factors will emerge as potential new grounds for competitiveness. You can find strategic possibilities by identifying critical success factors that your organization can bring to the industry for its competitive advantage.

Learning Sage Role Skills

Looking At The World Through Sage-Colored Glasses

Learning to Love Ambiguity

Use the following guidance for any situation where you are trying to understand more, are anxious about reaching a conclusion, and are feeling frustrated.

- Be specific about what you think is ambiguous.
- Try to do a relatively quick mental run-through using the different sage techniques to see how this affects your understanding. (If your frustration increases, it is due to a relative intolerance for ambiguity. Work on your sage skills.)
- Test some conclusions using what you currently know. (If your anxiety increases, you may be using increased understanding as an excuse for avoiding decisions. Work on your sovereign skills.)

Developing Mental Flexibility To See Things From More Than One Side

Frustrations

- Think of situations that you typically experience as frustrating or maddening.
- Adopt other perspectives to find logical reasons for such situations.

Problems of the World

- Choose a world problem.
- Map out or list different elements of this problem.
- Adopt different perspectives to see how the problem is understood.
- Think of solutions from these different perspectives.

You as Customer

- Think of different products or services you buy. If the seller were to take your perspective, what would he or she see and want to do differently?
- Take the seller's perspective to see what he or she should expect from customers.

Your Organization

- Identify some critical issues for your organization.
- Identify what you consider to be the key facts for these issues.
- Take the perspective of different people who affect or are affected by that issue.
- How do these perspectives alter your interpretation of the "objective" facts?
- Identify new strategic possibilities given your expanded understanding.

Perceiving The Possibilities

Mapping the Systems

- Construct a map with your job or organization as the starting focal point.
- The first layer is any person or organization with whom you have direct contact. For your job, it would be other jobs in the organization that directly influence the performance of your work or vice versa. For the organization, it would typically be suppliers, distributors, customers, and competitors. It helps to be specific rather than generic, identifying organizations by name or using some relevant form of segmentation to establish groups.
- The next layer has indirect contact with your job or your organization by having direct contact with one of the organizations identified in the first layer.
- Keep adding layers in the same manner until you run out of steam or you have identified layers that seem too remotely connected.
- In this technique, it is better to have too much than too little as it forms a base for the other techniques used by sages. Remember this is the expansive technique to map the whole terrain. The other techniques create focus.
- Determine if this mapping reveals any new insights about your job or organization.

Pattern Recognition

This is a somewhat intuitive process. You need to ask yourself challenging questions that are thought provoking and of importance to your organization. Do not worry so much about finding the correct answer; rather be willing to engage in an answering process. You will then find out the value of the information and knowledge you currently possess.

Scenario Planning

Use the phases described in the section to develop relevant scenarios depicting the environment faced by your organization.

- Choose a significant question or decision
- Identify key aspects of the environment that influence the question or decision
- Identify different states (or possibilities) and causal factors for these states for each key aspect
- Create distinctive scenarios based upon interesting and relevant combinations of states and causal factors

Gaining Competitive Advantage

System Dynamics

- Describe your job as an object. Do this by taking the perspective of a person who might observe you while you work.
- Describe your job as a system.
  - Think of the other systems connected to you—the way you influence them and the way they influence you.
  - Think about inputs you receive, the transforming process of your job—what you do to those inputs to add value and the outputs you must deliver.
  - Think about what those outputs help others do (including the customers of your whole organization).
- Contrast these thoughts with the impact on performance of people and the organization if you and others were to take an object mind-set for your jobs.
- Generate ideas for competitive advantage from taking the systems dynamics perspective.

Paradigm Shifting

Use this application for paradigms you have about everyday things, your own capabilities, management styles, or your organization.

- List your beliefs. This is simple to do by shifting statements from an absolute description to "I believe that _____."
- Depict the way you would view the world, think about things, and act as a result of each of those beliefs.
- Write a contrasting belief. You may find that you can slightly alter your belief to get a different paradigm, or you may want to write the polar opposite of your belief. In doing this process, try to avoid your judgments about which belief is superior; it will inhibit your ability to see things differently.
- Depict the way you view the world, think about things, and act as a result of each of those *new* beliefs.
- For organization paradigms or beliefs, think about the strategic possibilities of changing existing industry paradigms for your organization's competitive advantage.

Critical Success Factors

- Identify the different types of current critical success factors (as defined in the section).
- Identify new critical success factors that will emerge as the industry evolves and those you can create to gain competitive advantage.

Principal Focus of Managing Effort	Principal Leadership Process		
	Creating Order	Inspiring Action	Improving Performance
Systems	**Sage** Designs Strategy	**Visionary** Innovates the Future	**Magician** Orchestrates Change
People	**Globalist** Bridges Cultural Differences	**Mentor** Motivates Development	**Ally** Builds Partnerships
Work	**Sovereign** Empowers Decisions	**Guide** Achieves Goals	**Artisan** Pursues Excellence

FOUNDATION OF ALL ROLES
CORE VALUES

CHAPTER FOUR

Innovating the Future
Learning the Role of the Visionary

Profile of a Visionary

A *visionary* innovates a different future by pushing the capability limits of large groups of people and inspiring them to go beyond what they had previously accomplished. The role is akin to that of the person who looks at a desert, sees the possibility of a thriving community, and creates the means to bring that reality into existence.

In the dream side of the role, visionaries enjoy speculating and fantasizing about the future. They possess imagination to see completely new possibilities where others only see steady progression or worse, decline. A visionary is unbounded by the restraints of the past or what seems possible given the current state of things. However, this is not a role of fighting windmills; this Don Quixote can actually make the seemingly impossible dream become a reality. To a visionary, the dream future is clear and precise, and he or she knows why it is worthwhile. That future already exists in the visionary's mind.

The leadership strength of a visionary lies in having others share the excitement of pursuing that achievement and by clearly communicating the methods to accomplish the goal. Yet in this role, the focus of managing effort is not on people; rather it is movement toward the vision, the new future that occupies the attention of the visionary. People who are part of that future in its creation and in its benefits must work with the visionary to realize it.

Most importantly, a visionary has passion for that new future. This leads to the qualities of commitment and determination to face any challenges or impediments to making the vision a living reality. Commitment is a heart-felt belief that the path chosen is the right one, keeping on that path even when the actions or behaviors of others within the organization contradict the path, the core values, or the vision. Determination is the will to persevere, to resist any diversions that may make some short-run actions look attractive. People continually build capability to sustain commitment and determination as they work toward a vision.

Becoming a visionary is a fairly overwhelming aspiration. We do not mind setting goals and trying to achieve them, but the visionary approach raises this process to a level that evokes modesty and feelings of inadequacy. Vision is in the same terrain as dreams— dreams of the kind of life we want to live or the things we want to create. When we connect vision to dreams, we often relegate it to fantasy or useless daydreams; we talk about cold reality and being practical. We wind up with little expectation of dreams becoming real; they fade into the background, and we devote our attention to dealing with the problems and realities of the day.

Vision has more force in it. It occurs when we bring substance and detail to our dreams. The solidity of this dream creates direction and motivation to move toward reaching it. The "practical" vision comes from an inquiry, a question about the future rather than a question regarding a modification of the present.

I am always captivated by a quotation associated with Robert F. Kennedy, although he was quoting George Bernard Shaw: "You see things and you say, 'Why?' But I dream things that never were and I say, 'Why not?'"

In a simple form, that quotation encapsulates a major aspect of creating vision. "Dreaming things that never were" is the art of fully picturing a concrete possibility, experiencing its reality before it exists. It is not about idealizing or fantasizing. It stretches limits, boundaries, capabilities, and beliefs to get there, but it is possible to arrive. The question "Why not?" evokes, but does not guarantee, thinking about the initiatives or missions that must be tackled to get to the vision.

Wells' Field Guide—How to Spot a Visionary

Habitat

The visionary can be found gazing into the distance. Dwelling will be inundated with crystal balls and telescopes. Usually can be seen on the border between the real and the ideal.

Habits

Speculates and fantasizes about the future.

Pursues the seemingly impossible.

Clearly articulates a worthwhile future that capitalizes on the unique potential of the organization in its markets and community.

Chooses a future by attending to the needs and/or participation of all relevant stakeholders.

Generates enthusiasm and commitment in others to bring that new reality into existence.

Identifies specific missions—main areas of responsibility—that will move the organization toward its vision.

Identifies a purpose that describes why the vision is worthwhile and guides work on the missions.

Works with teams to create relevant visions, missions, and purposes consistent with those of other teams and of the overall organization.

Institutes actions in the present that are consistent with the desired future.

How the Visionary Helps the Organization

This role reflects the combination of the leadership process of inspiring action and the systems focus of managing effort. What does it mean to inspire action at the systems level? Inspiration always comes through actively reaching for something worthwhile.

For a system, this means everyone heading in the same direction toward a major accomplishment. To be truly inspiring and worth achieving, it needs to be a vision that *innovates the future.*

Visionary is probably the role most frequently associated with a leader who has charisma. That person inspires others to join in the venture of reaching a vision. They sense the vision has the full commitment of the leader and is a clear expression of the leader's values. In the business world, it is easy to see the strength of vision in galvanizing action in others. Business ventures are often means of achieving a vision larger than the business itself. Mary Kay's vision is one of women achieving success and independence; selling cosmetics was a way to do this. Steven Jobs has a vision of a world integrated through decentralized access to communication and information; the personal computer was a way to do this. Anita Roddick has a vision of self-help for less industrialized countries; a chain of retail stores selling products from these places throughout the industrialized world was a way to do this.

For many employees, everyday business challenges may have pushed the original vision aside in these ventures. Their customers may not share the visions, or even if they do, other factors may motivate their purchases. These businesses have high-quality products. The founders have become wealthy in the process. All these facts may make us cynical as observers, but they do not contradict the power of the vision. We cannot know in these cases if starting from a vision of personal wealth or a vision bounded by usual business ideas would have caused these businesses to reach the same rates of success. The original visions are quite challenging to achieve, but broad, long-term visions that are challenging to achieve may provide the highest level of motivation.

A visionary chooses and moves toward a desired future by creating and implementing powerful and inspiring vision, purpose, and missions:

- *Vision* depicts *what* the future will look like
- *Missions* are the major initiatives describing how the vision will be reached
- *Purpose* identifies *why* that future is worthwhile

In a *vision*, we describe the desired future in explicit, dynamic terms. We know what we are trying to create or bring into reality.

We can see the form, state, or condition and the interactions among people and things. Visions should have sufficient clarity so that it is possible to imagine living in that future. It is necessary to see how that future helps each person and the organization live according to core values.

Missions are the means by which individuals, teams, or organizations are able to stay on track toward a vision. Missions are specific major initiatives or types of activity that will clearly lead to the realization of the vision. They surround the whole thought process at the work level—the specific ways in which activities are organized to carry out different missions. Missions also have a personal side: When we say people have a sense of mission, we mean that they have a compelling inner drive that elevates their energy as they carry out the specific initiatives or types of activities.

Purpose is a crucial link between core values and vision. It defines why the vision is important and provides ongoing guidance to the different missions that achieve the vision. A clear purpose helps avoid the trap of believing the ends justify the means—that is, if the vision is worthwhile, then any action or behavior within any mission must be worthwhile. This kind of thinking often justifies some fairly damaging actions. Purpose can help make part of the vision a living reality even as work is being done to achieve that vision.

Realization of a desired future is dependent upon committed participation by all stakeholders. Involving people in articulation of the desired future is one method to gain that commitment. If the vision already exists, then the task for the manager is to generate enthusiasm for it. The manager may then try to generate appreciation of the vision's value and establish clear realms of responsibility to move the whole organization in the desired direction.

In this role, a manager looks at the big picture and asks, What future is worth pursuing? At its best, what can this organization create? How can we make real what seems impossible? On the other hand, managers in the sage role base strategies for the future on knowledge of the past and present. They work in the realm of alternative possible options, knowing how different forces influence events and other participants in their industry. They have creative leaps in their thinking when they coalesce multiple pieces of data and information into a smaller, concise set of conclusions.

It is possible for a visionary to use in-depth knowledge in identifying a desired future, but he or she is even more likely to make a major intuitive leap to a future that may not seem possible. Visionaries break out of modes of thinking that trap everyone else, including sages. They do not justify the vision of the desired future by a logical connection to facts because they do not find it necessary to rationalize the future; they feel that if the seemingly impossible vision is truly worth reaching, people will devote effort to make it happen. A good vision is never a general "feel-good" statement about the future; it always evokes a very clear sense of what the future will be even if the road to it seems nearly impossible or filled with hazard and struggle.

As with the sage, the qualities of this role seem more appropriate for upper levels of management. It is quite common, however, to have managers of various parts of the organization set visions that are in line with the vision of the entire organization. Even if this is not the case, it is imperative for such managers to be champions of the organization's vision. Vision statements are always very brief but have a broad perspective; thus the vision statement of an unfamiliar organization may appear too general. The visionary's special qualities are necessary to draw the inspiration to action from a statement that may appear unfocused to outsiders.

Some Examples of Vision in Organizations

We realize the challenge of communicating future direction when we read the value, vision, mission, or purpose statements of unfamiliar organizations. Often they seem to be rather general, overly optimistic, or too obvious. However, if the statements are useful within the organization, it is possible that the words serve as symbols to the employees. Carefully designed processes within the organization may give them a shared picture of the company's direction, which we on the outside do not perceive. Therefore, it is always important for an organization to decide if its statements are meant for internal or external use.

Nevertheless, as you read through the statements of various organizations in annual reports, advertising slogans, or company documents, you can get a sense of the impact of the statement within the organization by thinking about the following:

- Images you get from the statements
- Possible meaning for core value statements
- The core values embedded within vision, mission, or purpose statements
- Other ways to describe the future indicated by the statements
- The guidance the statements seem to give to the organization as it works to achieve its desired future
- The likely expectations or motivation of employees
- The likely expectations of employees

Here is an example of a typical statement: "We will sustain global leadership in the distribution of information by providing technology and accessibility that advances the flexibility, possibilities, and success of our customers."

This statement is similar to many statements that appear in internal company documents. It clearly includes mission and vision regardless of a company's label for it. The mission is the main work of the company: "*distribution of information.*" The vision describes what that work will create for its customers: "*providing technology and accessibility that advances the flexibility, possibilities, and success of our customers.*" There is even an element of purpose in it: "*sustain global leadership.*"

The statement may be interesting to those outside the company, but the real value is within. Each word must be significant to the way people think about their business, and there probably should be further statements that explain the meaning of them. For example, there would be clear reasons for the choice of *distribution of information* rather than *telecommunications,* or *advances* rather than *supports.*

Visions in organizations need to push the envelope of possibilities. They should have a broad, almost unattainable feel to them. There must be sufficient clarity so that people can imagine the future, but it does not need to be a measurable goal. Microsoft's often quoted vision of "a computer on every desk and in every home" and Apple's old vision of "changing the world one person at a time" have that sense to them. These companies could not be successful, however, without following these visions with very specific and more traditional organizational goals. Using goals allows the imagination to soar in the statement of vision.

How a Visionary Is Value-Driven

It is impossible to maintain commitment and determination to the vision without a strong foundation in core values. I would go further and say that no one can conceive a truly inspiring vision without a strong foundation in core values.

To innovate a future (not just a product) that inspires action in others, the visionary must truly care about the future. A major component of that level of passion is that we are able to live more closely in tune with core values in contrast to just talking about them. An inspiring vision creates that possibility for the visionary and others. This is why we continually hear about shared values and shared vision. You will never activate your own energy, let alone the enthusiasm of others, if the direction you are pursuing is in opposition to core values.

Meaningful visions, missions, and purposes always reflect core values. At any moment, there are many paths for an individual or an organization to follow—the world presents many opportunities and therefore many attractive futures. It can be seductive, quite easy to form a vision that is exciting but unrelated to core values.

When we pursue a vision or follow a path disconnected from values, we often find ourselves losing energy in a project because we realize that the result will not have us living by values. If the vision is exciting, we may have passion for it, but without the presence of values it will be very difficult to maintain the commitment and determination to bring it into reality. Sometimes we do not notice the impact until we finally achieve the ends we thought were important. Then the victory becomes hollow or meaningless. Often we rationalize that the ends justify the means, but such a concept really is a deterrent to successful vision work. It means accepting any path, even one that contradicts the values, as long as the ultimate end—the vision—seems worthwhile or exciting. But this approach is deceptive: If the vision is participation, operating autocratically to speed the process to get there will not work. If the vision is a learning organization, commanding people to change and learn will not work. If the vision is collaboration, putting people on teams will not be enough.

Warning Signs of Excess

You know you have overdone the visionary role if you

Discount new information that conflicts with your vision

Ignore pressing needs of the present, especially those that seem to delay movement toward the vision

Become impatient with the transition to the vision and force early closure

Expect a shared vision to resolve all conflicts

Do not tolerate development needs that delay the vision

Only consider decision alternatives that clearly support the vision

Would prefer to contemplate the future rather than act in the present

---

It happens so often that we continue to use the old means, the ones we know, the ones with which we are comfortable, the ones we can do automatically, to achieve a vision that contains new ways of behaving. Thus we never really get to that new state. The vision cannot remain purely in the future, or else tomorrow never comes.

The problem of the path not reflecting core values is particularly noticeable when the vision has some very significant statement about relationships among people, new leadership styles, quality of work life, or opportunities for personal challenge. Behavior that is inconsistent with that vision, meaning that it is probably inconsistent with the values as well, causes a rapid deterioration of people's faith. They become quite skeptical of visions and experience them as just good-sounding ideas with no real substance. The challenge for any manager is that most people have had this experience at some time. Even if we believe in a vision, we are reluctant to become too hopeful. We must all learn to overcome the inertia produced by our own cynicism. We must also learn to recognize that the path toward visions containing radical shifts in behavior will always have situations in which some people are operating from old patterns of behavior as they learn.

Building Visionary Skills

The three major visionary skills developed in this chapter are the following:

- *Seeing the Future*—different approaches to gaining a clear sense of desirable future states
- *Creating a Vision*—translating a desire for the future into a concrete vision (with some thought about purpose and mission)
- *Sustaining Commitment and Determination*—how to keep yourself and others pursuing the vision

Seeing the Future

We can understand vision on a quite simple, human level. Many people, when going on a vacation, think about—have a vision for—the vacation and plan accordingly. They may picture different types of vacations and match them with what is important to them—in other words, they have a value that they are trying to realize and experience through the vacation. For example, the vacation could reflect values of pure relaxation, bringing the family closer together, learning or further developing some skill, facing a physical challenge, or some combination of those. Values help to determine the form and choice of vision and then provide some direction for the activity. Obviously, an unplanned vacation can have enjoyment and benefit without the need for vision; spontaneity certainly has its place. Vision, however, is helpful when there is definite need to make a thoughtful choice ahead of time.

Athletes will often use a technique of visualizing a race or game to mentally attune and prepare themselves for competition. This visualizing process is anticipation of the experience itself; it is not a vision of some new reality desired from the experience. It is, however, a powerful process that builds capability for seeing things in the future and creating more significant, complex, and longer-term visions. Its aim is to develop mental clarity about a future event with an ability to anticipate different complexities and variations in the experience of that future. Visualizing physical activities is useful practice for that capability.

The visualizing process is an attempt to experience the process of reaching some desired end state. In more complex visions, we must also be capable of seeing specific qualities of the desired end state. When these two capabilities are strong, the ultimate creation can conform quite well to the original conception. There are times, however, when an artist will prefer to experiment and see what emerges rather than follow a vision. This approach is not different from that of the vacationer. We often prefer to embark on journeys or adventures in our lives because we have an emotional or intuitive sense that it is right. We will learn in the process and create what we can from that learning. We may not want to have a detailed vision.

Visions of future states in organizations need to include the people who will build and live in that future state as well as the desired relationships among them. There are also times when it is necessary to embark on new terrain in an organization. At such times, it may be necessary to operate without a complete vision for some time. Experience gained during that period will eventually lead to specific direction from a complete vision. Also at such times, it is necessary to have some clarity, or vision, about the relationships among people. This may prevent the possibility of their surroundings damaging their ability to work together until they have a detailed vision.

So far, these approaches to seeing the future may seem tame to you. But a good visionary needs to cross into unchartered terrain. Following are several ways people are able to imagine the future:

Wild dreams, unbridled speculations, and unbelievable possibilities for the future. This is a playful, brainstorming approach to seeing the future. It will give you the broadest possible view of the future and push you well to the right of the line of possibility. The idea is to ask questions, without judgment or criticism, to make the ideas more vibrant. You are not trying to be practical, only imaginative.

Hopes for the future that make it substantially different from the present. This is an approach to seeing the future you would really like to have. Frequently, people base their hopes on desires to have core values more evident in themselves and others.

Prophesies for the future. This is a more "serious" approach to seeing the future by using knowledge of economics, technology, cultures, sociology, and politics on regional, national, and global bases to think about where the future may be going.

Possible futures for your industry. This is the most specific approach for seeing the future. It is necessary to find the right definition for your industry. Narrow definitions will restrict thinking, whereas broad definitions will expand your thinking but may lose relevancy to your organization.

In seeing the future, you do want to avoid being what comedian Steven Wright calls a "peripheral visionary"—seeing into the future but way off to the side.

Creating a Vision

When you assume the role of the visionary to create vision for your organization, consider the following questions to keep the vision relevant to your business:

- What vision would our customers like us to have?
- What vision would our surrounding communities like us to have?
- What vision would our employees like us to have?
- What vision would our competitors fear?

People who create organizational vision, mission, or purpose statements know the process is energizing, thoughtful, and sometimes quite time consuming. Great weight is put on the words; small nuances in them can make a large difference because the words are being used almost as poetic images to create a wider range of thought and emotion than can be simply contained in dictionary definitions. Often this work results in a very brief statement or a symbol meant to evoke a rich tapestry of meaning. In using the statement or symbol with people outside the company, such as customers, the company is hoping they too will experience this imagery.

It is extremely important to make a fundamental decision when you create value, vision, mission, or purpose statements. You must choose between brief, broad, symbolic statements and specific, nearly quantifiable statements. Symbolic statements or images require more discussion within the organization to reach the same depth of interpretation among all employees. Without this process, broad statements do not have motivational appeal and may create a feeling of lack of direction.

Statements as simple as "beat the competition" are quite clear and quantifiable, and such simple slogans can be quite motivational: Everyone knows what the future should be. But these kinds of statements are more goals than visions. Once the competition has been beaten, core values are necessary to create a truly healthy organization that can reach the next goal or vision. Core values prevent people from falling in the trap of justifying any decisions or behavior as part of the "beat the competition" process.

Visionary management moves all individuals, teams, and work groups in the same direction; there must be alignment throughout the organization. However, sometimes the vision for the whole organization may be motivational but too broad to provide sufficient direction for specific systems within it. Managers of these subsystems must be sure that their efforts support and advance achievement of the organization-wide vision.

There is one typical major obstacle to alignment: Frequently, there may be a small team of people from the top levels of the organization who create the organization's values, vision, mission, and purpose. Dissemination to the rest of the organization occurs through mechanisms such as meetings, printed communications, specific guiding statements, new mottoes or slogans, and new symbols or corporate logos. The process of creating a new direction is usually a highly energizing process for the participants. But it is quite different to be on the receiving end of the communication of a completed direction and experience the same level of energy toward it.

There are obviously many ways to create values, vision, mission, and purpose in an organization. It may be the work of a small group of top managers or a group representing different parts of the organization. There may be widespread participation with a pattern of alternating between work by many groups of individuals and a single representative group that integrates the work and suggests the next step. Sometimes different work groups meet to establish their own specific values, vision, mission, and purpose in alignment with that of the organization. In those instances, it is best to include everyone in the work group. Organizations that are small enough in size (a few hundred people) can involve everyone with a well-designed process.

It is also best to design this work for the specific needs of a given organization. Seeing the future is a necessary first step to choosing a vision that you will pursue. The vision itself can comprise symbols, pictures, or other visual imagery in addition to words as a means to increase your flow of thoughts and the significance of this work to you. The aim in visionary work is to capture in a few succinct words or an image a multitude of complex thoughts for the future direction. Long statements or too many statements will never provide enough guidance. You may find after working through vision, purpose, and mission statements that you want to combine your ideas into a few larger statements.

Visions are a leap of imagination. You can think about the future in the manner suggested in the last few ideas in the previous section on "seeing the future." Those were only ideas for thinking about the future; they were not complete means of creating a vision. A vision must have some direct relationship to your organization; it is the way you want to respond to a possible future. A vision should reflect an aspiration related to your organization's current capability and the potential you see within it. Visions need to be specific and clear enough so that people can imagine themselves within it and can see real possibilities for efforts to attain it.

No matter how inspiring a vision may seem, it is still only a description of what the desired future is. It may be motivating but it will not provide sufficient guidance for the work needed to achieve it. *Purpose* is the reason why that future is valuable. If we think about the purpose as we work, we stand a much better chance of having our actions reflect our desire for the future. Keeping the purpose alive helps you make choices that will give people the experience of some of the vision's impacts in the present. People need guidance for more immediate work activities so they stay on the path to the vision. A purpose fulfills this need.

Purpose will provide guidance to the missions—the major initiatives or types of activities that you will need to achieve that vision. It is important to determine how well the current structure (functions, work groups, and job assignments) fits those initiatives and whether new structures are necessary. It is also important to have some useful detail on specific activities needed within these missions. At this point, you can see that all the fantasy, playfulness, and passion used to create a vision must be grounded in the reality of bringing the vision into being. A visionary is not an idle dreamer but a powerful force in making dreams real and facing the hard work that entails.

Sustaining Commitment and Determination

Creating a vision will evoke different thoughts, feelings, and energy. These reveal the level of commitment to a vision, your determination to make that future real, and the effort you are truly able to expend. One way to test the degree of commitment is to think about your determination to work for a vision that may be fully realized only after your own tenure with the organization.

Any vision worth pursuing will involve major changes. People will usually generate commitment and determination in proportion to how they will benefit from attainment of that vision. Few people, however, will be willing to undergo a change for a vision that is always in the future.

Any worthwhile vision is a serious departure from the present. To inspire and sustain commitment and determination may require time and an atmosphere where people feel free to express their concerns. Your task is to acknowledge the concerns at the same time you express the excitement that the future holds. Recognize that in the process of involving others, if your only concern is getting buy-in without considering employees' concerns, you may fail. You would be better off only talking about the meaning of the vision and your expectations for it. In some cases, this may be enough. In others, you may get understanding but not commitment and determination.

The organization's work or structure will be changed by the values, vision, mission, and purpose. People will probably need new capabilities or new job responsibilities for the vision to succeed. It is important to determine what is at stake from the perspective of different individuals or groups affected by the changes needed for this vision. People need to have faith that what they believe is at stake will be handled in a fair manner. They need to have hope for benefits that they can derive from their contribution to realizing the vision. A visionary role manager will think about how to help different stakeholders have that faith and hope, and will inspire their commitment and determination—in particular, by paying attention to opportunities that may not be apparent to individuals.

Developing Personal Visions

I believe that an organization with people who actively think about their own visions will be a more vibrant and productive workplace. Personal visions lead to commitment and determination. It is, however, a risky process to pursue in your managerial role. People value ideas about methods to be used to discover their own vision. They will resent ideas that tell them what that vision should be. Therefore, it is a somewhat delicate process that could anger people if mishandled. It is also possible that people (including yourself) will discover that work in the organization does not satisfy personal visions.

Sometimes it does happen that people see their own direction connected to the direction of the organization. If so, there is a powerful alignment. Often the very fact that an organization supports this personal insight for each employee demonstrates a different level of commitment that creates that alignment. In an organization permeated with control and compliance, personal insight is disruptive because people with it can be poor or very resentful followers.

The guidance for personal vision is the traditional set of questions actors use to fully understand the parts they play. You may find that the questions themselves are sufficient for your personal work on vision. They are certainly the major questions of life. My suggestion is to use these questions in any way that suits your needs.

- *Where Do I Come From?* This is the question for core values. It also addresses your heritage and life experiences as well as your perspectives or beliefs about how things are or should be.

- *Where Am I Going?* This is the vision or destiny question. It is about what you are trying to become or create, the kind of future you are trying to shape for yourself and others.

- *Who Am I?* This is the mission question. It addresses your uniqueness. It is about the behavioral patterns, personal qualities, capabilities, strengths, weaknesses, and continuing development needs that you bring to any situation. These can be seen in the "sense of mission" you bring to your work.

- *Why Am I Here?* This is the purpose question. It is the primary guidance for any activity. Sometimes people label it a calling. It is often the common element that make different experiences worthwhile. Maybe you can see it in your strongest managerial role. For example, mentors may have a purpose of teaching others regardless of their work assignment.

Learning Visionary Role Skills

Dreaming Things That Never Were

- Identify things as they are in your work life and personal life and ask, Why?
- Dream of things as they never were in your work life and personal life and ask, Why not?
- Contrast the responses to both questions.
- Whatever you see as vision for yourself, think about what you must do to make it real.

Seeing the Future

Here are three simple approaches to try:

- Get a feeling for how your own values influence your visions by thinking about something in the future such as a vacation or free weekend, and see how different values you hold influence your vision.
- Use the visualizing process with some simple examples meaningful to you, such as
  - A craft or art where you build or create something
  - A project around your home
  - A sport in which you will participate
  - An upcoming meeting or task at work

  Test the value of visualizing by seeing how it helped you or provided additional capability for you in the physical activity.
- Using examples from your business or personal life, contrast situations in which a concrete vision was useful with situations in which spontaneity and flexibility were useful. See if you can see patterns where specific visions are useful and where broad, hazier visions are useful. Test these ideas with some future situation to determine if you will benefit from a specific or broad vision.
- Try one of the more challenging methods for seeing the future
  - Wild dreams
  - Hopes

- Prophesies
- Your industry's future

Creating a Vision

- Use some of your images of the future from the previous practice, and then choose a vision for your organization within that. In choosing a vision, you can use the questions that began the section on this skill.
- Work with the vision until you can state it in as few words as possible. The vision should feel like a major aspiration, have sufficient breadth so it feels almost unattainable, and have sufficient clarity so you would be willing to pursue it.

Sustaining Commitment and Determination

- Look at current work processes to determine if there is a clear connection to the core values, vision, mission, and purpose. Find out what connection other people see.
- Specify the issues that deflect people from the vision's direction as they do their work.
- Consider what processes are in place or need to be in place to get people back on track.
- Look at the positive and negative aspects of the following:

  Work relationships among people on a team and across functions in relation to the vision's direction.

  The extent to which individuals feel that their capabilities are necessary for the vision's direction.

  The opportunities this direction seems to offer for development and career advancement.

  The extent to which people see their achievements effectively connected to the direction.

- Consider how frequently people discuss core values, vision, mission, and purpose.
- Determine what you need to sustain a high level of commitment and determination—altering the vision, getting current actions in line with the vision, or revisiting people's faith and hope in the vision's value.

Principal Focus of Managing Effort	Principal Leadership Process		
	Creating Order	Inspiring Action	Improving Performance
Systems	**Sage** Designs Strategy	**Visionary** Innovates the Future	**Magician** Orchestrates Change
People	**Globalist** Bridges Cultural Differences	**Mentor** Motivates Development	**Ally** Builds Partnerships
Work	**Sovereign** Empowers Decisions	**Guide** Achieves Goals	**Artisan** Pursues Excellence

FOUNDATION OF ALL ROLES
CORE VALUES

CHAPTER FIVE

Orchestrating Change
Learning the Role of the Magician

Profile of a Magician

I chose the role name *magician* to symbolize the ability to make change occur in a seemingly effortless manner. Magicians have a fundamental belief that change is for the better—especially when it is deliberately chosen. The lifeless wand becomes a dove; lead is turned into gold. Magicians focus on change that is necessary, real, and proactive rather than change for the sake of change.

Turbulence always exists in the transition from the existing state to the desired state. If the trapeze artist is not willing to hang in space momentarily, there is no way to leave one swing for another. The old conditions are left before the new conditions are completely in place. When a caterpillar undergoes metamorphosis to become a butterfly, it is not slowly gaining butterfly characteristics and shedding caterpillar characteristics. If you open the cocoon, you will find an amorphous mass—not a caterpillar, not a butterfly, and not some combination of the two. So it is with change in the organization: The old state must be gone while the new state is not yet fully formed. Fear and anxiety over these disruptions often lead to a premature clinging to order or an outright resistance to change. Calmness in the face of this turbulence enables the magician to face the tensions caused by change.

Wells' Field Guide—How to Spot a Magician

Habitat

The magician can be found in surprising places that are always in motion. Dwelling will keep changing appearances and never remains stationary. Usually can be seen over there in the next place.

Habits

Transforms systems from one state to another.

Sustains momentum in the turbulence of the transition from the current state to the desired state.

Leaps the gap between where the organization is and where it needs to be by bringing about necessary, useful, and consistent shifts in people, processes, products, and systems.

Implements each phase of the change effort at a rate corresponding to the capability of people and the organization to bring about the change.

Understands and manages the causes of resistance to change and fear of change while acknowledging the reality of change in organization life.

Orchestrates the relationships among things that must be changed, things that accelerate change, and things that inhibit change.

Differentiates between necessary and unnecessary change, real and cosmetic change, and proactive and reactive change.

Sustains calmness, patience, focus, excitement, acceptance of risk, and tolerance of failure in any change.

Magicians pay simultaneous attention to a multitude of different but related things. With apparent effortlessness, magicians keep several things in motion at the same time for the trick to work. They do not complete one activity before moving on to the next. Similarly this magician quality in the organization is a juggling of changing processes, systems, and structures—dynamic balancing. Each element is changing at its appropriate rate but is coordinated with the other changes.

The manager has many components in motion because they are no longer in their initial state but have not yet reached the changed state. This is the turbulence that so many people find hard to endure. No matter how bad the present is, it is at least familiar. Many people resist taking the plunge into change because they fear the unknown. Even people who are quite amenable to change will resist change imposed upon them by others. But a person who possesses the magician's quality of simultaneous attention thrives in the turbulent condition of change. It is not the excitement of the change that motivates this manager as much as the belief that improved performance is possible. This optimism is driven by the willingness to live through the sacrifice of the present state, the turbulence in the transition, and the uncertainty of achieving the desired state. Unlike people who may prefer the comfort of the status quo, magician role strength means comfort in change.

How the Magician Helps the Organization

This role reflects the combination of the leadership process of improving performance and the systems focus of managing effort. Continuous improvement, reengineering, total quality management, organizational transformation or renewal, and paradigm shifting are among the many valid approaches to moving a whole system from the status quo to an improved level of performance. At the core of each of these is coordinated systemwide change.

In this role, when a manager *orchestrates change* there is a need to leap the gap between where the organization is and where it needs to be by coordinating shifts throughout the organization. Change at the systems level is all-encompassing as it is usually connected to some major competitive need such as moving into global markets, incorporating new technologies, changing product lines, becoming more efficient, or merging with another organization. Systemwide improvement or change needs to happen at a rate that matches the existing and improving capability of the people and the organization to bring about the change. However, the change must also proceed at the pace dictated by the factors that led to the need for change. Balancing the need for change with the ability to realize the change is one of the major challenges to this role.

The language of systemwide change certainly will lead to the impression that this role should be confined to the top levels of management. Although it is obviously relevant to that level, it is also important for this role to permeate management levels of the organization. Sometimes systemwide change does not involve the whole organization but rather a particular division or group within it. Sometimes change for the whole organization has very uneven impacts with some parts barely experiencing any effects and some parts experiencing a complete overhaul. Managers in any position who bear responsibility for bringing a change to its completion will need to use this role.

The only constant is change. This ancient statement has always been true. We either face entropy or evolution—systems are either deteriorating or improving. Clinging to the status quo is hopeless. Entropy is unmanaged change, allowing things to happen to lower system performance levels as well as undermine individual motivation. It is allowing technological change, market needs, and competitor capability to create an ever-widening gap with the performance of the organization. Evolution is managed change. It is recognizing that change in the organization's environment is inevitable, focusing the efforts of the organization on those changes that keep it in balance with or leading its environment. Magicians orchestrate change in many areas simultaneously so that the organization reaches higher standards of performance.

Organizations often make product changes: product modifications, new products, and deletion of products. Significant systemwide change invariably involves some major reengineering, restructuring, reordering, or redirecting of the roles and responsibilities of people in the organization in addition to product and process changes. In that change, people usually must give up something with which they were comfortable or that they valued in the initial state.

Meanwhile, the surrounding environment is not static; it continues to change and adds to the challenge. As the change effort unfolds, some of the assumptions driving the change may not be valid. The course of the change effort may need alteration.

Change will create disruptions and evoke resistance; obviously, one would try to avoid making a change solely for the sake of having something different. But in a world filled with change, an individual or an organization cannot remain isolated and unaffected; change is inevitable. It is amazing to see energy expended by individuals or organizations trying to maintain the status quo and then rationalizing this effort, even as the world is putting increasing pressure on them to change.

On the other hand, one cannot become caught in the reactive web of constantly mandating change to respond to every shift in the environment or problem encountered. Many organizations go through wave after wave of restructuring and change in a search, often desperate, to find the right way of operating. They will jump on the bandwagon of the latest management fad, try to mimic the success of others by copying what they believe to be the new rules. The effort fails because they did not fully understand what the others did to succeed. This process can be quite disruptive.

Too often the change occurs because of some flash of insight on the part of top management. There are many instances where managers have received some training or idea about new ways of operating and instigate an organization-wide effort to change everybody, but it is an error to try to apply one's own experience to a larger organization. In other circumstances, newly appointed managers at any level try to make their mark by changing things. But when their need for achievement rather than the needs of the organization motivate the change, problems will occur.

All these experiences, many of which fail, lead people to believe that any change effort is really temporary. If they keep their heads low and participate, it will pass, and they will return to business as usual. Magician managers reduce these hazards by choosing the right changes and making those changes permanent. To a magician, there is no going back, no value to return. If you have changed lead into gold, why return to lead? If the wand becomes a dove, why go back to the wand? It is important to be able to identify when change is necessary, to understand the real meaning and significance of the change, and to have the will to manage appropriately the challenges of resistance.

Change is not always a top-down mandate or direction. In fact, it is very frequently the case that someone further down in the organization notices the need for change. Strong resistance to change can come from the top of the organization's hierarchy as well as from its middle or bottom. Managers in the middle of an organization are often confronted with a strong desire to change but a sense of futility and powerlessness because of their position in the organization. They face a choice of trying to convince top management to make the change, of waiting for top management to get some insight and initiate the change, or of beginning to initiate changes on their own.

Choosing the third alternative is to embark on a challenging, sometimes perilous, and often frustrating journey. As a first step, managers identify something over which they have some influence or control, even though lack of change in the environment hampers this change. The environment is operating according to the conditions of the initial state and does not value or understand the new state; thus the pressure of the environment will keep pushing the attempt at change back to the initial state.

Some people are able to sustain this path because they can picture their success and the accolades they will receive. Others sustain momentum by being clear about core values and how those values aid the organization. Without self-awareness, it is possible to get lost in the challenges of change or get caught in debates with others on their resistance. Setting oneself apart from others by losing compassion for their experience of change creates winners and losers but not collaborators.

Once you see the need for change, it is hard to ignore. There are countless reasons why people avoid change, such as the timing is not right, the change is too complex, or they feel they lack the power to succeed. More often, however, the true reason is a lack of magician qualities. Change must be managed, but it cannot be controlled; this frightens many managers. Change will always unleash unexpected forces. It is similar to the story of the sorcerer's apprentice: Once the magic is released, anything can happen. It takes real wisdom to keep the change on course.

The most important unleashed force is the raised expectations of people once they overcome their own resistance. Nobody is going to join willingly in a change effort unless there is a clear benefit to the new state. The more challenging the change and the deeper it cuts into the organization, the higher the expectations. The risk of disappointing these expectations is a powerful deterrent to embarking on a journey of change. Managers at all levels may avoid change because of this fear of failure. Indeed, there is no

Warning Signs of Excess

You know you have overdone the magician role if you

Do not see the need for some degree of order in the change transition

Become more enthralled by the process of change than by the state you are trying to reach

Ignore information that does not directly relate to the change effort

See any expressed concern as unwillingness to change

Believe change should take precedence over other personnel and work needs

Believe all change is for the better

See most cultural traditions as a major impediment to change

View change as so encompassing that you could throw out the baby with the bathwater

Have difficulty staying focused in relatively stable conditions, believing they are too dull and predictable

---

guarantee of success. One aspect, however, resembles magic—carefully planning and setting up the trick precedes its performance. The same situation exists in the organization. Planning does not mean controlling; it is informed anticipation.

How a Magician Is Value-Driven

Core values are crucial to the process of change. Most change leaves the core values intact. The values then provide the foundation from which the magician is able to bring some stability to the turbulence of change. Products, processes, and job responsibilities may be changing, but the organization's core identity remains.

Sometimes a need to revitalize core values dictates the change. Perhaps the pressure of business has caused the organization to drift from its own values and operate in ways that contradict its original desires. The magician may need to orchestrate change in many parts of the organization to ensure that the values are once again providing the desired identity.

There are times, perhaps in a merger, when change cuts deeply and requires a shift in core values. The magician orchestrates the change based upon that shift in core values. If the core value change is the result of merging two organizations with two different cultures, there is work needed by the globalist role, to which we turn in the next chapter.

Building Magician Skills

The three major magician skills developed in this chapter are the following:

- *Knowing When and What To Change*—choosing change when it will improve performance
- *Handling Resistance to Different Phases of Change*—understanding and facing the natural and changing nature of resistance to change
- *Maintaining Balance in Change*—orchestrating the multitude of factors that are in simultaneous motion during a change

Knowing When and What to Change

Change is going to be disruptive whether we are in a transition between an initial state and a desired state or we are in circumstances that cause us to be in some constant state of change. Therefore the questions of when and what to change are critical to success in the magician role. Let's start with some negative responses to these questions:

Don't initiate a change because you just attended a seminar or read a book that captivates your interest. First, test the ideas with others. See the meaningfulness of these ideas for your organization.

Don't initiate a change because it has become a fashionable topic and you are inundated with examples of organizations that failed to change. Take a look at the environmental conditions they faced and then look at your own—changes in technology, customer desires, competitor strategies, government regulation, etc.—and determine if these require a fine-tuning response or a major change.

Don't initiate a change because you are losing market share or face declining profits. Too often the responding change is to cut costs and reduce efforts when in fact you may need to make different investments, alter the organization, and take very different risks.

Don't initiate a change to shake things up or make your mark. Your sense may be quite accurate on the need to inject new energy or improve performance, but too often we assume that the problem is in the people rather than the organization.

When to Change

When should you change? Most of the answers are obvious, but we seem to continually ignore the writing on the wall.

Change when an opportunity exists that you cannot seize with the current mode of operation.

Change when the environment poses a threat that you cannot face with the current mode of operation.

Change when you confront a problem and have become fully knowledgeable about the difference between symptoms and causes.

Change when your existing organization will not allow full implementation of a new strategy or achievement of a new vision.

What to Change

The answer to the question of what to change also becomes obvious:

Don't try to change people. Even worse, don't demand that people change. There is no surer guarantee of failing in the magician role and defeating a change effort than centering it around changes in people. Will people have to change when the organization changes? Inevitably. Any serious change is going to disrupt existing work patterns and alter people's responsibility; that is a fact of life. People may need new skills or development. You cannot properly address this need from the magician role when your attention is on moving the system to a new state.

Let us be realistic. Nowadays many changes also involve substantial reductions in workforce. The fact that there are layoffs associated with change puts even greater stress on the change. You must redefine work processes and responsibilities; you cannot have the same amount of work with fewer people. This is why reengineering has become so popular: It is a change directed toward a very important response to the question of what to change—the key operational processes of the organization, the ones that would greatly enhance the success of the organization if they were better, faster, or more effective. I am sure many organizations are paying lip service to reengineering while they are merely trying to cut costs and shed people. There is no inherent reason for this. Reengineering can increase the level of employment by freeing resources to pursue other activities and expand the business.

To know what to change, you must get at the source, and the source is never people. Whether you lower or raise employment levels, it is a consequence of change, not its essence. If you are not working on the following question, you will not get to the source: *How do we need to operate in order to effectively do those things most critical to creating the value we want to deliver to our customers?* This question will enable you to operate in the magician role and choose what to change. Perhaps other things will change as a consequence of this emphasis, but you must devote attention to the critical items for improving performance.

Making Change Worthwhile

You'll never win if all your change efforts are in response to problems, declining markets, competitive pressure, or cost pressures. The magician role is about the leadership process of improving performance—proactive, planned change; it is not about desperately trying to hold on to a position—reactive, forced change. If most of your change effort is in the latter category, you will expend the capital needed to bring about proactive change. People get worn out by wave after wave of change and cynical about its necessity; I have spoken to too many people whose cynicism and distrust have increased. Their experience of change: They are worse off.

The idea of change from the perspective of the magician role is not to make people better off; it is to improve performance at the system level—get an organization to be more successful. As you need people to make the change work, you must get ahead of the situation and devote effort to proactive, planned change. A change is going to be a challenge; you must choose your battles carefully.

What gives you a strong sense of organizational identity? What does your organization do really well? What do you really want? There is so much current emphasis on cutting back, reducing, and eliminating that we forget there are important things we need to build on. There is turbulence in change, and the magician role is one that demonstrates remarkable proficiency in the face of this turbulence. If you are going to sail into a storm, you better have a strong rudder to give you some semblance of stability in the midst of the turmoil. There is a simple secret to this apparent calmness in the magician role: a strong sense of the organization's identity, clarity about what the organization does well, and an absolute conviction that the destination is worth the journey.

Many change efforts begin with work on organizational core values to gain that strong sense of organizational identity. If core values are already in place, you have a large jump on the change process. If they are not present, you will need to depend upon your own core values to provide that sense of stability. Change is often planned to work only with products and what I call organizational activities—processes, systems, structures, and people's responsibilities. But less observable cultural patterns and core values can be a major restraint if people see them as incompatible with the desired change. Putting more energy toward the activities will not work. Instead, make the cultural patterns and core values explicit, and test for consensus about their meaning; a lack of consensus can easily inhibit change if people experience the change as violating important values. With luck, this situation is managed by gaining consensus on interpretations. Alternatively it may be necessary to modify the change to remain in tune with existing cultural patterns and core values.

Nobody will have much enthusiasm for change if the focus is on correcting things that are wrong. It is very different to highlight the strengths and then use the change effort to build upon them. Therefore make those strengths—the areas where people feel most successful—the center of the changed organization. If you want to eliminate or reduce something, get rid of those components that hamper the full exercise of the strengths.

Increasing your ability to thrive in turbulence does not mean seeking an adrenaline rush but being better able to handle the journey of transition to reach the destination. On a personal level, it is a wonderful idea to think of life as a journey, not a destination. But this doesn't work for an organization: Performance must reach higher standards; that is the destination. It does not matter if this destination implies a somewhat fixed new state or a somewhat fluid state in which there are ongoing adaptations to meet shifting conditions. You must raise the standards high to make the journey worthwhile.

Handling Resistance to Different Phases of Change

From outside an organization, it is often difficult to understand why change is so difficult. For example, in the often cited example of the American automobile industry in the 1970s, people wondered why they did not meet the changing environment and customer demands, why they did not repeat in their own plants the success of team efforts in production plants in other countries, why, in the face of falling profits and market share, change did not come sooner.

There are many answers. For purposes of this chapter, we merely need to understand how deeply embedded we can become in the status quo and ignore the need to change even when all evidence points to its necessity. It is hard enough for a single individual to move from the current comfort zone, the known parameters, into the unknown, where the chance of failure seems so much greater. Multiply that by the number of individuals in an organization, and the result is a strong desire to remain in position, entrenched in the familiar, even though this recalcitrance ultimately carries a higher risk of failure than venturing off into the unknown. When change reaches the level of core values or beliefs about basic operating parameters, it disrupts our thinking patterns. In the automobile example, new product design is not enough until there is a willingness to conform to the new realities about the industry, shift paradigms, and form a new set of beliefs about customers, quality, and product line.

It may seem odd to talk about change creating disruptions and resistance. That is obviously not the intent of change, but inevitably change implies resistance. Each change phase has a different type of resistance. To properly develop magician capability, it is important to examine the elements of a standard change model with the corresponding resistance (see Table 4).

The three-phase change process is a specific metaphor relevant to most changes. Change may be quite complex, but the first two phases (unfreezing from the status quo and moving through a transition) are always present. The third phase of refreezing can be the achievement of some fixed final state or a more fluid state in which things are kept in a constant state of change—an experience of always being in transition and never re-creating complete stability.

Unfreezing

Unfreezing is the process of dissolving bonds with the initial state. It is more than rearranging the furniture, a procedure that is always reversible for very little cost. Unfreezing is more akin to removing the old furniture and giving it away. It feels like the end of an accustomed way of operating; parts of the initial state that are no longer useful for the organization's future are discontinued.

Obviously this phase encounters the most severe resistance because the process of unfreezing means that people will experience *sacrifice* of some kind. People often become comfortable with the status quo, even when they want it to change, because it is known; their "comfort zone" will be dislodged by the change. People may have spent a long time building capabilities or establishing themselves within a particular position or role in the organization; the change will often be experienced as a threat to this

Table 4   Change Model

The three phases in this model with the type of resistance are

Unfreezing	Transition	Refreezing
releasing, unlocking, or disengaging from the current state	the time between states when neither state is on firm ground	structuring, locking, or engaging the desired state
Sacrifice	*Turbulence*	*Uncertainty*

individual's expertise. The manager in the magician role does not experience the processes as sacrifice but as a welcome relief from conditions that are no longer interesting or have any chance of meeting the improved standards of performance.

Transition

The second phase of change is transition. The initial state is no longer useful, and the new state is not quite settled into place. Things are unstable and uncertain. As the initial state is disappearing, elements of the new state begin to appear, and as the transition continues, these elements come into ever sharper focus. As mentioned earlier, there are many aspects of the organization that may remain in a constant state of change, always in transition. The ongoing pressure to improve products, keep costs low, and effectively compete will keep some parts of the organization constantly in flux. Transition is not about reaching a final stable state but a fairly well-managed state of flexibility, adaptability, and responsiveness.

People experience *turbulence* in this phase. To some people, it may feel like being in the cocoon, neither a caterpillar nor a butterfly. It is not a smooth shedding of the old and slow building of the new but rather an immersion into turmoil until the change itself emerges. As resistance increases, there is sometimes a tendency to retreat to the initial state or rush the transition to the new state because of a strong preference for stability and seeming order. But a retreat can never fully return things to the initial state because much has been dislodged by the unfreezing. Thus there is a change, but it is not the desired one. Similarly, rushing the transition often misses the essential elements requiring change, and the organization finds itself with a change that does not meet its expectations.

It is impossible for people to be productive when everything seems to be in a state of turbulence. Some stability is important; it gives people a sense of security and predictability and also helps to focus attention on the items most crucial to a successful change. If the organization is going to remain in a constant state of change, it must have some elements that are stable. Of course, the manager in the magician role does not experience the turbulence but rather the joy of managing many things in a state of change.

Refreezing

Refreezing is the final phase in which the organization is able to settle into a new state, fixed or fluid. The new state may be desirable, but it also creates *uncertainty* because it is a departure from what is known. Resistance in the final phase is interesting because it can block the change from ever starting. Resistance may occur if

- People have not been a part of the creation of the future direction
- People are not clear about the meaning of the future direction
- People are unable to see a valuable role for themselves in the future described by that direction
- People believe that challenges within the desired future are beyond their capabilities and that they will have difficulty duplicating their past successes
- People do not believe that the future direction is enough of a change from the present

Some Ideas for Managing Resistance

The manager with strong magician qualities is experiencing not uncertainty but optimism about the promise of the future. This is not a Pollyanna attitude but rather a willingness to accept the possibility of failure in order to reach a higher standard of performance for the organization.

The manager in the magician role obviously experiences each change phase differently from those who experience resistance. They experience sacrifice; the manager experiences liberation from the status quo. They experience turbulence; the manager experiences the challenge of balancing many elements in transition and in coordination with each other. They experience uncertainty; the manager experiences the promise of the future. What people see as a problem that causes them to resist change, the manager sees as a natural part of the process of change. In the magician role, the manager has patience for the change process but not necessarily patience for resistance to it. Yet success in the change is dependent upon an ability to move people past their resistance into a state of commitment to the change.

If you are strong in the magician role, you may need to develop increased empathy for people's experience of resistance. If you are increasing competency in the magician role, you will be shifting away from your experience of resistance. In either case, it is important to work with some of your past experiences with change, particularly those times when you were swept into someone else's change initiative. If you can view your experience of resistance—why it existed and what did or could enable you to shift from it—you have an improved chance of creating the conditions under which others can make the same shift.

During the unfreezing phase, it is helpful to induce people to turn from the sacrifices of the present to the promise of the future. One approach you can use is increasing dissatisfaction with the status quo by publicizing problems people are having and challenges being created by changes in the environment. Help people to see that the initial state has become increasingly untenable. Show them that escape from the present is an exciting adventure. Clarity about the benefits of the future are important as change often involves short-term sacrifices for long-term gains. It is not uncommon to have a continuing stream of crisis situations indefinitely delaying a change. Appeasing these pressures keeps you locked in the initial state.

People do not want to linger in the transition phase. Its turbulence evokes tension that can create excessive stress and make change a huge burden. Make tension creative by defining problems during this phase in "bitable chunks," and have confidence in solving those problems. This shifts the experience of change during the transition phase: Instead of turbulence between two states, it becomes a journey through a series of tests and challenges. A magician performing on the stage succeeds by drawing people into the experience—otherwise people sit, watch the tricks, acknowledge the cleverness, but ignore or reject the illusion, more interested in analyzing it than enjoying it.

When you reach the refreezing phase or the desired state, the change is not going to be perfect. Not all your hopes for something better will be met; some expectations will be unsatisfied. Refreezing means some sense of stability, some solid ground. Focusing attention on what went wrong or what remains undone throws you back into the transition phase, so do this only if you really believe there is energy for it. It is preferable, however, to generate energy for further challenges of change by gaining consensus on the value of what you did achieve. Assuming people have been reaching for their best efforts, a miss is not a failure; it simply points to an area for further learning. Transferring learning from the successes to the gaps is a fruitful approach. Identify what worked well, acknowledge how that was achieved, and then apply that approach to remaining challenges.

Maintaining Balance in Change

We return at the end of this chapter to the most significant magician quality: sustaining simultaneous attention to multiple activities. This is the heart of the ability to maintain balance in change. Think about all the aspects of a business that would possibly be in a state of change. The focus of the change may be new products, new markets, a change in corporate direction, a merger, a divestiture, a reaction to competitive pressure, or a need to reduce costs. The focus of the change may provide a good rallying point for people, giving them an incentive to try to stay the course through the change, but that is not the same as the capability to orchestrate change.

The orchestration of change provided by the magicians can be seen as a balance among the other leading-edge manager roles. The magician-role manager does not need expertise in all of the other roles but must coordinate essential system, people, and work issues associated with change. Quite frequently, an innovative and compelling strategy for gaining competitive advantage involves significant change in operations in the organization, leading to new products, new markets, or a shift in the basic structure of the organization. Similarly one could say that any vision that inspires action will also involve a departure from the current state. If not, the vision will not generate the energy needed for people to strive to reach their collective potential.

Although the manager in the magician role is addressing the resistance and tension related to change, it is not a role particularly focused on people. It may be necessary to reform or re-create the organization's culture to bring people together in the changed organization. This need is particularly important whenever the change effort includes the increased interaction of different cultures, for example, greater diversity in the workforce, increased international operations, a merger of two organizations, or an internal restructuring such as a shift from a functional structure (divided by marketing, operations, engineering, finance, etc.) to a product group structure (people from different functions, and presumably different minicultures, now working in the same part of the organization).

A truly significant change can have dual impacts on people—it displaces the status quo in which they have established themselves and creates new responsibilities in which they may be unsure of their success. Too many change efforts involve large-scale training sessions or meetings to get everyone on board for the change. But you only get complete commitment, or buy-in, if there is a very practical effort to be sure people have the capability needed for success in the new organization.

Change may require the dissolution of previous teams or work groups and the formation of new ones. Clearly it may lead to new work relationships among people within the organization as well as the possibility of new partnerships or alliances outside the organization. The success of the change and the speed of its completion depend upon the ability to establish productive, collective work.

Regardless of the clarity of the desired state and the plans to achieve it, uncertainty will occur. We can plan for the future and for change, but we cannot control all the circumstances surrounding that change. There may be unanticipated difficulties, or assumptions may prove to be incorrect. Regardless of the cause, it is quite likely that new decision points and unforeseen alternatives will arise as the work continues during the change.

Maybe you can shut your organization during a change and reopen when everything is in place. Most of the time, however, life goes on, business continues, products must be produced, services must be available to customers, so it is imperative to meet current performance goals at the same time processes are being put in place to meet new goals. A change is not worth the effort if it does not lead to higher quality standards, but quality standards will not magically improve once a change is complete. The meaning of change is not waiting for completion but rather improving the competitive viability of the organization. Work quality standards must improve during the change.

Ultimately, to fulfill the focus of change one must face the transition-experience challenge of maintaining balance among changes occurring throughout the organization in various activities: processes, systems, structures, and people's responsibilities. Among all these things in motion, there are several different types of balance needs:

- Balance among things that change at different rates—some change activities can be completed more rapidly than others.

- Balance of interdependencies among different change activities—progress in changing one process, for example, is dependent upon progress made in changing another one.

- Balance among the things that are changed and the capability of people to succeed in that change—an activity can be changed on paper, redesigned, and even have a new investment in equipment and materials, but it can only be activated if people have the necessary skills.

- Balance in attention to activities at the center of change, activities at the periphery to support change, and activities that must remain unchanged.

This is a tall order. You need to be a magician to juggle so much without having something come crashing down. Throughout this chapter, I have given various forms of guidance for increasing your ability in the magician role including things such as reconfirming a commitment to core values, igniting a greater sense of dissatisfaction with the current state, maintaining clarity about the promise of the future, and most importantly, responding to various forms of resistance. Those qualities are relatively easy to improve. Achieving balance is more difficult.

Certainly you face multiple responsibilities—within your job alone but even more so if you include home and family. The normal experience is to see these as competing demands on our time, and we often feel that it is impossible to satisfy the needs imposed on us. This is why so many people feel under stress and overworked. You may be able to draw on some of the magician's capabilities to address this challenge to your personal and professional time, which is often a more difficult challenge than the problem of achieving the balance needed in change.

When time is an issue, there is competition among activities, and you may need to discard some or let performance slide. This is not the case during change. The multiple activities that you are coordinating are not in competition with each other but are integral parts of the whole change pattern. If you were going to completely remodel your home, you might experience the different activities as challenging but integrated; they fit together. You would start with a plan that encompasses all the remodeling activities, but as you progressed, your learning in the change process could cause you to see smaller changes that improve your performance—the refreezing state of the type of home you want. If you decide to alter one activity, you can trace the rippling effects through other activities and make the necessary adjustments. Thus in a change effort you must break from your experience of competing demands on time and see how progress in multiple activities is mutually supportive.

Coordinating the different activities is important to change. However, you cannot coordinate them all simultaneously. Maybe you can walk and chew gum at the same time, but you cannot keep your attention focused on both. A similar allocation of effort exists in the transition: You need to have several things in motion at the same time, focusing attention on one at a time. The important thing in change is that you shift among activities without feeling a need to complete any one activity. It is the completion of change that you need to target. Sequential completion of change activities is unlikely to be the best path to bringing about the total change, so if you want to learn more about balance, you need to work on your compulsion to finish one thing before you do something else. This is a challenge, because seeing things through to completion is normally a desirable trait. It just happens to be one that could interfere with your efforts in the magician role.

Learning Magician Role Skills

Knowing When and What To Change

Use your own experience of change and consider the following:

- Your perception of your environment (within or outside the organization or your immediate sphere of influence)—things you ignored and things that helped you see the need for change
- The main reason for the change—capture an opportunity, meet a threat, satisfy someone else's ideas, etc.
- Focus of change through the use of questions such as,

    If we could only change a few things, what would they be?

    What if we do not do _____? How does that affect the change?

    What if we do _____? How does that affect the change?

    What do we need to do to substantially improve performance?

    How do we need to operate in order to effectively do those things most critical to creating the value we want to deliver to our customers?

- Differences in your thoughts and behavior between those changes during which you quickly accepted movement to the new state and those during which you were more reluctant to change

Handling Resistance to Different Phases of Change

- Choose change experiences where your resistance was highest.
- Describe the specifics of your resistance and connect it to the three phases of change—unfreezing, transition, and refreezing. Identify things you considered important enough to lead to your resistance in these phases.
- Identify people or events that helped you manage your own resistance in each phase.
- Think about change resistance you have observed in others. Connect the resistance to phases of change and try to identify the source of this resistance. Accepting the validity of the reason for resistance, try to determine what could be done to reduce resistance.

Maintaining Balance in Change

Using some of your experiences with change,

- Identify instances where the change seems to have activities competing for time.
- Determine how to relate the activities to each other in the overall change effort.
- Identify instances where you or others are driving efforts to completing changes in a sequential fashion.
- Determine natural breakpoints where you could pause in some activity to reallocate efforts to another activity to further its progress.

Principal Focus of Managing Effort	Principal Leadership Process		
	Creating Order	Inspiring Action	Improving Performance
Systems	**Sage** Designs Strategy	**Visionary** Innovates the Future	**Magician** Orchestrates Change
People	**Globalist** Bridges Cultural Differences	**Mentor** Motivates Development	**Ally** Builds Partnerships
Work	**Sovereign** Empowers Decisions	**Guide** Achieves Goals	**Artisan** Pursues Excellence

FOUNDATION OF ALL ROLES
CORE VALUES

CHAPTER SIX

Bridging Cultural Differences

Learning the Role of the Globalist

Profile of a Globalist

The word *globalist* implies an ease in operating in different cultural environments. Perhaps the most important quality of the globalist is a high value for, appreciation of, and interest in all types of cultural diversity. This goes far beyond simple toleration: The globalist has a genuine desire to benefit from the different ideas and perspectives this diversity brings. Globalists respect the uniqueness of each culture and are attuned to the cultural consequences of doing business on a global basis. They are highly capable in creating cohesion within all forms of diversity. On the other hand, they will be quite willing to make judgments about relevant cultural strengths and weaknesses in different organizational situations.

Language is a good metaphor for the many differences among us, including cultural background. After all, it is sometimes said that Americans and British are two people separated by a common language. The globalist's role is to appreciate individual or cultural "language" and use understanding of differences to create a common ground for everyone within the organization.

According to the Bible, there was a time when all people spoke one language. Globalists were not needed. Because they were able to cooperate so well through a single language, the people organized to build a tower to heaven. For this act, they were dispersed throughout the world and given different languages so they could not understand each other. This is our heritage—we do not understand each other, and we have difficulty working together because of our differences. Sometimes we do not want to try to understand or bridge these differences; sometimes we are brutal to each other because of them. Full appreciation of each other's language seems to evade us.

Berlitz, the founder of the language schools, grew up in a household of many family members and servants who spoke several languages among them. Each person was instructed to speak a different language to the child, so he grew up fluent in eight different languages. He also developed a belief, as he was growing up, that everyone speaks in a personal language.

I recently read an article written by a hearing mother of a deaf, college-age daughter. She feels that unless we learn American Sign Language to converse with the deaf, we will never be able to fully understand the culture of the deaf. Her daughter refers to herself as a "deaf," that is, part of a cultural group of people. People accustomed to auditory communication cannot fully comprehend the experience of the world created by sign language. Simply translating words does not capture different thought processes, reasoning, and interpretation of meaning.

Somehow our human need for self-worth leads us to compare ourselves with other cultures and judge ourselves superior, and our own cultural background leads us to believe that our thinking, values, and actions are the right way. We believe that how we see reality is the way it really is, that the truth is an absolute based upon our own construction of it. We have become unconscious of the basis for our definition of right, reality, and truth, forgetting that we see the world through the filter of a particular cultural perspective. We may find other cultures to be interesting or quaint, but we often do not use globalist insight to see that other cultures can provide a different, and valuable, approach to understanding the world.

Why should all of this matter to a manager? This situation is the history of the world since ancient times. Can a manager change the course of history? Probably not, but this history continues to play itself out within organizations. Many people feel that the subject of diversity will inevitably lead to further splits and problems; people identifying with some group affiliation—race,

Wells' Field Guide—How to Spot a Globalist

Habitat

The globalist can be found wandering from place to place. Dwelling will contain artifacts from many sources. Usually can be seen trying to communicate across barriers erected by differences.

Habits

Has the interest and capability to operate within a wide variety of cultural contexts.

Savors the cacophony of diversity among cultures and different individuals as they work to bring focus to a common ground.

Judges the situational value of cultural and individual diversity without using bias from own background and capabilities.

Seeks to understand the perspective and thinking of others.

Creates a climate of appreciation for differences to move others past their biases and past the simple level of toleration of differences.

Builds and maintains a productive organizational culture.

Uses the strengths of the diversity and individuality of people in the organization.

Enhances the competitive effectiveness of the organization to work with the cultural diversity it faces in its global operations.

Develops a unifying corporate culture to access the strength and manage the conflicts of diversity within the organization.

Manages the cultural dynamics of any merger of organizations.

Addresses the subculture friction that exists among different departments or groups within the organization.

---

gender, religion, ethnicity—will have less commitment to the larger, mixed group. We see nations around the world struggling. Why open the same topic and undermine organizations? This is a tough issue, but do we really want everyone to be the same? Do you not prefer life in the natural forest to one on a managed tree farm?

Ignoring diversity does not suppress its existence. Furthermore, managers have responsibility to alter the dynamics of cultural distrust and create a change in the way people behave with each other. If you are a managing in an American company or if your organization has any global business, then you need to understand something about the globalist role to bridge cultural differences. Globalist managers can help organizations operate on the leading edge by reversing the socialization patterns, lack of awareness of cultural perspective, and inability to appreciate cultural difference that permeate so much of our behavior. With globalist skills, we can traverse this rather delicate and challenging terrain.

A danger in seeing cultural differences is having people fall into stereotyping: Then individuals feel trapped by their group or cultural affiliation. It is absolutely important to recognize the tremendous diversity that exists among individuals regardless of their cultural background.

A globalist will take the risk of bringing cultural diversity into sharp focus because he or she knows that within all of these differences we have common bonds as human beings. Within any particular organizational context, these bonds can help to form an organizational culture that channels the differences in productive ways and avoids the destructive desire for homogeneity, sameness, or conformity. Diversity in the hands of the globalist moves from apparent chaos into a much higher order.

How the Globalist Helps the Organization

This role reflects the combination of the leadership process of creating order and the people focus of managing effort. Culture, a learned phenomenon, is the major source of chaos among people within an organization. To our disadvantage, having a large country with a large market and little need for most people to ever learn a second language protects us from the challenges of culture. To some extent in the United States, we are quite provincial. More of the world using English for business purposes further lulls us into believing that sharing a language implies sharing perspectives. It does not. We do face a multitude of challenges—

operating a business among different international cultures, the cultural backgrounds of employees, the subcultures that form in different parts of the same organization, and the conflicts of culture that often exist in a merger.

Although I have been emphasizing cultural diversity, it is necessary to restate that globalist skills are aimed at *bridging cultural differences*—the creation of a unifying culture that allows expression of differences. The globalist is not an idealist but rather a realist. Individual and cultural differences exist; they will not go away. If you try to suppress or ignore them, you will create resentment and a less productive work environment. On the other hand, if you bring them to the surface and give them too much attention, you will create divisions and a less productive work environment.

Therefore, we need to use this role whenever a clash of cultures has the potential of creating disorder and damaging effective and productive operations. Improving the functioning of the organization may be an important result, but we must remember that in the globalist role, the manager's focus is on people and their cultures with the desired result of creating order by building bridges—maintaining a productive organizational culture that draws on the strength of the cultural backgrounds of the people. It is a common ground that is inclusive and unites people without homogenizing them and losing the value that is contained in diversity.

The work of the globalist takes place whenever people face the possibility of separation by culture:

- The diversity of cultural backgrounds of people within the organization
- The diversity of cultures the organization faces in its environment, especially if it has global operations or national operations in countries with very diverse populations
- The diversity of culture that frequently exists when two organizations merge
- The diversity of culture that can exist among different departments or functions of the organization
- The need to change a culture when it is no longer effective within its environment

The first of these items captures most of our attention when we speak about cultural diversity. Unfortunately, the issue has become politicized, with people taking strong stands and halting meaningful progress. I do not want to ignore the powerful convictions and emotions associated with different viewpoints. But to me, the simple practicality is that a manager must learn to work in the seeming contradiction of understanding diversity and establishing a common ground. It is not enough to respect and celebrate the differences. It is nearly impossible for an organization to function without a culture that pulls people together. The products, the profits, the work are not enough in the long run. People are drawn to organizations that have cultures they respect.

The second bulleted item should be quite obvious to any organization conducting business across national boundaries, whether it has production facilities or is marketing its products in other countries. The issues faced are similar to those in the first point: developing an appreciation for the differences and finding effective means to create bridges so there is a common ground to support the work people are doing.

Because we often relegate the matter of cultural diversity to ethnic, national, religious, or even, gender differences, we miss the important but less obvious problems of the third and fourth items. We do have different cultures because we have different backgrounds, but our backgrounds reflect our human desire to form communities that have some basic rules of operation. We need this predictability so we know how our fellow citizen is likely to behave. We did not need a Tower of Babel to cause our separation; we would have done it on our own. As soon as you have an organization, you will have a culture. Any person who has worked for more than one company or for more than one department in a company, or who has even been a sufficiently aware observer as a customer or visitor to organizations, can easily detect real differences in behavioral patterns. Let's face it—marketing, accounting, financial, production, and engineering people all have different views of the world. The longer they work in their area of expertise, the more they begin to become part of the culture of that expertise. These problems are magnified and the need for this role is intensified when there is a merger between two organizations with very different cultures.

Cultures do not form for arbitrary reasons. They are natural responses to environments as people try to collectively solve the problems they face and work productively toward the ends they desire. It would be unreasonable to expect the culture of people facing different geographic environments to be exactly the same. Life experience varies tremendously from the Arctic to the tropics, from the desert to the forests, from the plains to the islands, etc. We are all humans, we have similarities, but the cultural differences that evolve to confront the environments are dramatic. Climatic environments influence people's attitudes toward nature and their relationship to it and can affect their ideas about time and space as well. Frequently, environment influences religion or spiritual life. Cultures also form values and beliefs about human nature, the role of men and women, and the boundaries and meaning of community.

Organizations face different environments. Do electronics firms face the same conditions as fast food restaurants? Do hospitals face the same conditions as mass media organizations? Although we are all in the same general business climate, on a day-to-day basis we need to respond to very different issues. Over the long run, the nature of competition, rate of technological change, effects of economic conditions, and many other forces in the environment also lead to very different experiences. It would be irrational not to have a culture—a consistent pattern of behavior among people in the organization—that helps address these issues.

We form organizations around a few people who exert tremendous influence over the way the organization evolves. We all have values, and it is quite natural to form organizations to reflect those values. Over time, it is easy for a culture to solidify around its origins. When two organizations merge, we have cultural differences from two sources: the environments and the origins. Many mergers fail because we lack the globalist skills to bridge the differences and create a culture that pulls people together.

It is similar within an organization. If your organization is large enough, think about the different departments and the work atmosphere of different groups. You will probably see quite quickly that you fit more easily into some departments than others. This kind of comfort reflects subcultures within the organization. Things go well when each of these cultures is well attuned to the issues and environments it faces. The globalist challenge occurs when people from these different cultures must collectively solve the same problems or pursue the same results. This is not very complex or mysterious: Finance people have a view of the world, a way of thinking, and a language that differs markedly from marketing people, production people, human resource people, or engineering people. To say that one of these ways is best is ridiculous. Many organizations remain locked in interdepartmental warfare; the language we sometimes use about our co-workers in other departments can be startling. We need globalist skills to rid the organization of this terrible waste of energy.

The fifth bulleted item brings up one of the most important needs for globalist qualities. If cultures emerge to effectively confront environmental conditions, then they must evolve to deal with major shifts in those environments. The agrarian society culture, regardless of how admirable or interesting, is not fully able to address the problems of an industrial world. An industrial society culture must evolve to succeed in the "information age." An organizational culture that has its origins in its founders may no longer be effective if its industry has changed dramatically. In the globalist role, therefore, we have the ability to handle the apparent contradiction of appreciating cultures and making judgments regarding their appropriateness for changing environmental conditions.

A quick note on the mentor and ally role: At this point, it would not be surprising if you were experiencing some difficulty resolving overlaps among the three people roles. The globalist role focuses on the structure of cultures that bind and separate people. It addresses diversity on a broad level. Although culture influences part of our individual makeup and behavior, the mentor is tuned into people on a purely individual basis. The mentor addresses differences by focusing on personal needs for development and motivation. You do not need to know much about cultures in that role; you are not trying to use stereotypes or more universal patterns in order to understand and counsel one person. Only a fool would believe that knowledge about a culture completely predicts the behavior of a particular individual. For example, individual differences in preference patterns for these nine leading-edge roles is not a cultural issue. Therefore, effective leadership development requires the mentor to solely concentrate on individuals. Globalists do not consider development or individual motivation as a key

Warning Signs of Excess

You know you have overdone the globalist role if you

Focus on cultural issues as the chief reason for divisions among people

See people as members of cultures rather than as individuals

Try to explain complex phenomena in terms of culture

Want culture to be the focal point of any vision

Focus on culture and diversity as a main development need for most people

Place greater emphasis on resolving cultural issues than work issues

Believe that experience or background inevitably conveys wisdom or insight equivalent to knowledge-building efforts

Think that multiculturalism means that all beliefs have equal validity for the organization's success

issue in bridging cultures. The mentor is a very personal role; the globalist is more universal. The mentor inspires action, the globalist creates order.

In the ally role, managers improve performance by concentrating upon the effectiveness of collaborative work. Work on culture forms a base for this work, but it should be quite evident that even within a relatively homogeneous culture we are not guaranteed successful teamwork. Clearly issues for the ally, such as trust and conflict resolution, can have origins in culture. We cannot, however, explain all group problems by culture and it would be de-energizing to always reexamine culture as a way of improving teamwork. There are many other barriers to effective teamwork beyond the limits of possible cultural biases. The ally must be knowledgeable about and adept at handling a variety of restraints to building trust and transforming conflict to progress. The ally is working with specific individuals who collectively have a practical business issue or goal. The globalist's concern is on a larger scale—cultures that unite and separate large groups of people. The ally is a very interpersonal role to some extent; the globalist role may seem impersonal.

How a Globalist Is Value-Driven

This is very straightforward: A unique set of core values is the base of any culture. These values lead to different perspectives on the world and different cultural patterns, regular, predictable ways of operating that can differ among cultures. It is meaningless to be in the globalist role without being able to understand and appreciate these differences in values. The globalist has no way of effectively bridging cultures without addressing the differences in values, nor of building a culture within the organization without a firm rooting in values. There is no functional organizational culture without clear sets of values.

Building Globalist Skills

The three major globalist skills developed in this chapter are the following:

- *Appreciating Cultures*—identifying and understanding the different patterns that constitute the strength of a culture
- *Bridging Cultures*—assessing the organizational relevance of different cultural perspectives
- *Choosing a Culture*—designing a single culture for the organization that binds people together for their collective success

Appreciating Cultures

Culture bonds a group of people through shared values and cultural patterns. Patterns are repeatable ways that members of a culture interact with each other to produce some degree of conformity, predictability, and stability. This creates social cohesion, traditions, and norms to which people adhere and methods to cope with changes in the environment or typical problems they face. People in the culture use their common bonds to work together in socially and economically productive ways to achieve what they desire.

Whether we are looking at a national culture or an organization's culture, we can see a similar structure. Core values lead to cultural patterns. These patterns are usually readily observable to outsiders; values help us understand the meaning of those patterns. A whole series of words such as *taboos, customs, status, myths, rites of passage,* and *rituals* typically describe these cultural patterns. When people consciously use these patterns and understand the connection to values, the patterns can be very meaningful ways of guiding the culture and the people within it. A pattern change in an organization's culture is often necessary in situations in which two cultures meet—increasing diversity within the organization, increasing international operations, merging of two organizations, or increasing interdependency of departments within the organization.

When people become automatic about cultural patterns or core values, they may severely inhibit their ability to change. The patterns and values are so habitual that people fail to recognize their presence. The more one understands the existing culture, the greater the possibility for creating a new culture that would fit a new environment or bridge existing cultural differences. We often find, however, that people cling tenaciously to their culture regardless of its relevance because it is familiar and comfortable.

If we know the values of a culture, we can observe the patterns and determine if there is a consistency among them. Often, however, values are not stated, and we can only surmise them from the patterns we are able to observe. This skill of appreciating cultures means observing a culture nonjudgmentally and with the intention of learning. The idea is to see the culture as an integrated whole. Cultures are not quaint or amusing; they serve the people within them, whether or not it is the way we ourselves would choose to live. Without this depth of appreciation, there cannot be a useful bridging of cultures or choice of a unifying organizational culture. The patterns described here can be used as a simple checklist of what to look for in appreciating a culture. As you use this checklist to understand cultures, you can accelerate your appreciation by trying to determine why the culture has those patterns. An inquiry of that type will help you understand the way those patterns reflect values, environmental conditions, collective problems, and aspirations of that culture.

Checklist of Patterns for Appreciating Cultures

Communication

❑ Special language or jargon used to rapidly convey ideas among members of cultures

❑ Influence of different people when they speak and the manner in which people listen to each other—the relative weight or importance given to the ideas and thoughts of different people

❑ Symbols used to signify achievement or success

❑ Kind of analogies or metaphors people use to convey ideas

❑ The stories they tell about people in the culture (even heavily embellished) to convey behavior and actions the culture highly regards or shuns

Behavior

❑ The rituals—regularly followed steps or procedures—used in any part of the culture

❑ Customs—expected or encouraged behavioral norms

❑ Taboos—banned or discouraged behavior

Progression

❑ The reasons for gaining status

❑ The use of titles or other means to convey status

❑ The rites of passage or well-defined criteria to acknowledge progressive movement in status

❑ The types of rewards and punishments used

Relationships

❑ Subgroups within the culture and whether they establish any cultural distinctiveness

❑ The way people obtain, access, and use power

❏ The use of hierarchy and peer relationships among people

❏ The manner in which people are included in or excluded from significant decisions or power

Bridging Cultures

Cultural values and patterns are not innate. Move a child at birth from one culture to another and he or she will not have memory of or affinity with the original culture. Although it is learned behavior, we often feel that our background is a natural and normal part of ourselves.

Some people believe that gender differences are so strong that the two genders have two different cultures. Our life experiences of men and women reflect stereotypes about gender as well as real differences. Are these differences learned or genetic? There is ongoing controversy about the cause of the differences. There are certainly chemical and physiological differences, but it is not easy to decide whether these also lead to qualitative differences in personality, psychology, behavior, or traits. Perhaps all our assumptions about men and women are simply stereotypes, but we seem to have a strong interest in the subject—there is a continuing stream of best-selling books on the topic. Therefore, I will happily jump into the topic as an example of a method for bridging cultures. In this approach, it does not really matter if the stereotypes are true or not as we are only using them as a springboard to distinguish between different approaches to the same topic in business.

For example, given a list of qualities of men and women, do we get different insight into approaches to decision making, strategy, or team building? Seeing the way cultural background—gender, national, ethnic, or religious—translates into organizationally relevant behavior provides the necessary ground for the bridging skill of the globalist role. Consider the following quick grouping of qualities associated with men and women based on various studies in psychology, sociology, and anthropology. I label them *apples* and *oranges* so we do not have to expend energy worrying about the accuracy of the qualities. What is important is that the qualities are positive in both groups and are in sharp contrast to each other. We are appreciating cultural differences in order to bridge them. I will translate these lists of qualities into approaches that each culture would take to a variety of business topics. This can serve as a model for your efforts in the globalist role: Understand the qualities of the culture, then determine the possible contributions to an organization.

People in the *apple culture* are process oriented, include others by seeking their participation, are driven by personal connection, value interdependence, seek support and give it to others, build relationship through interpersonal concern, show strength by revealing vulnerabilities, use subjective thought process and emotion to guide action, see systemic relationship among people and their responsibilities, create networks to enable people to evolve, value multiple perspectives based upon diverse experiences, are aware of possibility of multiple answers, see life as continuous cycles, work from personal examples, utilize principles related to specific situations, view fairness as treating people according to their needs, use synthesis to relate and connect, interact through building upon thoughts of others, see order in simultaneity, and sustain contextual awareness.

People in the *orange culture* are result oriented, include others when they show desire to participate, are driven by purpose, value independence, prefer self-reliance, build relationship through participation in activities, show strength by hiding or ignoring weaknesses, use objective thought processes to drive action, see systemic relationship among things and tasks, create networks to increase individual effectiveness, value multiple perspectives from alternative theories, focus to find the right answer, see things as discrete events, work from abstract concepts, utilize universal rules and principles, view fairness as treating everyone the same, use analysis to segment and categorize, interact through articulation of thought and challenge to ideas of others, see order in sequences, and sustain focused awareness.

Table 5 captures the translation of these contrasting groupings of cultural qualities into approaches to specific business topics. The way to do this is simply think of the topic, for example, strategy, and ask, How would people with this group of cultural qualities approach strategy in an organization? If you can develop this skill, you can take an understanding about another culture and discern the positive impact on an organization.

Table 5 *Translation of Cultural Qualities to Business Topics*

Business Topic	Apple Culture	Orange Culture
Strategy	Uses multiple perspectives to discover possibilities	Focuses on complexity of environmental analysis
Vision	Includes others in creating vision and considers effect of vision upon them	Seeks vision to extend organization boundaries, sustains focused pursuit of vision
Change	Manages personal impact of change and resistance to it	Tolerates turbulence of change and seeks to use change to make a difference
Cultures	Listens to and appreciates differences in perspective	Establishes common ground among cultures
Development	Matches development possibilities with individual needs	Identifies organizational personnel needs and helps people fit those needs
Collaboration	Focuses on relationships among people and seeks different ideas	Creates dynamic team spirit in desire for rapid conflict resolution
Decisions	Sees full context of decision and multiple consequences	Seeks to understand value of alternatives and willing to take risks
Projects	Maintains connection to other project needs in organization	Identifies specific tasks, schedules work, and sequences activities
Quality	Manages quality in relation to customer needs and organization's ability	Establishes clear, definable quality standards and pushes to improve upon them

The example on gender diversity demonstrates a method of approach for dealing with cultural diversity within the organization and diversity met in global operations. It enables you to approach the apparent contradiction of appreciating cultures for their differences and establishing a common ground. Naturally, appreciation of a contrasting perspective requires your ability to approach things with an open mind to understand and see value before you judge. In this case, we are simply seeing the business relevance of different cultures.

The approach can be reversed when you need the globalist role to work with mergers or different departments in the organization. We can often infer the cultural patterns from the more readily observable organizational behaviors or handling of typical business topics. If we can see the organization's process, why bother with culture? For the simple but important reason that culture is a powerful force operating below the surface. You need to think about what sort of culture would drive the approach you observe to these business topics.

We all become tuned into the cultures of the different groups we join, social or business. Yet culture is rarely discussed. In a merger or controversy within an organization, cultural differences will cause an instinctive reaction to things that violate accustomed cultural norms. The established ways of doing business have roots in deep-seated cultural differences. To complete a merger and resolve controversy, it is necessary to understand the cause of the observable behavior.

There is a second apparent contradiction, that of appreciating cultures for their differences yet making necessary judgments about the appropriateness of different cultures to changing environments. We must judge the appropriateness of different cultures for the specific conditions faced by the organization. If you follow the processes we have discussed, you will first list qualities of a culture. Use the checklist on page 116 for appreciating cultures to put qualities or cultural patterns in the most positive and nonjudgmental light. Then translate these cultural insights to business topics. Finally, look at the organization's environment and determine relevant responses for organizational success. You then have a basis for appropriate judgments about the degree to which the organization must establish a common ground or can tolerate different perspectives. Remember that when you are judging, your cultural background or the patterns with which you are most familiar may not be the best sources for approaching the business challenges of the future.

Choosing a Culture

Regardless of the degree to which the organization can tolerate different perspectives, there ultimately must be a single unifying culture for the organization. There can be great degree of latitude for individual or cultural differences, but this degree of flexibility must be a clear and accepted part of the organization's culture. The globalist's role is to create order among people through establishing a culture that best allows people to use their capabilities in the organization's interest. To see how this skill of choosing a culture operates, it is best to return to the simple model from Chapter Two.

> **VALUES drive BEHAVIOR**
> **BEHAVIOR leads to RESULTS**

In this case, we would simply say that behavior has two components—cultural patterns (the way people work) and work processes (the work they are doing).

> **ORGANIZATION CORE VALUES drive**
> **CULTURAL PATTERNS**
> **which provide a ground for**
> **WORK PROCESSES**
> **WORK PROCESSES lead to GOALS, STRATEGY, VISION**

A globalist uses core values and the desired results—what the organization is trying to accomplish as expressed in strategy, vision, change, or major goals—to create a culture. The culture must suit the work needed to achieve these results while fully reflecting the organization's values. We can use the business content focus of the other leading-edge roles to provide the realm of issues that a globalist must address. You can use the checklist from the skill of appreciating cultures to help you identify the desired cultural patterns. For example, ask the question, In order to imple-

ment the strategy, what rituals, customs, and taboos does the organization require?

Issues To Consider in Choosing a Culture

Results

Strategy—The strategy should reflect the best way to approach
the cultures of the organization's customers. The organization's
culture must be the best means to implement the strategy.

Vision—The vision should inspire the action of the different
cultural groups within the organization, be one means to bridge
cultural differences, and reflect the desired benefits to cultures
within the organization's environment. The organization's cultural patterns must best enable realization of the vision.

Change—The culture must make the desired change successful.
The culture may need to adapt if successful change must permeate cultural patterns and core values. The culture must be managed during the change.

People

Individuals—Culture should not be the only means used to
understand different individuals. The organization's culture
must allow for the appropriate degree of individual differences
to best achieve the organization's desired results.

Teams—Culture should not be the only means used to achieve
diversity of perspectives in a team. The culture must facilitate
the necessary collaboration to meet the organization's desired
results.

Cultures—Use your skills in appreciating cultures and bridging
cultures to choose an organizational culture that best incorpo-
rates the strengths and abilities from the organization's cultural
diversity.

Work Processes

Decisions—The culture should provide a sufficiently consistent
approach to decisions. Cultural diversity may create different

perspectives for insight but should not lead to different results reflecting people's subjective cultural bias.

Tasks—The culture should enable people to organize and implement tasks best suited to the organization's desired results.

Quality—Quality should reflect awareness of the effects of customer culture on desired product or service features. The culture should ensure that there is equivalent commitment to quality among all people in the organization.

Learning Globalist Role Skills

Appreciating Cultures—A Playful Exercise

- Choose one of the environments mentioned earlier—desert, Arctic, etc.
- Sit for a few minutes and think about what life was like in that environment long before industrialization, maybe 10,000 years ago.
- Living in that environment, identify the values and beliefs that you would form about religion, the meaning of life, human nature, the way the world works or things happen, and the role of community.
- Try to determine some of the cultural patterns that would flow from those values. Use the cultural checklist.

Appreciating Cultures

- Look at your own cultural background and identify its core values. (See if you can identify the ones that have become more implicit and not within daily conscious awareness.)
- Identify some of the cultural patterns based upon these values.
- Choose an organization you know well.
- Identify the different cultural patterns.
- Think about how these patterns reflect core values.
- Describe the benefits of or detriments to the organization due to these patterns.
- Determine necessary changes in patterns to be more consistent with core values.
- Think about different national or ethnic cultures represented within your organization and by those with whom you conduct business, and use the checklist approach to appreciate those cultures.

Bridging Cultures—A Playful Exercise

Continue with the playful exercise on appreciating cultures. Now we need a great leap of imagination. Skyrocket to the present and use those values and patterns as the foundation for an organization, and determine how it would operate.

Bridging Cultures

You must first have an appreciation for the different cultures represented in your organization. Following the approach used in the skill section, choose significant business topics to assess how someone from that culture might make the best contribution to each topic.

Choosing a Culture—A Playful Exercise

If you have viewed more than one culture in this playful exercise, determine what you can extract from these cultures to choose an organizational culture that best meets the necessary goals of your organization.

Choosing a Culture

Use the issue list in the skill section to determine the most effective culture for your organization. Use your work from appreciating and bridging cultures represented in your organization to define a culture that best encompasses the relevant strengths you have observed.

Principal Focus of Managing Effort	Principal Leadership Process		
	Creating Order	**Inspiring Action**	**Improving Performance**
Systems	**Sage** Designs Strategy	**Visionary** Innovates the Future	**Magician** Orchestrates Change
People	**Globalist** Bridges Cultural Differences	**Mentor** Motivates Development	**Ally** Builds Partnerships
Work	**Sovereign** Empowers Decisions	**Guide** Achieves Goals	**Artisan** Pursues Excellence

FOUNDATION OF ALL ROLES
CORE VALUES

CHAPTER SEVEN

Motivating Development

Learning the Role of the Mentor

Profile of a Mentor

I chose the name *mentor* for this role because it best captures the necessary one-to-one relationship. The kind of mentoring defined in this chapter is analogous to the medieval guild systems or the training received by most classical artists. Traditional crafts have masters who teach and help people through their development (novice, apprentice, practitioner, master). Biographies of performers in classical music, opera, or ballet frequently acknowledge people who teach them their art. These two examples illustrate the depth of true mentoring and how such a process develops artisans and artists to the stage of mastery. People in these disciplines recognize that development can be a lifelong pursuit with clear standards for continuing progress; they are inspired to take action for their own growth by their mentors because they see value in achieving mastery.

Modern mentoring in organizations is a different experience. There are few masters; mentors are still on their own path toward mastery. This is not especially problematic because mentors are not necessarily teachers of development; they support individual development paths according to each person's goals. A manager can still be learning and support the right situations for others' development. Managers who recognize their own lack of complete mas-

Wells' Field Guide—How to Spot a Mentor

Habitat

The mentor can be found encouraging someone across a boundary. Dwelling will contain toys, games, and other experiments. Usually can be seen turning everything into a learning opportunity.

Habits

Champions ongoing individual development as a cornerstone of the organization's competitive effectiveness.

Supports a variety of practical methods to help people progress on their own development path recognizing individual differences in capability, learning needs, and learning styles.

Ensures that individuals have opportunities for learning, challenge, and advancement.

Matches organizational needs with development and capabilities of specific individuals.

Enhances individual ability to make a unique contribution to the organization.

Inspires and enables others to achieve personal goals.

Manages own self through continued learning and maximum use of own capability.

Manages the performance of others by clearly setting goals and expectations, using practical and timely feedback, and providing appropriate compensation, promotional opportunities, and development.

Ensures balance of personal and work life.

tery understand that they cannot directly motivate someone else. Mentors can, however, create situations that enable or inhibit others' opportunities for motivation. A mentor is more likely to help individuals find the best learning opportunities than be a teacher for others.

Looking at the nine leading-edge roles, we see that people are always in various stages of their development journey: We are novices in some of the roles and masters of others. Mentoring can be a process in which people learn from each other, but it does not need to be a purely hierarchical process of someone more advanced in the organization helping someone who has just arrived. People possess capability they can use to help others learn even if they are in the early stages of their own career.

This chapter addresses the type of workplace the organization envisions for its employees and the role of managers and others in creating that workplace. My approach may seem idealistic; after all, "realists" feel that people just want to be left alone, do their work, draw their paycheck, and go home. To the extent that this attitude exists, it is difficult for an organization to be a flexible, responsive, effective competitor that has a clear focus on its value-adding role for its customers.

The kind of workplace created by mentors is not the result of good ideas or intentions alone—it requires dedicated, long-term effort on the part of many people. Top levels of the organization cannot decree it. Mentors help others develop according to their needs and support people on their individual journey to realize their potential in the workplace. Connecting potential to an individual's uniqueness does not imply that idiosyncratic behavior is valuable to the organization. Contribution to productivity and adding value to the work of others is always a part of developing individual potential.

How the Mentor Helps the Organization

This role reflects the combination of the leadership process of inspiring action and the people focus of managing effort. Motivation means people inspired to act, so it would seem this role must be about motivation. It is, but not in the way you may think. I want to reverse the unfortunate notion promoted by most motivational techniques, that motivation is a way to get someone to do a job better. This approach focuses on managing *work* rather than *people*. Traditional motivational techniques, based on behavioral psychology, are quite similar to Pavlov's experiments motivating dogs with stimulus and response. Rewards (stimulus) encourage desirable behavior (response), and punishment (stimulus) discourages undesirable behavior. Motivation techniques will fail when they focus only on work the manager wants someone else to do. People feel manipulated by such techniques.

Motivation is about inner drive; it is within the person. No motivational techniques, especially those with ulterior motives to cause the person to do what you want, will have long-lasting impacts. In this role of inspiring action and focusing on people, you do not have a *result* in mind, you have the *person* in mind. This distinction is easy to understand; simply consider your own experiences in being motivated. I am sure you will find the more manipulative techniques to be short-lived compared to the times you were motivated by your own inner drive.

Motivation is inevitably a person-to-person phenomenon. Motivation exists when people have work opportunities or responsibilities consistent with their stage of development and when they experience relevant expressions of appreciation for their efforts. The more traditional motivational techniques try to directly influence people; a mentor focuses on the conditions that help or hinder an individual in finding inner motivational drive.

In this role, the manager *motivates development* by helping people to learn and work to their potential. A highly motivated person is going to have self-generated energy to achieve. That is why it is unnecessary to test the latest motivational techniques on people. Ultimately, we all experience those approaches as manipulative because there is no apparent personal concern. Personal concern occurs when the manager tries to help individuals find that motivation within themselves regardless of what job they have to perform.

Motivated people push themselves and their capability. Ongoing development is important to them. Given that people are trying to improve and high levels of motivation will lead to high levels of achievement, you may feel that this role belongs in the leadership process column of improving performance. Most people do welcome the opportunity to learn. However, they experience the idea of someone trying to improve them as condescending and often resent it. You know how it is when people are sent to a workshop because they were told it would be good for them rather than being given support for the development opportunities they choose. Individual differences in learning needs cause people to seek choice in their development and resent any efforts, regardless of how well intentioned, that tells them or forces them to participate in learning. In these conditions, people feel wrong and the workshop's intention is to make them feel right. There is little inspiration to act. Mentors make leaving possibilities available, not because people are wrong but recognizing that ongoing learning is a natural part of personal growth and career advancement.

The standard mentoring approach helps an individual learn, adapt to, and fit in with the inner workings of the organization. Mentoring to "learn the ropes" is useful for people first entering the organization and people whose own cultural background differs from the dominant culture within the organization. Many people do need the guidance provided by an experienced individual who knows the organization's norms—its particular ways of operating, how to get things done, and the processes for judging individual capability. People do want career advancement. With excessive adaptation, however, people may lose or suppress the unique capabilities they can offer to the organization. Motivation is highest when people have clear opportunities to satisfy their desire to develop, grow, learn, and change to reach their potential in contributing to an organization's success.

This chapter's view of motivation, focusing on the person rather than the work, evokes doubt in some managers. They feel this approach to motivation could be detrimental to the organization when the work is mundane and bereft of challenge. People motivated by challenge and development will seek their satisfaction elsewhere—either at a different company or outside the workplace. After all, there are significant turnover problems at all ranks in many organizations. These concerns are justified.

A true mentor, however, motivates development of individuals so that they can successfully advance their career even if they eventually choose alternatives outside the organization. A mentor is willing to extend effort for that person and take that risk. A good mentor is able to let go—if a person needs to leave the organization, a mentor will support that decision. Mentors help people gain a new perspective on an existing situation and find meaning for themselves in their job. The mentor absolutely understands and considers the organization's personnel needs but more as an option for the individual rather than the sole reason for being a mentor to that person. They have complete faith that this focus on the needs of the individual will benefit the organization for whatever length of time that person chooses to remain. By this attitude mentors alter the entire climate in the organization. It is quite practical, not idealistic, that truly motivated people will be most inspired to act in an organization that continually demonstrates an ongoing commitment to development.

Promotions, advancements, changes in job responsibilities, and performance evaluations are all a regular part of organizational life. Fear of disrupting their own career path often has people trying to hide their development needs, but mentors can manage these apparently contradictory demands of career and learning. The learning organization evolves from this climate of individual learning.

Mentoring is a serious demand on a manager's capability. As a mentor sustains focus on individuals, working with them on a one-to-one basis, there is a natural limit to the number of people any one manager can effectively mentor. The challenge inherent in this role shows us why there is such a tendency to use traditional motivation techniques and ignore the wide range of individual differences.

How a Mentor Is Value-Driven

Motivation is linked to the values we use in a situation and the way the environment or circumstances affect that choice. You can test the relationship of motivation and values for yourself by taking one of your own core values and thinking about how that value motivates you to behave.

Development partially consists of the ability to make behavior more consistent with core values. People are more motivated when they have opportunities to live by their core values. Too often we experience fear used as a motivational device; any system that uses rewards and punishments is relying upon fear as a motivator. When people are fearful, they usually have other values displacing their core values, and they will do what is necessary for the expediency of the situation.

A successful mentor must understand an individual's core values in order to help that person make the best development choices. Part of that development is strengthening the capability of people to withstand challenging situations that may divert them from their core values. Although the mentor may lack the expertise to always uphold his or her own core values regardless of the circumstances, demonstrating a high value for learning for oneself may be an effective substitute for expertise in guiding others.

Warning Signs of Excess

You know you have overdone the mentor role if you

Regard a systems perspective as too abstract and impersonal

Emphasize people's learning rather than their accomplishments

Subordinate organizational needs to individual needs

Restrain change so rate of change does not seem to exceed people's rate of learning

Only value a vision that has clear learning possibilities

Building Mentor Skills

The three major mentor skills developed in this chapter are the following:

- *Motivating Others*—observing behavior to connect people's motivations with the values they currently hold and choosing actions to influence the use of values you would like them to hold

- *Understanding Individual Development Needs*—understanding the value of alternative assessment techniques to judge individual differences

- *Creating Learning Opportunities*—ensuring that learning goes through all necessary phases to make it usable and practical

Motivating Others

Traditional Approaches and Values

How do you motivate people? Managers' most frequent response is, salary, promotion, or some other reward or recognition. Many managers, thinking further about the question, will realize they do many other things to provide motivation. They may solicit input on complex issues, trust people to effectively represent their team to other groups in the organization, respond rapidly to individual or group needs, or create a work atmosphere that is enlivening. Looking at a wider range of things that have motivational appeal reminds us that each person has many intrinsic needs the manager can address. Moving among this spectrum of possibilities and shifting external things to satisfy the needs of each person is the manager's challenge.

As individuals, we seek to satisfy values that we hold. Conditions in a given situation can cause our focus to shift among a wide variety of values. Motivation at any moment is the choice of behavior that satisfies the prevailing values. A manager cannot set values for another individual; values are *always* a matter of personal choice. It is possible, however, to create conditions that make it relatively easy or difficult to satisfy particular values. For example, money is probably important to people but may not be a powerful motivator to improved performance; other values may drive behavior. Treat people unfairly in regard to pay, though, and you may find that it is a powerful demotivator. People get pulled away from other values in order to focus on their money values when money values are not being satisfied.

People do not respond to motivators or demotivators in a uniform manner; identical conditions will affect individuals differently. For example, the pressure of a deadline may cause some people to value completing the work and devote energy to getting things done, whereas others may continue to value achieving high standards and risk being late on a deadline.

Although values are personal, there can be external influences on the values and behavior of an individual. Criticize someone and they may use a value for achievement to find a way to improve their performance, but alternatively, they may fall into a value of survival and try to defend themselves or lose motivation because they do not believe they are capable of meeting the implied standards. Conditions can also influence values: Some people find competitive pressure inspiring and they move to achievement values; others find this pressure threatening and they move to survival values.

The internal source of motivation can be stronger than the external influences. Individual development always involves increased self-awareness and greater clarity about one's own capabilities and behavior. This opens the door for attaining greater alignment of behavior with the values we want to express and achieving the results or consequences we desire. Development leads to increased mastery of our own motivation. We know that external conditions do not force us to behave in a particular way and that our behavior is always our own choice. When we choose unconsciously, our behavior may not be what we truly want.

The job of the mentor is three-fold in this scheme:

- Give appropriate feedback so people can have "objective" information on their behavior and its consequences.
- Concentrate on the conditions that could affect people's values and behavior.
- Support the development of individuals so that they have increasing capability to manage their own response to external conditions and to be conscious of their own choice of values and behavior.

Possibilities for Influencing Values

Traditional behavioral approaches to motivation have a dominant focus on rewards and punishment, with little attention to conscious behavior. The anticipation or experience of a stimulus leads to a response of automatic behavior. There is no conscious thought between stimulus and response; we behave in ways that bring us rewards and help us avoid punishment. Externally set rewards and punishment seem to have little effect, even for people who seem relatively unmotivated. If they did, nobody would be fired for poor performance, and everybody would be devoting their efforts to receive the financial rewards offered by the organization.

Rewards will motivate when they match the individual's desires and standards of success. "Punishment" may work from the outside but is stronger when it is "self-inflicted," when people perceive they have failed in their attempts and decide to try harder. We use punishments as a threat if someone fails. Is that what we want in an organization? When people are working to avoid punishment, they are not exemplifying inspired action. You inspire someone when you help them move to higher stages of personal values.

I spoke about core values in Chapter Two, but we need to recognize that there is a whole continuum of personal values that can influence our behavior. Do not view this continuum as a hierarchy in terms of good and bad, because all values are relevant to us throughout our lives. It is preferable to look at the continuum representing the breadth with which we engage with the world. At the lower end, there are fewer things that we think about or that fall within our scope of attention; we are limited in our outlook, less willing to take chances, and less likely to work to our potential. At the higher end, we have a wider range of issues we believe important.

To give you a way to deal with the use of values in motivation, I will discuss four relatively distinctive stages along this continuum, define the values at each stage, list behaviors you are likely to observe in others, and suggest some managerial actions you can take to reinforce the values of this stage (see Tables 6 through 9). The four stages focus on values related to protection, acceptance, achievement, and challenge. (I have chosen to use Maslow's hierarchy of needs as a basis for this approach to values in motivation.)

Critical Ideas About Using These Four Stages in a Continuum of Values

- Each stage is significant to us and we can experience each on a daily basis.

- It is possible to shift very rapidly from one stage to another and to perceive simultaneously being at more than one stage in a given situation.

- External conditions—our situation or circumstances—can influence the stage of values dominating our behavior, but we can ignore this influence and make our own choice.

- Unfulfilled values at a lower stage can pull us to that stage.

- We all seek to have experiences at the highest stage because we are more productive and able to live more in tune with core values when we are at this stage.

- Regardless of how well a manager or organization satisfies values or rewards behavior stemming from values at a lower stage, we will ultimately feel demotivated if we see no possibility of moving to the highest stage.

- We have little or no motivation for learning and development at the lowest stage of values.

- There is a decreasing need for external rewards as we move up the range.

- Inspired action stems from values at the higher range.

Table 6   *Protection*

This table shows a value for protection—keeping things as they are, maintaining tight boundaries around one's job responsibilities, experiencing change as a threat to one's existence, treating ideas as if they were unalterable doctrine and absolute truth, and remaining within one's comfort zone.

Observable Behavior

What You Are Likely to Notice in the Behavior of People
Being Motivated by the Value of Protection

- Aggressively defending self against any criticism of work

- Being easily defeated by any criticism

- Demonstrating extreme aversion to taking any risk

- Seeking clearly defined boundaries for jobs

- Resenting when others interfere with their jobs

- Blocking anything that will alter the status quo

- Choosing to work alone rather than share responsibility with someone else and lose control

- Refusing to listen to ideas that diverge from their own

- Being overly critical of others and easily falling into difficult-to-resolve debates

- Ruling out any suggestions that deviate from normal company operating policies

- Repeating organizationally sanctioned thoughts or perspectives without fully understanding their meaning or intent

- Avoiding new situations

- Being unwilling to accept any responsibilities in which they have any risk of failing due to what they believe is a lack of necessary skills or knowledge

- Having little interest in learning anything new

Table 6 *Protection (continued)*

Managerial Action

What You Can Do If You Want to Influence People
to Use the Value of Protection

- Make sure that people are continually aware that their job is on the line.

- Publicize any information that creates a crisis condition for the organization.

- Propose changes to existing jobs in which people perceive they need a dramatic change in their skills or normal mode of behavior to succeed.

- Attack any ideas that deviate from the norm.

- Create a climate in which the first thought about anything is always what is wrong with it or why it will not work.

- Enforce company policies without any deviation—work from the exact detail of them rather than the intent.

- Offer no challenges, and insulate people against changes.

- Treat any challenge or change as an insurmountable mountain.

- Place very high stakes on any deviations from "comfort zones" so people experience a high level of risk if they try to move beyond their self-imposed boundaries.

- Expose any failure that occurs when someone attempts a movement beyond those boundaries.

Using Values for Motivation

You must never forget that the choice of values always remains with the individual. You may create conditions that are likely to evoke lower-stage values, but people are capable of avoiding external influences on their values. They can retain core values in the most adverse conditions and act in ways consistent with those values. On the other hand, you may create conditions that you believe will absolutely support higher-stage values, but people may have no interest in those values or feel they do not possess the capability to act from those values.

Table 7   Acceptance

This table shows a value for acceptance—seeking to fit in, doing tasks that inspire the respect and admiration of the manager and group members, adapting one's thoughts and ideas to those generally accepted by the group, and supporting the social norms of the group.

Observable Behavior

What You Are Likely to Notice in the Behavior of People
Being Motivated by the Value of Acceptance

- Taking actions only with prior permission or consent

- Needing praise for motivation

- Seeking clarification to know what is required rather than trying to figure things out for themselves

- Avoiding conflict or controversy

- Seeking agreement rather than asserting differences

- Putting more energy to gaining agreement for an acceptable idea than championing a radically different idea

As we discussed in the earlier part of this chapter, there are many kinds of extrinsic conditions that a manager can use for motivation within any team or organization. These include but are not limited to salaries, benefits, promotions, bonuses, job assignment, inclusion in decisions, interactions to improve performance or raise standards of performance, and acknowledgment of work efforts. Extrinsic conditions are only relevant when they are consistent with the value of the individual being motivated. For example, an increased salary will not lead to more effective work if the individual is seeking more challenge. Here are some suggestions for alternative approaches using values in motivation:

- Choose managerial actions consistent with values people hold or values you desire them to hold.

- Alter the circumstances or conditions facing an individual to allow satisfaction of the value that person chooses.

- Without changing any external conditions, help the individual change a personal state so that a value is no longer dominating behavior.

Table 7 Acceptance (continued)

Managerial Action

What You Can Do If You Want to Influence People
to Use the Value of Acceptance

- Give people tasks in which they have a high likelihood of success.

- Whenever you delegate responsibility, be sure people check with you before proceeding.

- Retain final authority for any decisions.

- Create a sharp distinction in your treatment of people with praise and criticism so that people take it as a personal assessment rather than an evaluation of the work.

- Maintain a competitive environment with other groups.

- Be quick to criticize the actions of other groups when they seem to have negative impacts on your group.

- Place greater emphasis on the team or work group than on the organization; expect loyalty to your group.

- Exhibit low tolerance for ideas or questions that do not demonstrate agreement with the direction of the group.

- Resolve any differences rapidly by emphasizing similarities or connections among ideas.

- Pepper your speech with phrases such as "That is not the way we do things around here."

- Structure any new situation or responsibility so that it does not conflict with the value that the individual is currently satisfying.

- Threaten an individual's ability to satisfy a value if work is not done to an acceptable level.

- Create new responsibilities and situations that allow a person to satisfy values at higher stages.

- Create an environment that is consistently aimed at values at higher stages, and put no energy to values at lower stages.

- Provide ongoing support to individually designed and implemented development paths using self-assessments from some model of individual diversity.

Table 8 Achievement

This table shows a value for achievement—operating to high standards, performing one's responsibilities with a high degree of proficiency and competency, forming work relationships with other highly motivated individuals, and committing to a high level of contribution to the organization.

Observable Behavior

What You Are Likely to Notice in the Behavior of People
Being Motivated by the Value of Achievement

- Dealing with roadblocks to the completion of their work

- Showing tenacity and determination to do work in the way it is necessary

- Seeking out learning or development if it will raise the standards of their work

- Staking reputation on the quality of their work

- Bringing people together who share common interests or who would benefit from each other

- Trying to help others reach higher levels of motivation

- Withholding judgments and opinions when they are unsure

- Listening carefully to gain understanding from others

- Enjoying having their knowledge and capability tested

- Being available when others need their knowledge or capability

- Offering and accepting criticisms that constructively lead to high performance

Managerial Action

What You Can Do If You Want to Influence People
to Use the Value of Achievement

- Make sure work assignments fully use an individual's strengths.

- Reduce boundaries among work responsibilities to avoid "turf" issues.

- Gain clarity about desired results, and leave the means to individual discretion.

Table 8   Achievement (continued)

- Give specific information about areas of success and areas for improvement in performance.

- Seek understanding about people's thoughts and actions in different situations.

- Encourage people to seek advice and trust advisors to have insight into their problems.

- Make sure people know what strengths you see in them and what you expect them to contribute to a taskforce or project team.

- Gain consensus on standards or principles to guide all work within the group and interactions among people.

- Conduct evaluations to determine how things can be improved or what has been learned from previous experiences.

Understanding Individual Development Needs

People have different strengths, capabilities, and styles. Therefore their development needs differ. Learning styles also differ. A mentor assists individuals with diverse needs to reach potential. This is quite a challenge—there is almost no end to combinations of development needs and learning styles. The mentor also maintains awareness of the vision, mission, and purpose as well as specific task assignments to determine a practical realm for development needs of the organization.

Certain questions provide an organizational context for development: Based upon the proposed strategy, what are the necessary capabilities to ensure success? Based upon the organization's future direction, what are the necessary leadership and management skills to provide guidance? These questions are important, but the mentor's main focus is on individual strengths and weaknesses. A mentor will help an individual follow his or her own development path and will champion organizational financial support for development regardless of its connection to organizational needs. This is not idealism but rather a practical mentor belief that a climate of support of individual development leads to people working from the highest stages of motivation and therefore better productivity for the organization.

Table 9   Challenge

This table shows a value for challenge—seeking responsibilities that go beyond present capabilities, taking risks in new or unfamiliar situations, especially when learning is required to succeed, creating something new, operating in ways that fully reflect an ethical and moral base, and desiring to participate in things that make a difference in the lives of others.

Observable Behavior

What You Are Likely to Notice in the Behavior of People
Being Motivated by the Value of Challenge

- Being excited by tough assignments

- Having higher energy levels when there is a real question about the likelihood of success

- Showing a high level of ability to understand the perspective of others

- Behaving in ways that serve the best interests of others

- Downplaying unnecessary constraints to thinking and using different ideas that have benefits to the organization

- Actively seeking alternatives to actions

- Confronting restraints or boundaries that stop others

- Having a high level of integrity in all of their endeavors

- Confronting the ethical implications of decisions

Managerial Action

What You Can Do If You Want to Influence People
to Use the Value of Challenge

- Role model the behaviors.

- Act from a state of trust in individuals' capabilities, judgments, and decisions about their own development and the way they conduct their work responsibilities.

- Provide necessary resource support consistent with this trust.

- People with these values are not easily influenced by external conditions. As these conditions become more adverse, the development level of an individual will determine whether these values remain valid or the person moves to a different level. A manager's best action is supporting individual development to strengthen ability to handle tough situations.

Mentors seek understanding of individual strengths and weaknesses. Using a variety of methods for assessing differences among individuals, the mentor helps individuals create relevant development plans. These plans identify the capability or skill focus of the individual's learning and the methods for achieving the desired state. Methods can include participation in various workshops or seminars, individual coaching, and self-study. Organizations spend too much time and money on companywide programs that do not address particular needs of individuals and in their breadth fail to recognize the details of practical applications. Individuals who attend workshops outside the company often receive insufficient support to bring their learning back to the workplace.

People are likely to resist development any time they are told what they need to learn or treated as if they needed to be changed. Mentors reduce this resistance; they use various assessment devices to help each individual gain a clearer picture of areas of strengths and weaknesses or areas of preferred styles. With these assessments as background data, and always remembering the organization's needs, a good mentor helps the individual create and implement his or her own development plans.

I have found that people enjoy various methods of self-assessment. When they use a few different approaches, they often find that the composite picture of themselves is integrated. The leading-edge roles form a clear model explaining individual differences in management style; you can certainly use this model to help individuals determine their development needs. Lower-preference roles can become the focus for ongoing development.

There are many other assessment methods on the market that you may find useful, including the *Myers-Briggs Type Indicator®*, Herrmann Brain Dominance Instrument, and *Benchmarks®*. I mention these as I find them quite useful and chose to become certified in their use. When I work with people to create their development plans, I like to use a variety of instruments in addition to my own. My experience is that these instruments create a cohesive picture of preferences, strengths, and weaknesses, making the assessment process more realistic and useful in helping people choose their own development path.

Creating Learning Opportunities

Understanding differences in styles, preferences, skills, and capabilities is an important part of creating development plans. Perhaps the most overlooked part of development is the different ways in which people learn; unfortunately, most learning situations do not reflect understanding of these differences. People are expected to adapt to the situations they face. It is important for a good mentor to understand different learning styles, helping individuals identify their own and then seeking learning opportunities where they have a better chance of success.

For example, consider which of the following best represents your learning style:

- Using data or fact-based content and case studies
- Synthesizing ideas or discovering concepts
- Learning through doing or applying ideas or knowledge
- Interacting in groups and sharing ideas or perspectives
- Conducting experiments or simulations
- Analyzing past events
- Using visual or auditory input
- Introspectively contemplating your own responses, experiences, or ideas

Clearly, this list could go on. We would also find that we each have more than one approach to learning and that we vary our approach depending upon the situation, type of material, or skill. Reading this book and others like it indicates that you have some preference for using written material, usually ideas, as a part of your learning.

It is a challenge to know the range of learning-style possibilities, accurately assess individual preferences for learning, and ensure that development experience has clear learning-style objectives. Although I have been emphasizing the mentor's quality of individual focus, I also want to suggest a deviation from this in regard to learning. I have spent too many years in universities and consulting to believe that satisfying individual learning-style preferences is sufficient. Learning must pass through a few significant phases to be complete and usable. Even though individual preferences may favor one phase over another, we need to ensure that all phases are taking place. Organizations spend billions of dollars on training and development each year, but I think much of it is poorly spent because there is never an opportunity to complete the cycle of learning. It is your responsibility in the mentor role to be sure that every person has a clear opportunity to fully engage with each phase of the learning cycle.

Using the mentor role's sensitivity to individual needs, you may want to help people identify learning situations that best match their preference. You must also help them move into phases for which they have lower preferences. I hesitate to use the expression, but it is important to "learn how to learn." Regardless of our individual preferences, we all need to engage with all phases of the learning cycle.

In Figure 1, based on David Kolb's *Learning Styles Inventory,* the cycle of learning is drawn with arrows to indicate that the phases have no fixed order; they are dependent upon each other. I will describe them briefly with some ideas about possible learning situations. An important mentor skill is ensuring that people receive the full range of learning opportunities represented by the learning cycle.

It is very easy to see the value of all phases of this cycle. Although I personally have a strong preference to start with some degree of conceptual understanding, I have also found myself in many situations in which I prefer to start elsewhere. For example, when computers started to appear on our desktops, we went to basic training sessions where we would sit in front of a terminal and be subjected to a long talk about CPUs, memory, and many other things that were irrelevant at that particular time. What we needed was some low-risk practice and answers to questions such as, Are there ways we might damage the computer? With appropriate warnings, we wanted a chance to play around to see what happened. After experimenting, it would then be possible to go back to conceptual understanding to get some ideas to help us in more challenging situations. We also needed hands-on experience— using word-processing to prepare something important to us, spreadsheets to work with real numbers, etc.

Figure 1 Complete Cycle of Learning

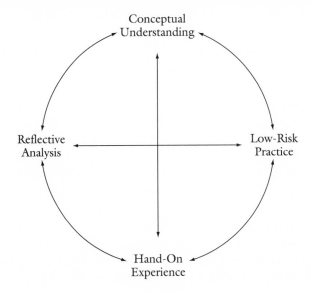

A low-risk practice is a controlled situation, frequently struc-tured by a trainer, to give people familiarity in using some part of the skill or some piece of knowledge. Less control exists in the real-time exposure of hands-on experience. You can practice a skill in a workshop, but you need to get some experience with it in real work situations. In the practice and even more so in the experi-ence, problems arise and questions come up that better help us to engage with conceptual understanding. We need this conceptual understanding whether it is complex theoretical or abstract knowl-edge; we need a mental model or precise ideas so that we are able to face real situations that are even less structured than low-risk practice or hands-on experience. We need to be able to deal with ambiguous situations with unforeseen consequences.

It is hard to go from training to real problem solving. In the university, many students are quite adept at solving any problem presented to them in the classroom or on a test, but real life always throws us curve balls. Problems and challenges we now face appeared neatly structured when we were first learning. Without conceptual understanding, we would have absolutely no chance of transferring knowledge from the structured past to the less well-defined present. Theory and real world are not incompatible; they depend upon each other. We cannot ignore either one.

The fourth phase—reflective analysis—is a useful mediator between the theoretical and the practical. We engage in this phase to evaluate our response from the practice or experience phases to come up with questions, insights, patterns, or problems. We use that evaluation to delve further into conceptual understanding or engage in more complex or challenging practice and experience.

I hope it is once again clear why I started this book with an insistence that you take responsibility for learning what you choose about these roles. A book can do no more than further your conceptual understanding and give you guidance on engaging with the other three phases. I have tried to provide this guidance throughout the book. I am not, however, acting as a mentor, because I have no personal contact with you. I am merely providing general forms of guidance that work in groups but frequently need modification to accommodate individual differences.

Workshops and seminars can only cover the two phases of conceptual understanding and low-risk practice. In the mentor role, you have an obligation to support the availability of learning opportunities in *all* phases. What this means quite simply is learning on the job and learning away from the job. Every dollar spent on a seminar or workshop is wasted if there are no opportunities at work to use the skill—hands-on experience—and no opportunity o take the time for reflective analysis. You must create opportunities where the penalties for failure are low or where there is sufficient backup to solve problems before they escalate. Then the learner, who has a higher risk of failure than an expert, will be motivated to try newly learned skills at work.

Learning Mentor Role Skills

Motivating Others

- To reinforce the relationship of values to behavior at the different stages, keep track of your own experiences for a day or two.
- Determine which stage seems to dominate different situations.
- Try to see the extent to which external conditions or the actions of others influence your experience of the different stages.
- Take deliberate action to move yourself to desired stages.
- Use the checklists to observe the behavior of others.
- Observe how your actions influence the motivation of others by experimenting with the different methods discussed here.

Understanding Individual Development Needs

Use this exercise for your own development and then try to help others go through a similar process.

- Determine your preferences for the leading-edge roles.
- Complete the "Leading-Edge Portrait" in the Appendix.
- Judge how well the portrait results match your preferences.
- Seek out other assessment instruments that you can use where you have a value for the underlying model of the assessment.
- Judge how well the assessment results match your opinion about your preferences or abilities on that model.
- From the formal assessments or your own judgments, identify key learning items for yourself.

Creating Learning Opportunities

Use this exercise for your own development, and then try to help others go through a similar process.

- Determine your preferences for phases of the learning cycle.
- Determine what personnel skills your organization needs to move it toward its desired future.
- Choose specific learning goals that reflect your development toward your desired position within the organization.
- Identify learning content—desired leading-edge role skills.
- Use the learning cycle to design your development plan by identifying development opportunities for each phase of the cycle.
- Implement it.

Principal Focus of Managing Effort	Principal Leadership Process		
	Creating Order	Inspiring Action	Improving Performance
Systems	**Sage** Designs Strategy	**Visionary** Innovates the Future	**Magician** Orchestrates Change
People	**Globalist** Bridges Cultural Differences	**Mentor** Motivates Development	**Ally** Builds Partnerships
Work	**Sovereign** Empowers Decisions	**Guide** Achieves Goals	**Artisan** Pursues Excellence

FOUNDATION OF ALL ROLES
CORE VALUES

CHAPTER EIGHT

Building Partnerships
Learning the Role of the Ally

Profile of an Ally

Ally is the best choice for a name for this role as it symbolizes a person devoted to working with others, enabling them to achieve high levels of performance. If we remembered what we learned in kindergarten—play nicely together—we would not have as much need for this role.

An ally has confidence in the capability and responsibility of others, building interdependent work relationships in which each person contributes to the efforts of others. Respecting a desire for independence, the ally maintains a place for individual action, thought, and contribution and holds individuals accountable for their actions.

Treating others as peers, the ally develops a climate of trust and commitment among collaborators. Team spirit is not just limited to regular work teams; it is an important component of all partnerships at work whether inside or outside the organization. The ally's method of conflict management creates honest dialogue to handle issues that threaten the effectiveness of collaboration.

An ally is different from a coach. Good coaching usually focuses on task accomplishment. That important quality of coaching is the guide role—managing the work and achieving goals. The guide organizes people to implement missions, meet obstacles, maintain

Wells' Field Guide—How to Spot an Ally

Habitat

The ally can be found at water coolers, coffee pots, cafeterias, and other meeting places. Dwelling will be noisy and communal, filled with all kinds of living creatures. Usually can be seen in the midst of a crowd, herd, flock, pack, or swarm.

Habits

Enjoys collaboration and treats others as peers.

Enhances the quality of collaboration within the organization and with external groups.

Improves the value of collaboration in formal work groupings as well as informal work assignments.

Supports interdependent work partnerships where members rely upon each other's capability and sense of responsibility.

Builds team spirit, trust, and commitment and enables resolution of conflicts that challenge these.

Uses a high level of interpersonal skills in a variety of situations.

Creates a high level of team involvement without unnecessary competition with other teams or work groups.

---

flexibility, and achieve those goals most critical to the success of the organization and its overall vision.

An ally focuses on the people rather than the work, believing that powerful partnerships achieve high-standard results. In this aspect, it is similar to the other people roles. In the globalist role, a manager understands the structural aspects that distinguish people, pull them apart, and bring them together. Even though the role is about people, it borders on being impersonal by taking a cultural perspective. The mentor role, on the other hand, displays an intense focus on individuals—their unique combinations of strengths and development needs. It is the most personal of all roles, placing the individual above the organization, although mentor managers do attend to the organization's personnel needs.

The ally role places interpersonal relationships in the foreground of attention. As with the other two roles, the background is the organization, and effort is directed toward how people are working together rather than what they are trying to accomplish. Every single instance of two or more people working—brief discussions, organized meetings, ongoing groups with mutual responsibility—requires the interpersonal skills of the ally role.

It is quite easy to see the kinds of qualities and skills a manager must bring to the ally role. Think of a time when you would describe your work relationships with others as absolutely excellent. You do not need to think about the group's achievements as well-functioning partnerships easily create the necessary results. Think instead about how people were working together—with shared commitment, a high level of trust, and an ability to extract the value from conflict among other things. It is that high level of experience that the ally role must duplicate in every work partnership. Please remember the remarkably loose definition I am using for a work partnership—*every single instance of two or more people working together.* Ally work is not confined to team building.

How an Ally Helps the Organization

This role reflects the combination of the leadership process of improving performance and the people focus of managing effort. We can easily understand the nature of this combination by identifying the biggest daily energy drain among people in an organization: the widespread lack of effective interpersonal skill and the wasted effort caused by misunderstandings, debates, inattention to others' ideas, and unresolved conflicts.

Beyond the work inside the organization, there are innumerable instances of contact with customers, suppliers, distributors, strategic alliances, joint ventures, and others outside the organization. We constantly form work groups, task forces, committees, and project teams. I use the terms *teamwork, partnership,* and *collaboration* interchangeably throughout this chapter as I think of the ally role more in the process sense—building partnerships or improving the performance of working relationships among people. The need for this role exists in several places within an organization:

- Formal work groups or teams with a relatively fixed place in the organization's structure whose existence remains until there is a major organizational change

- Special assignment project teams or task forces whose existence remains until a specific mission is accomplished

- Committees with representatives from different groups to form or oversee policies

- Necessary ongoing work relations among different groups

- Informal or occasional needs for assistance or cooperation

- Regular work relationships with suppliers, customers, and others outside the organization

- Formal cooperation among different organizations for a specific business purpose—strategic alliances, joint ventures, and virtual corporations

- Any meeting for work purposes

A manager in this role sees each instance of collaboration as an opportunity to *build partnerships*. Organizations and communities exist for similar reasons: People acting in concert can accomplish more than individuals operating independently of each other. The motivating force for communities may have simply been survival. For modern organizations, survival in highly competitive markets requires a wide range of skills beyond the capability and knowledge of any single person. Most organizations have a hierarchical structure; people often have specific, nearly individual responsibility. In the past, if you managed a group, you had relatively complete authority. Although we recognized the need for collective action, we tried to divide work as much as possible. The emphasis on teamwork is a more recent phenomenon. Increasing numbers of organizations have shifted to team-based models of production and thus saved costs and increased productivity.

Disregarding the meetings that you consider wasteful, how much of your day is spent in contact with others? How much of your job can you do without ever working with someone else? We spend significant amounts of time working with others, and lack of strong collaborative skills is a serious waste of resources. With this broad definition of teamwork, the opportunities for advancing collaboration and improving performance are enormous. Think of all the energy expended to deal with interpersonal problems and ineffective collaboration in your organization. If you could measure the financial consequences of this waste and inefficiency, it would astound you. Proficiency in the ally role is a crucial competitive advantage to minimize wasted energy and channel people's collective responsibilities toward improved performance. With the large number of collaborative interactions among people, there is tremendous untapped potential for this improvement.

Despite such clear potential, there are many types of resistance to teamwork in the organization. Although we desire the benefits of collaborative partnerships in organizations, we do not seem willing to put the necessary effort into building team effectiveness. We derail attempts to improve collaboration by labeling them too "touchy-feely." Many find teamwork or collaborative work to be tedious if not detrimental; they perceive too much need for consensus and too many meetings whenever there is a need to work with others. To some extent, collaboration is such a foreign idea that organizations often find that the effort devoted to generating strong relationships within teams can lead to competition and conflict among teams.

The ally role is necessary to alter these experiences and create strong collaborative partnerships in which there is a high degree of efficiency and effectiveness, thus eliminating many of the negative experiences of teamwork. Therefore, to improve performance, managers need to focus on the way people work together and eliminate the wasted energy. I am not advocating seemingly endless discussions about how people are feeling and examination of every nuance of interpersonal relationships. I am saying, however, that explicit work is necessary to bring the ally role to its full strength. The paradox is that when people are functioning powerfully in the ally role, there is much less time spent on explicit discussions of interpersonal relations because there are fewer interpersonal problems, trust levels are high, and conflict is a positive force to advance the performance of the group.

How an Ally Is Value-Driven

Shared values are an important mechanism by which these different collaborative efforts operate more efficiently, effectively, and equitably. Values are not a subject for discussion in every work

Warning Signs of Excess

You know you have overdone the ally role if you

Ignore individual contributions and needs

Choose values or vision that are sufficiently broad so everyone agrees

Restrict or downplay differences to obtain greater harmony

Would rather talk with others about views on the work than divide it up

Shun independence

Restrain change that disrupts work relationships

Would rather reach a consensus than take a definitive personal stand

Spend more time on way people are working than what they are doing

Set work standards so everyone can feel included

---

interaction among people, but groups who work together for some time need some discussion about values. Knowing the personal values of each participant leads to greater trust and understanding of each other. Setting values for a group provides a platform for its work together.

Disconnecting from core values causes group loss of interpersonal energy. Conflict, lack of trust, failure to listen to each other, among many other things, will drain energy from a group. These behaviors only occur because of core value displacement and lack of the ally role. A group with a strong ally manager and clear connection to core values will have plenty of disagreements, different perspectives, and alternative ideas, but they will experience enlivened dialogue rather than energy-draining debate. Improved performance only occurs through honoring differences and encouraging the exploration of people's perspectives. With core values firmly in place, an ally can probably move a group to greater but more productive differences.

Building Ally Skills

The three major ally skills developed in this chapter are the following:

- *Lowering the Barriers to Teamwork*—removing the individual restraints that turn teamwork into drudgery for everyone
- *Building Trust*—constructing the bedrock that determines the strength and longevity of any collaborative effort
- *Transforming Conflict to Progress*—recognizing conflict as a natural, even desirable occurrence, and transforming confrontation to benefit from useful differences in perspectives

Lowering the Barriers to Teamwork

Despite all the clear benefits to better work partnerships and all the wasted energy on weak interpersonal relationships, there are still many barriers to teamwork. I have worked with large groups of people on this role and asked people to divide themselves into two groups, allies and non-allies. We need to recognize the validity of the non-allies desire for independence, but it is unlikely that anyone in an organization can remain completely isolated and perform his or her job.

Invariably there is a fifty-fifty split between the two groups—large numbers of people dislike teamwork and would avoid it if they could. The ally role is the only one that seems to raise a powerful negative emotional response. People with lower preferences for the other roles recognize the role contributions in a more objective fashion. That is why it is important for the ally role to focus on lowering some of the barriers to partnerships.

Nevertheless the ally role's purpose is *not* subverting individual freedom for the benefit of the group, *not* suppressing the power of individual responsibility, creativity, entrepreneurship, and leadership and subjecting it to rule by committee, *not* freezing all action in the pursuit of consensus, *not* filling everyone's schedule with endless meetings. Some of these misconceptions create barriers that are unnecessary and counterproductive. It is an important ally quality to reduce the effects of barriers that come from negative experience, lack of experience, and images that *only* elevate the value of the individual.

Negative Experience

Many people have had a variety of negative experiences with teams:

- Team relationships may have been overemphasized so people have more loyalty to the team than the organization.
- For the sake of team cohesiveness and consensus, it becomes increasingly difficult for individuals to express differences as the group experiences such expressions as restraints to its actions.
- There is collective involvement so no individual feels personally responsible for any team decisions.
- The desire for collaboration and consensus requires participation by all so the team begins to have excessive meetings, spending time on group process at the expense of effective action.

Lack of Experience

Managers asked to lead teams often lack skills to be effective team members. When they speak of "my team," they are usually referring to their responsibility and the people who report to them rather than their own participation on a team. There are many published case studies of successful teams, but very few of these are at the managerial level, across different functions, or across vertical levels of the organizational hierarchy.

Most managers have experienced some type of task force work within organizations. These task forces have the possibility of developing effective teamwork but usually do not emphasize that need because of the following reasons:

- They are often established for short time periods.
- They are usually only part of the total work responsibilities of any individual on the task force.
- The people on the task force may be in competition for future promotions.
- The people on the task force see their primary loyalty toward their original work group.
- People feel they have too many items on their calendars, are pressured for time, and experience the meetings necessitated by

task force work as one of the primary causes of their time pressure.

Traditional Images

A dominant theme in American society has been a strong value on individual freedom, challenge, struggle, and achievement. Many of our images of success glorify the individual inventor, entrepreneur, or charismatic leader. We joke that a camel is a horse designed by committee. Consequently we often believe that being on a team means less attention to the individual. Our literature and movies glorify the individual and have the hero defying the restraints imposed by the group. The main Americans myths are those associated with the individual succeeding against all odds. For example, we remember our frontier heritage in the form of the lone adventurer who explored the wilds; we forget that the real building came when wagon trains brought women and men with their children. Frontier communities demonstrated the spirit of cooperation as families helped each other when necessary to pool resources for challenging tasks.

Our dualistic thinking tells us that our choice is to either glorify the individual or elevate the relationships of the team. We do not think that both are possible. If individual work is right, we believe, then teamwork is no more than a necessary evil that circumstances force us to accept. Such thinking leads us to fear loss of freedom in a group or team setting.

Creating New Images

Our approach to competition reinforces this dichotomy of individual versus team. The organization needs to compete with other firms for customers. Inside the organization, too, we see ourselves competing for jobs. Collaboration is the antithesis of the traditional approach to competition—exploit the weaknesses of the competitor. But in collaborative competition, individuals strive to improve their own capability rather than attacking the weakness of their competitors. I remember watching the women's marathon in the 1988 Olympics. Somewhere past twenty miles, the two leaders were running right next to each other at the same pace. I am sure that each wanted the gold medal. When they passed the water table, however, the woman closest to the table picked up a cup and handed it to the woman next to her. She then took her own. In an organization, this analogy implies that people collaborate to help each other succeed and simultaneously seek their individual triumphs through improvement of their own capability.

Each business or organization creates images of the accepted path to success. We need both types of images in organizations: *individual strength, perseverance, and responsibility;* and *collaborative efforts throughout the organization based on team spirit and relationships.*

Create images of effective work partnerships by circulating stories that show how:

- Partnerships provide new and valuable opportunities for each participant to extend the impact of individual capabilities and talents.
- Resolving conflicts to strengthen the team and building trust lead to a heightened experience of team spirit that elevates the quality of individual and collective action.
- Teamwork, with the active involvement of each participant, creates something worthwhile to others beyond the partnership. Improved performance would not be possible if people tried to operate independently or with completely divided responsibilities.

We will find that partnership is a liberating experience that increases rather than restricts our freedom and creates more opportunities for doing worthwhile work than we could ever find on our own.

Developing a Common Interest for New Experiences

Adding stories of collective achievement to the organization's folklore is an important step to lowering the barriers. It is more important, however, to articulate a clear common interest. You must assume there are many people whose attitudes range from a marginal willingness to tolerate teamwork to outright antagonism toward it. There is no reason for these people to even contemplate committing to collective effort if they do not see the partnership as a path to satisfy personal needs or desire. If the personal needs are purely self-serving, however, you will not be able to establish a stable partnership; people will withdraw as soon as they see their personal benefits evaporate.

On the other hand, despite the spiritual appeal of altruism or self-sacrifice, they are unlikely grounds for partnership for most people in a typical organization. There must be some middle ground between self-serving and self-sacrifice. One skill for an ally is balancing the satisfaction of one partner's personal needs with a common interest in collective problem solving and achievement. There must be a commitment to something outside the group. Any partnership must be able to answer this question: *Is the nature of our common interest significant enough to demand the same level of commitment among all participants?*

Many discussions about teamwork identify shared values or vision as a necessary binding component. As I believe you are familiar with those ideas and as I have already discussed values and vision elsewhere in this book, I prefer to concentrate upon the commitment of partnership members. The topic of building trust will follow. Although I recognize that some people can enter a new work partnership with a powerful willingness to immediately operate from trust, it seems that most people feel that trust flows from experience in working with others. Therefore I want to use the level of commitment as a base you need to construct in order to elevate the level of trust.

Commitment is the level of effort people are willing to put into their work responsibility in a partnership. It is a binding of oneself to the common interest and experienced as a relatively unalterable pledge or obligation. The expression *half-hearted enthusiasm* refers to a lack of commitment. It may seem odd to talk about the commitment to work in a partnership when the ally is a people role. It seems as if it should be commitment to *people*. But the ally role is about the quality of interpersonal relationships in the work environment; it is not about friendship, regardless of how desirable or useful that may be. It makes no sense to talk about an ally role managing interpersonal relationships among people who have no clear work purpose to their partnership. There may be important social roles that people desire, but there is no degree of friendship or socialization necessary for success in the ally role. It is quite possible that some people find a focus on this aspect of interpersonal relationships a detraction from effective work partnerships.

If the level of commitment seems to be, *let's define the work, allocate the tasks, and get it done,* you do not have the kind of commitment conducive to partnerships. Almost without exception, this attitude occurs when the partnership assignment is seen as an intrusion on the normal flow of work. What can you do in the ally role when faced with this level of commitment? It is your job to offer them the possibility of expanding their view. Drop the rhetoric; they do not need inspirational "halftime" speeches. What they need is your demonstration of ally capability to articulate your views, really hear their perspective, and be willing to continue the discussion. If you resort to your hierarchical power, abandon the essential peer relationship quality of the ally role, or try to win a debate by the force of your argument, you will lose the opportunity for a partnership.

Building Trust

Trust is the confidence or faith that people have in each other. It may seem that commitment and trust are only important or possible in a long-term relationship. For a short-term job assignment, people tend to feel they can overlook the relationship and use the pressure of the work to mask any deficiencies in commitment or trust. People also tend to believe that trust only happens when people know each other for a long time, that time is necessary to know each other's values and be able to predict or rely upon the behavior of the other.

Managers cannot command people to have commitment and trust. Rewards and punishment will have no effect. It may cause people to work together, but they will not form a partnership. A true partnership requires the free will of each participant. Nonpartners may get the task accomplished, even to a high standard, but they will not be developing the necessary capability to enter other work partnerships or collaborative efforts that will also meet high standards. They will be dependent upon a "coach" to take charge and make things happen.

There is no simple or single method for building trust. It is not merely a matter of working together for a long enough time to build familiarity with each other. It does not occur if the partnership faces complexity and ambiguity and gives mutual support only to vent frustration about the shared adversity. It *does* occur through the attitude and intention of each partner.

The manager can support the growth of trust by acting from a complete trust in the ability of each person. Such a situation occurs when each person feels that he or she still has the trust of the manager despite mistakes or errors and that the manager will provide personal support even when there is a need to be critical of performance and place a higher demand for better performance. Trust does not exist when judgment is present.

As an ally, the manager's role is one of creating an environment for the partnership to develop its own path rather than acting as the leader and delegating tasks regardless of the overall complexity and ambiguity that the group faces. Trust is not present in a manager who delegates responsibility and then feels compelled to continually check on the work. You know that you lack trust when you worry or have sleepless nights thinking about the actions of the members of the partnership. Trust does not exist when fear is present.

As an ally, the manager's role in building trust is to exhibit complete honesty. Tell people what you are thinking, share information that you possess and they want to know, tell them when you cannot share information and why, ask and accept challenging questions, give clear responses or make a clear commitment to a future response. There is no trust-building exercise—climbing ropes, blindfolded walks, rafting—that will substitute for your strength in acting from a state of trust. I have hesitated to use the clichés of role-modeling and "walking the talk," but they are the most applicable in this part of the ally role. Trust does not exist unless it exists in you.

Use the following discussion of different levels of trust to honestly assess your own position in a work partnership. After you are clear about your own motives, you can use the levels of trust to determine the state of the group. Your only hope for altering the level of trust in a group is to be at that level yourself. Every aspect of your behavior must be consistent with the level of trust you desire.

The four levels of trust are as follows:

- *Negotiated trust*—you only trust what people state in formal agreements.

- *Conditional trust*—people earn trust by proving themselves.
- *Cooperative trust*—belief in other people is not easily shaken by occasional mistakes, lapses in judgment, or errors.
- *Unconditional trust*—unquestioning faith is placed in the values, intentions, actions, and decisions of another.

Negotiated Trust

This level of trust exists in relationships that are mostly adversarial; in such relationships, people need formal agreements. When negotiated trust exists, there is basic distrust of each other—people do not trust each other's values or motives, that the other will consider their interests in an equitable manner, or that behavior and task performance will be adequate. This level is labeled *negotiated trust* on the premise that in reaching agreement, each participant assumes that others will honor the agreement; trust exists to the extent that things are explicitly agreed upon.

The group is certainly not a true partnership at this stage. It is likely that each individual is thinking about protecting his or her own interest. There is no true joining of spirit. The process for being successful at this level of trust is to have each individual bring up the items he or she feels will deter from the group's performance and the items he or she feels are necessary for the group to succeed. Form agreements that explicitly address the concerns of all people in the partnership. If you are unwilling to address legitimate concerns, you are not at the level of negotiated trust, and you will not move a group to this most basic level of trust.

Conditional Trust

This trust exists when people are willing to give each other the benefit of the doubt but reserve full judgment until they see how everyone behaves. They are adopting a wait-and-see attitude, and each person has an image of various expectations for other members of the group. This trust is conditional because a failure to meet those expectations will lead to a reduction in trust. This is a stage beyond the negotiated trust because there truly is an attitude of goodwill combined with the wariness. People do not feel that they are adversaries; they believe that they have interests in common. They are truly willing to give each other a chance; they believe that other members are starting with good intentions about the work and the relationships.

When expectations are not fulfilled, the trust begins to erode. One could say that trust in this situation is in a fragile state. When things go well, there is no challenge to this level of trust. People might have a good partnership experience, but they will not know if they created the capability of the team or the circumstances were simply fortuitous for that team. Outside adversity, deadline pressure, unexpected complications, or unanticipated setbacks place strains on the partnership and the level of trust.

One process for building this level of trust is having each person state his or her expectations, hopes, desires, and values. Creating values, vision, purpose, and mission for the team may also help. Coming to some common understanding of individual and group expectations and direction is useful to alleviate some of the fear blocking conditional trust.

Cooperative Trust

This level of trust is a significant stage beyond conditional trust. People have expectations of each other but failing to meet these expectations does not automatically erode the level of trust. It leads the person to assume that there is some misunderstanding or miscommunication. When this level of trust pervades a partnership, each member is actively seeking ways to further understand the other and reconcile differences.

In conditional trust, one could say that there is a quid pro quo: If you are doing what we expect, then we will continue to trust you. In cooperative trust, there is no real quid pro quo. People do not extend cooperative trust on the basis of expecting something in return. They have a strongly held belief that people will act with the right intentions and the interests of the partnership in mind. There is also a real knowledge that people will make mistakes, do things unintentionally that may cause harm, and fall back on their own needs, putting their own interests ahead of the group. These are not violations of trust but merely human frailties. People in the partnership will protect each other when their weaknesses strike, and they will also trust each other to develop past these weaknesses.

As the partnership faces more challenging responsibilities, it may be pushing other team members to the limits of their capabilities. At such times, judgment of each other may become more of an issue. When people feel judged, they do not feel trusted. As the perception of judgment increases, the trust level of the partnership may decline. In the face of increasing fear and judgment, a strong partnership has processes that pull the group together. They know how to sit down and talk things out. If the desire to cooperate and be conciliatory is still present, the group can restore its level of trust.

Creating cooperative trust requires an explicit emphasis on building relationships. People in the partnership will create mutually held values, vision, purpose, and mission that not only relate to the work they are doing but to the kind of partnership they want to build among themselves. They will also discuss their personal values, vision, mission, and purpose.

Unconditional Trust

This trust exists when people rely on the word of each other without questioning it. It is trust unaffected by individual weaknesses. It exists among adults when they are truly willing to take responsibility for their own actions and their own state, and they fully trust that others will do the same.

Such trust may seem too idealistic or impossible for people in an organization, but it is not. Think of this level of trust as a worthwhile aspiration, not beyond our capabilities. It is simply that state of trust that is nearly unshakable, in which people completely trust each other's actions. If those actions produce undesirable results or harmful consequences, they trust the other person will find ways to improve. For example, suppose this level of trust existed in physical team-building exercises. If someone failed in a responsibility, putting someone else in a hazardous position that person would be completely willing to trust him or her again. That person trusts that he or she acknowledges the mistake, recognizes his or her own deficiencies or weaknesses, and makes an honest assessment to continue handling the responsibility. People trust each other to be conscious of their decisions, responsible for their own actions, willing to seek help when confronted with situations beyond their capability, and improve actions when there are problems.

Part of unconditional trust is that people are not suspicious of the motivation or intentions of others in the partnership. They accept that problems can occur when people are operating in areas beyond their capability, and they believe that people are working from intentions that serve the whole partnership. All members are willing to receive help from each other. If someone questions someone else's actions, these questions are seen as help in developing strengths and overcoming weaknesses.

Processes to move toward this level of trust are both individual and collective. Unconditional trust is a state individuals reach when they do not depend upon the level of trust of the other. People in this state are neither idealistic nor naive; they know there may be situations when people violate their trust, but they are willing to take the time and responsibility to work to improve those situations. They would rather risk the problems caused by extending unconditional trust than the problems caused by a lower level of trust.

Transforming Conflict to Progress

Conflict among people is inevitable. Normal human foibles—trivial concerns, misunderstanding, poor communications, fears, judgments, failure to appreciate different perspectives, inflexibility, the need to win, or the need to be right—cause conflict. Even if we transcend all these issues, we can still expect that conflict will exist. Inevitably, people will have different opinions, ideas, or interpretations of situations. Conflicts will occur at any level of trust.

Teams lose some of their effectiveness when they avoid conflict. If everyone already thinks the same way and has the same ideas, why bother with meetings? Positive conflict can lead to totally different solutions than any individual could discover independently.

Conflict resolution is of major importance when people are working collaboratively. The processes used can raise the level of trust. As people reveal and resolve their differences, they begin to have more confidence in each other.

There can be an upward spiral between the use of conflict resolution and the levels of commitment and trust. There can also be a downward spiral. Groups can become stalled in their conflict; surfacing differences can anger people, and they find more items to disagree upon. They may resent the issues that others want to discuss and start losing their commitment and trust. Nevertheless most people know that if a serious issue remains hidden, not consciously addressed, it will often affect many aspects of collaborative work as it keeps manifesting in different forms. People may choose the risky strategy of ignoring things and hoping they will go away when they feel their ability to complete the task is tenuous. They may fear that any time spent in conflict resolution will not succeed and only delay their work.

In all levels of conflict resolution, there is an assumption of a basic goodwill among team members. If the attitude is win at all costs, resolution will be quite difficult. The way you handle conflict is a tremendous clue to other participants about your level of trust and your skills as an ally. Assess your own capabilities by the way you use these four types of conflict resolution:

- *Arbitration*—using a third party to make the decision resolving the conflict
- *Mediation*—using a third party to counsel the conflicting parties toward a mutual resolution
- *Compromise*—the parties to the conflict conducting their own negotiation to make trades that reach a resolution
- *Dialogue*—the parties to the conflict conducting discussion until each fully understands the other and a resolution emerges

Arbitration

The people involved in the conflict have no way to truly hear each other and reach an agreement. They turn to someone else to present their sides and have that person make a decision. This is a challenging situation for a manager as an ally. People are dependent upon the capability of the manager. Many managers like to fix problems when they hear about them, and as people are asking for advice, it would be natural to give it—the desire is to reach a decision that seems to resolve the conflict. But often a decision quickly chosen does not involve sufficient effort in getting to the true cause of the conflict. If the cause remains, it will manifest in other ways at other times. The immediate issue is resolved, but the cause of the difference may remain unresolved.

Mediation

The role of the ally is to help the people in the conflict gain an understanding and, if possible, an appreciation of the perspective of each other. The mediation process is one of helping the conflicting parties find their own resolution through discussion. People need mediation when their attempts to resolve conflict without help break down and inflame the conflict. This is an opportunity for the ally to resolve the immediate conflict and get to the cause of the differences to minimize future conflicts.

Compromise

There are obvious possibilities for compromise in arbitration and mediation, but the word *compromise* in this instance means those circumstances in which the conflicting sides work out their own resolution. A compromise often has both sides making concessions, and this is not always satisfying. In resolving the conflict, each person feels he or she has sacrificed something to gain agreement. Compromise does not work if one person has more power and forces concessions from the other—that type of imbalance is no longer a compromise.

In addition to this process of trading, there is another process that sometimes works in compromise: the appeal to higher values. The parties find the ground that they hold in common. They may return to the core values of the group or the organization; revisit purpose, vision, mission, and principles; find something of more fundamental importance to themselves, the group, or the organization. This approach can create a "win-win" situation: Both sides feel they have gained from the compromise.

On the other hand, resolution of the conflict may require the parties to find a third path that neither had chosen prior to the compromise. This compromise path may not be as favorable as either of the original positions, but the parties agree in order to resolve the conflict.

Dialogue

A dialogue is an open, frank, and honest discussion of ideas and positions to reach mutual understanding and harmony. There is no intention in this approach for either party to compromise, nor is there a desire for concessions from any participant. There is a very different atmosphere in a group that uses this technique. The ally manager actively participates in these dialogues but does not bring resolution, facilitate the discussion, or remain as an observer.

This form of conflict resolution takes place when there is a high level of trust, and it also fosters a high level of trust. In a dialogue, people know that they disagree, but they do not allow the disagreement to affect their basic relationship with others. They assume that there is a common bonding with deeper values, and they assume that each person has good intentions. They want to avoid compromise that exists just for the sake of finding a resolution.

In a dialogue, they actively seek a solution, which could be the position of one of the parties or a completely new idea. A dialogue is not a debate; each person may have a passion for his or her idea but does not resort to using powerful debate skills to overwhelm others' thoughts. Nor are people trying to find the weaknesses of each other's ideas. They are trying to find the strengths and the meaning behind those ideas. They acknowledge that there is a reason that the other has a different perspective and honestly want to understand how that perspective led to the opinion. In a true dialogue, they may be more willing to see problems with their own ideas than to actively seek problems in the ideas of the others.

Learning Ally Role Skills

Lowering the Barriers to Teamwork

- Try to identify barriers to teamwork that you personally experience and that you notice in the organization.
- Identify images that do or could support more collaborative work in your organization.
- Identify a common interest that could elevate the desire for teamwork.
- Define the nature of commitment needed to make the collaboration more successful.
- Determine how you can best blend individual needs, responsibility, and accountability with collaborative work.

Building Trust

- For your team or any collaborative work, identify your level of trust.
- Identify the conditions on the team that lead you to that level.
- Identify your own state—the existence or lack of fears, judgments, patience, tolerance, capability—that leads you to that level of trust.
- Assess the level of trust of others in your group.
- Determine what you could do as an ally to move them to higher levels of trust.

Transforming Conflict to Progress

- Think of different conflicts in which you have a vested interest.
- In these conflicts, determine what it is about the other person or his or her position that would cause you to seek one method of resolution over another.
- Determine how your own level of trust leads you to select one method of resolution over another.
- Identify what you need to learn to further develop your own ally skills so that the dialogue approach becomes your method of choice.

Principal Focus of Managing Effort	Principal Leadership Process		
	Creating Order	Inspiring Action	Improving Performance
Systems	**Sage** Designs Strategy	**Visionary** Innovates the Future	**Magician** Orchestrates Change
People	**Globalist** Bridges Cultural Differences	**Mentor** Motivates Development	**Ally** Builds Partnerships
Work	**Sovereign** Empowers Decisions	**Guide** Achieves Goals	**Artisan** Pursues Excellence

FOUNDATION OF ALL ROLES
CORE VALUES

CHAPTER NINE

Empowering Decisions

Learning the Role of the Sovereign

Profile of a Sovereign

The role name *sovereign* is the best choice to indicate a person who makes decisions, takes responsibility for the outcomes, and empowers others to do the same. When a crisis or opportunity arises, the response is often, "Let's establish a committee (team, task force) to study this situation further." This is a perfectly rational approach and a good shield for indecisiveness. In the sovereign role, a manager will also ask, "Based upon what I know now, what would I do? What are the consequences of not deciding now? What do I hope to learn during this delay and how do I expect that to influence the decision?" The manager uses clear and comprehensive decision-making techniques, sees the way further study aids that method, and determines the best time to decide.

The future will always remain uncertain and carry risks; no amount of study will ever create absolute certainty. Life seems to be filled with decisions. You go to a restaurant and have trouble ordering because choosing one dish means you will have to give up eating something else, and how do you know you have made the best choice without more taste information? You are standing on the threshold of the airline door about to jump for your first sky dive. If you decide not to jump, what will people think of you? If you do jump and do not like it, you cannot get back into the plane. As Yogi Berra says, "When you come to a fork in the road, take it."

Maybe you learned to be rational and logical in your approach. If you delay a decision, it is because you need more information, are judiciously weighing the facts, or are making sure you have accurately analyzed all pros and cons. Or you are trying to test your decision in a manner similar to using a test market prior to national distribution. This is the conservative, cautious approach to decisions: Care, not speed, is the issue. You believe using the right analysis leads to intelligent decision making. You probably went to business school. Unfortunately, you are only using the analytical side of your brain—the intuitive side simply does not fit in this approach to decisions.

You may feel that making decisions is not a problem for you. You use "gut feelings," "shooting from the hip," or "intuition." You are action oriented and would rather do something than "beat a dead horse" with too much discussion or thought; you are impatient with those who dawdle because you know that by delaying a decision you can miss significant opportunities. You are a risk-taker, willing to pursue a path despite little information; you believe that "the one who hesitates is lost." Yours is a free-wheeling, aggressive approach to decisions. You may have gone to business school, but that did not develop your basic skills. For you, the analytical approach does not fit because "time is of the essence."

In a typical significant decision, there are two or more attractive alternatives. Avoiding procrastination, sovereigns will decide. They employ a useful combination of judiciousness and gut feeling. This decisiveness results from a willingness to face uncertainty, commit to the chosen alternative, and let go of the possibilities embedded in the rejected alternatives. Sovereigns will never hide beyond company policy or group decisions as a shield for personal responsibility; they will take a clear stand. Their power comes from their decisiveness and unwavering responsibility for the consequences of their choice.

In empowering others to decide, the sovereign is helping them become accountable for their actions and giving them the power to make decisions without imposing excessive conditions. If you have no scope for decisions, you have not been empowered;

Wells' Field Guide—How to Spot a Sovereign

Habitat

The sovereign can be found at the crossroads. Dwelling will contain several versions of the scales of justice. Usually can be seen roaming the lands of the intuitive and the analytical.

Habits

Welcomes accountability in situations with attractive and complex alternatives even when there are high stakes and risk.

Uses power responsibly to make decisions.

Empowers others by increasing the range of their decisions.

Creates order by choosing a definite course of action in response to immediate time pressures.

Balances this response to significant immediate pressures with the organization's longer-term interests.

Minimizes delay of decision and delay between decision and action.

Considers a range of outcomes and consequences of the decision including the unexpected, unintended, and undesirable.

Confronts own response to uncertainty or any other issue leading to procrastination.

Relies on innovative thinking to bring creativity to problem solving and decision making.

Will take a stand and decide on own when it is necessary.

Will carry out tough and/or unpopular decisions.

Moves quickly and directly to solve problems and make decisions.

Takes responsibility for any decision made individually or as part of a group.

---

accountability without decision authority is a deception. Furthermore, decision-making authority without the willingness to accept responsibility is cowardice.

How the Sovereign Helps the Organization

This role reflects the combination of the leadership process of creating order and the work focus of managing effort. Different things occur to destabilize work; some are predictable, and some are completely unexpected. In fact, the reactions to them often create further disorder. Order is not routine, procedures, rules, and conformity at work; it is created by a manager with a willingness to choose a course of action and be responsible for that choice even in the face of uncertainty, a manager who ensures that other people also have the power and accountability to act.

It is potentially disruptive and disorderly to centralize all power and decision making in a few hands. When several different levels of management are needed for approval of actions, we have bureaucracy with no guarantee of true order. This type of system provides too many opportunities for people to hide and avoid decisions or shift responsibility for decisions. As a sovereign, the manager *empowers decisions* to create orderly decentralization.

One could say that it is through decisions that managers earn their pay. Much of a manager's work and responsibility is preparing for the next decision or implementing a previous decision. A decision will put you on one path at a crossroads, but as you proceed down that path, other crossroads will appear and other decisions will be necessary. Keeping the organization operating as a well-balanced and synchronized system requires a connecting link among decisions. A decision is an investment in the future of the organization, and we can never fully know what the future will bring; thus decisions in organizations are complex, as shown in Table 10.

As you can see, this is a complex number of characteristics to consider in a decision. This should not be unexpected: A manager is not a jet fighter pilot, and there are no significant split-second decisions; there is time to think. Nevertheless there is a decision point, and all the preparation comes down to that one instant. *A decision is a particular moment in time in which an individual or a team becomes committed to a path of action leading to a future with the expectation of attaining desired outcomes.*

How a Sovereign Is Value-Driven

Decisions are challenging when the alternatives are complex and have complex impacts, both positive and negative. A decision is

Table 10   Decision Characteristics in Organizations

Choice among attractive alternatives, each having valuable consequences

Choice among alternatives, each having costly impacts on the organization or on different groups of people

Complex sets of advantages and disadvantages

Lack of complete information

Unknown or unintended hazards or consequences

Irreversibility of the chosen path

Loss of other paths

Different levels of risk

Personal state that leads to impulsiveness or procrastination

Personal response to uncertainty

Need for well-structured analytical thinking

Need for free-flowing intuitive thinking

Networks of organization decisions that affect each other and the overall success and health of the whole system

Aiming people and the organization toward some desired but uncertain future

significant when it has far-reaching consequences that are important to the organization or to people or to both. Core values provide a beacon for serious choices. The appropriate exercise of the power to decide requires that the chosen alternative embodies core values.

We often think that attention to core values will effectively guide choice. We expect someone strong in the sovereign role not to compromise core values and make decisions purely for expediency. Obviously, there are also some decisions where core values are not important to the choice. Perhaps the most difficult decisions occur when two alternatives represent different but equally valid core values. Each alternative leads to a completely different path of action, incorporating one core value and violating the core value embedded in the other alternative. There is no simple, fully

Warning Signs of Excess

You know you have overdone the sovereign role if you

Avoid information or opinions that will delay a decision

Lack patience for people who cannot decide

Have little concern for people defending stakes in alternatives that are less desirable

Are intolerant of delays to implementing a well-chosen decision

See cultural differences as putting unnecessary subjectivity into decisions

Would rather make decision or empower one person than build consensus

Cannot sustain energy for changes or visions that are too long term or seem detached from more immediate work pressures

Would rather choose than contemplate

Prefer analysis to synthesis

---

satisfactory resolution to this dilemma. Chapter Two contains some suggested guidelines for facing this decision in the section on managing values conflict for an individual. A sovereign will venture into this situation.

Core values gain their significance when we are able to live by them. Decision making is the crucial point at which to consider values as providing the guidance we desire; therefore values must permeate the decision process. However, under the pressure to reach a decision, it is often possible to neglect values.

Core values bring our spirit, a sense of a meaningful life, into decisions. Without core values present, people become fairly mechanical in their way of dealing with situations. They justify their actions by rationalizing that any organizational decision should pursue one purpose—enhanced profit, for example. To all organizations, profit is an important outcome for any decision, but it is not a core value.

It seems reasonable to say that if an individual's core values are not present, that individual has little at stake in the decision. Therefore the decision should belong to someone else, someone with a stake, whose values are affected by the implementation of the decision or the outcomes. If an organization's core values cannot be present, the decision process will be weakened. In the long run, decisions inconsistent with core values will begin to undermine the organization itself. The fabric of that organization, the cohesiveness that keeps people together, begins to tear.

The intention is to choose that alternative that most closely aligns with desired core values; therefore it is important to identify the core values relevant to the decision. It is also always important to think about the core values of the people empowered to make the decision, the people affected by the decision, and the organization itself in order to determine what is really at stake. If the decision seems to have little relationship to values, then there is less at stake and less need to agonize over the decision.

Building Sovereign Skills

The three major sovereign skills developed in this chapter are the following:

- *Empowering Others*—ensuring that accountability for performance is appropriately matched with the power and responsibility to decide
- *Deciding*—following a sufficiently comprehensive approach to making significant decisions
- *Facing Procrastination and Impulsiveness*—addressing the time-tested blocks to effective decision making

Empowering Others

Sovereignty is about power. There is little doubt that the power to decide is one of the ultimate powers within an organization. For example, think of the times that you have been part of a group in which someone has asked for your input but has retained the right to make the final decision. Also consider situations when someone has given you some authority but has retained the final say, approval, or veto. Decision-making authority is the final power in any major undertaking within an organization. Decisions put people on a path toward the future and reflect the degree of control they exercise over themselves and their environment.

All the current talk about empowering employees is complete deception unless people have the power to make significant decisions. Too often, empowerment simply means being held accountable for the results of one's work, but without the power to decide, it is not true empowerment, and accountability is inappropriate. A trick in raising small children is to give them highly restricted choices rather than rules: for example, choosing which parent will read a story rather than telling them to go to bed. Restricted choice is not empowerment and is inappropriate for responsible adults. Effective sovereignty means sharing power to decide and removing as many restrictions as possible.

There are times when the manager is going to make the decision independently, perhaps with some input from the group. It is necessary to keep the boundaries clear and for the manager to assume the full responsibility for the consequences of the decision. This responsibility does not preclude acknowledging the contributions of others. If things do not go as planned, the manager is responsible and does not rationalize the difficulty by blaming others for the poor quality of information or advice they provided.

There are other times when a group will decide. Frequently, people avoid personal responsibility for the decision. Empowerment means each person in the group accepts personal accountability for the decision. For this, they must have full participation in the decision process; if not, the manager has failed to empower others on the team, individuals have failed to be clear about their own intentions and attitudes toward the decision, or the opinions of some have dominated the opinions of others.

Sovereignty in decision making means that no individual in the group can simply "go along" with the decision if he or she has true reservations about it. It also means that taking a vote to resolve a conflict when there are significant differences will result in a decision but not necessarily in all group members feeling personally responsible. Under these conditions, it is possible for any member of the group to derail the decision process by refusing to be responsible. Because of these kinds of complications, many managers will fall back on individual decision making. Frustration with "participatory management" and other forms of inclusion in decisions occurs because it is difficult to get everyone to fully agree to a single decision. A full agreement means that each person takes a stand on the decision and will accept responsibility for it.

This role is quite challenging and is probably the one most frequently subject to excessive emphasis because it is the role that is the center of power, the role from which an individual is able to take charge, retain control, and preserve command of most activities of a group. Obviously, developing sovereignty in the whole group is a challenge because it inevitably means a sharing of power.

Who should be empowered to make a decision? Those affected by the decision? There are major decisions that can affect large segments of the organization; it is neither possible nor practical to have people involved in every decision that affects them. We live in a representative democracy; do we really want everyone participating in every decision? Consensus is an attractive idea but has very practical limitations. Even with smaller groups, it is often cumbersome to have each individual participate in every decision, whereas it is reasonable to have representatives of different stakeholders participate in the decision.

On the other hand, we often form a task force to study an issue, come up with alternatives, and make a recommendation, but the power to decide lies elsewhere. This can be frustrating for the participants. It may be a good principle to have those involved in understanding the alternatives and the different components make the decision. If they are doing the work, why exclude them from the power? You only have power when your choice sticks and you are held accountable for the consequences. When people have no power, we call them disenfranchised—being excluded from power, they may not feel part of the system and will tend to have a lower level of loyalty.

There is tremendous merit in moving decisions down in an organization as far as possible. How do you know how far down? When the next level up cannot have any more information or insight into the decision and would only retain the decision power out of a desire for control—that's how far down. Therefore, in deciding whom to empower, you have two major criteria: the person's position in the organization and the person's attributes. Judge the position first, and determine if it provides sufficient perspective and access to the relevant information to make the decision. Next, think about the person occupying the position: Does that person have sufficient experience, capability, and acceptance of responsibility to properly use the perspective from that position and make a decision? Clearly, you can use a similar process with a group.

Remember, if you have empowered someone to decide, you are no longer the final arbiter on the decision. You do not have veto power; your approval is not necessary. If you are uncomfortable with that degree of empowerment, participate actively with that person (or group) in the decision process, and make the method for reaching the final decision absolutely clear.

In order to have responsibility, we need to be committed to the alternative we choose. We need to believe in it. One thing that interferes with the strength of this commitment is that rejected alternatives will contain some features we desire, and the chosen alternative will contain some features we find less desirable. We do not live in a perfect world, and the nature of the decision was a choice among alternatives with relative advantages and disadvantages. Furthermore desirability is not the same thing as likes and dislikes. For example, one alternative may have you working with people you do not like. Another alternative may place you in an environment that you like. These likes and dislikes can distort your decisions. Qualities or characteristics of alternatives are desirable when they connect with what is truly important in the decision, for example, deeply held values or significant outcomes. If you focus on your likes and dislikes, you will often lose contact with what is really important to you.

Anticipation or imagination about what others will think of us if we succeed or fail in our decision can affect our willingness to accept responsibility. It is natural to want responsibility when others' thoughts would be positive and avoid it when those thoughts would be negative. Unfortunately, we need to accept responsibility prior to the decision, not wait to see what happens and then try to get or avoid credit. A decision requires us to take a definite stand and accept accountability up front. Responsibility links us back to empowerment, and anyone who wants the power to decide must accept accountability.

Deciding

A major attribute in the sovereign role is the ability to make difficult decisions. Tied to this ability is the quality of taking responsibility for the consequences of decisions and the willingness to empower others by giving them increasing authority to make decisions. Therefore the major focus of this section is a fairly rigorous and challenging decision process. By following the various components of this process, you will increase your competency in the sovereign role.

There are several components to this decision process, which you can approach analytically or intuitively. Analysis develops knowledge about each component in which you can communicate reasoning to another person; intuition often relies upon prior experience. The latter is a more challenging approach because it is often difficult when using intuition to articulate specific reasons to another person.

The major components to decision making are the following:

- *Alternatives*—the choices you face
- *Uncertainty and risk*—the inability to ever know the future and your attitude toward the risk
- *Linkage*—the way any single decision must be part of the larger context of the organization and consistent with other decisions
- *Outcomes*—the entire set of potential consequences of implementing the decision
- *Implementation*—the effort and resource commitments necessary to carry out the decision

These multiple components create a fairly complex decision process, but each is important to significant decisions. It is often difficult, however, to give full attention to all components; choices are often necessary to emphasize some components and ignore others. Such choices depend upon the situation and how sensitive the choice is to the particular component. Sensitivity means that the decision could easily change as one develops information regarding a component. If there is little likelihood the decision will change, then it is less important to focus on that component.

This approach is similar to the approach used when deciding to delay a decision for more information. If new information is likely to affect the decision and the cost of attaining the information and delaying the decision are acceptable, get the information. If the decision is relatively insensitive or the costs are too high relative to a decision error, do not seek additional information.

A relationship exists among these components because it is frequently necessary to work through several of them before feeling complete on any one. Thought in one component will affect thoughts in other components, and each component will give different insights into the decision. There is no single linear sequence for going through these elements; it is possible to start with any of the components and then move through the other components.

Inability to decide and dissatisfaction with decisions are usually a result of an incomplete decision process. These components assure us that we have been as complete as possible given the information available to us at the time we make a decision.

As you read through the different ideas about components, do not feel constrained to follow them in the written order, and do not be concerned about whether you are putting your thoughts in the "right" component. It is more important to improve your sense of the interaction among components and what each is distinctively adding to the quality of your decisions.

The decision process is iterative; you may need to return to some components after you have worked with other components. It is also possible that as you work with one of the components, you will gain some new insight into the decision and that the insight will lead you to a decision without the necessity to do work on more of the components. Nor is it necessary to do detailed work on each of the components. The essential reason for this whole model is to improve decision making and help you make decisions in challenging circumstances.

A decision is the selection of one alternative. As you work through this model, some of the alternatives will diminish while others will increase in their attractiveness to you. You may find that you thought you had several alternatives that were strong possibilities, but by the time you complete the process there is only one left that has any real value. This decision process does not depend upon weighing pros and cons; rather it improves clarity about the alternatives, your own attitudes toward those alternatives, and the process of choosing. It is possible to say that the decision emerges by working on this process.

Decision making is a major difficulty faced by every group. Teams quickly find that voting is an expedient but unsatisfactory method when there are significant differences among people on the team. As you improve your understanding of these decision process components, you will be more likely to make decisions acceptable to all team members and better understand the source of differences when you seem unable to agree on one path. Rather than debating the decision and having the strongest team member win, you can find the different blocks that people have to decision making and their different perspectives about a variety of issues connected to the decision.

Alternatives

The whole decision process is one of choosing among alternatives, and each component of the process is one of the means for helping this choice. There are a few ways to think about alternatives that will help you choose among them.

First, there is the inspiration that leads to the initial ideas of possible alternatives. Second, there is the thinking that designs more details for each alternative. Third, there is the effort to be sure that there is an equivalent level of comprehension of each alternative by everyone participating in the decision. Fourth, there is the thinking that leads to modifications of alternatives. As you start to analyze the alternatives, you may find that by modifying one alternative you can include some of the desirable features from another alternative.

The first step is a creative process of identifying alternatives. You can think about a wide range of possibilities or imagine the best possible circumstances. You should not allow judgment to come in at this point and lead to an instantaneous evaluation and rejection of alternatives. Sometimes this judgment process moves so fast that you will reject an alternative when it is only a seed of an idea in your head. Include the ideas of others, and think about their preferred alternatives. Think about alternatives that have been possible for other decisions you or others have made, and consider if these alternatives are relevant at this point.

Once you have identified a range of alternatives, try to choose the ones that have the strongest possibilities for you or your team to pursue and accomplish. In designing an alternative, you are trying to become as informed as possible about its different characteristics and qualities. Any alternative is likely to have some uncertainty; you will not be able to design or know every feature of every alternative. In many decisions, you have control over these features. Try to notice if a bias is entering your design that reflects an underlying preference for one of the alternatives. If this preference is strong and accurate, you may already have your decision and need not waste more time on the rest of the decision process.

To participate in the creation and design of alternatives, each person should have sufficient understanding. Make sure everyone shares the same interpretation of the alternatives. This should be an objective process, but it is possible for people's preferences to come into play, giving them different impressions of the alternatives. When you evaluate the alternatives with the different components that follow, it is quite easy for your preferences to create more favorable views of some alternatives. In a group, it is useful to get these preferences identified early on; otherwise the group will be debating an evaluation when people are really trying to find a way to defend a position they already hold.

The step of modifying alternatives occurs when you work through the other decision process components and gain new insights. These insights may lead to new combinations of alternatives or redesigning an alternative to shift it to a more desirable state.

Uncertainty and Risk

Any decision involves a path of action you will pursue in the future. You cannot perfectly predict the experience of being on that path or your success in attaining your desired outcomes; uncertainty exists because of hazards and unknowns in the future. Of course, you can "measure" uncertainty, use probabilities, and quantify the risk you face. But your response to uncertainty and risk in any decision may be quite different from the answer you get from the quantified approach. Decision makers experience uncertainty as apprehension, anxiety, excitement, or fear, and this affects their attitude toward risk in that situation. There are times when you are willing to embrace risk and times when you go out of your way to avoid risk.

If the stakes are high for the organization, is there greater or less willingness to take risk? What about if the personal stakes are high, such as a promotion or a career-damaging failure? In a group decision, everyone sees the same risk numbers, but does everyone have the same attitude toward risk? These are all subjective questions—your responses vary depending upon the circumstances, and different people will have different responses. If the personal rewards are higher and the punishment for failure lower, that will encourage people to take more risk.

You need to be clear about the attitude toward risk of the people making the decision as well as of the organization itself. Try to articulate the apprehensions, anxieties, excitement, and fears you and others experience regarding this decision. If you can identify these responses, you can identify the source of your attitude toward risk in the particular situation and determine if you will allow that attitude to drive your thinking and choice.

I suggest you also conduct a quick risk assessment to determine your exposure to problems in the different alternatives. When we say there is uncertainty in the decision because it is about the future, we are also saying that each alternative could have different types of uncertainty. To design an alternative, you have probably made some assumptions; it is these assumptions that contain your uncertainty. Quickly separate the assumptions that have a high level of uncertainty from those that have a low level. Then assess the relative impact on your organization if the assumption proves wrong. It should be clear that your greatest risk is with those assumptions in which the uncertainty and impact are highest. Determine if you are willing to accept such risk or if it is worth pursuing additional information to reduce some of the uncertainty.

Linkage

Decisions of significance are usually not made in isolation. A decision is a move into a different kind of future, and in any organization, a decision in one part will link with other decisions of current importance. If a production department makes a decision that changes the process of building the product, there may need to be corresponding marketing decisions. If a marketing decision is made to enter new markets, there may need to be corresponding production and finance decisions.

It is also realistic to assume that a decision is not set in concrete. Things will happen in implementing the decision that will require further decisions in the future. If we are at a fork in the road and choose one path, we know that each path will lead to different forks and further decisions. Picture the decision as a rock tossed into calm water. As the decision ripples outward, there are many effects. Identify possible effects of your alternatives on other parts of the organization, and determine if they are prepared for the consequences of your choice. Try to identify other concurrent decisions and how they link into your alternatives; plot out the future decisions you will face for each of the alternatives, and remember, the decision you face is affected by the ripples from other decisions.

Outcomes

When you think about outcomes, you are thinking about the particular benefits of the decision you are facing. A decision is always about placing yourself on one path of action chosen from different alternatives. Sometimes different paths can lead to the same outcomes, but we often find that as we vary the paths, the outcomes will also change. It wouldn't be much of a decision if each alternative led to the same outcomes or if one alternative was most favorable on all outcomes. The most likely case is relative advantages and disadvantages for each alternative. We need to weigh the different impacts on outcomes; when we identify outcomes, we can seek those most directly connected to what we value and avoid those that conflict with our values.

Some outcomes are specific results you are trying to achieve for yourself, others, or the organization. You need to determine how this array of results varies with the different alternatives. If there were only one desired result, you would choose the alternative with the "highest score." Expect, however, that you will face multiple results. An array of new opportunities (and problems) can accompany any alternative. The whole purpose of the decision can be to put the organization in a different position where it will have a better chance of pursuing the benefits or results it desires.

Decisions can also have unintended or peripheral consequences such as beneficial or harmful effects, although they are not the main intention of the decision. Simply ignoring them because they do not fit your intentions is an inappropriate response. Ignorance is only bliss in George Orwell's fictional world. Suppose an alternative will lead to the results you desire but will negatively affect others. In such a case, you are in a difficult position. Operating from self-interest will make the decision much easier, but your decision will not accurately represent reality. On the other hand, sacrificing your interests to avoid the undesired consequences may be too great a burden. There is no doubt that this is one of the most difficult challenges in major decisions, and you must find your own path through this maze; there are no simple rules to follow.

Implementation

We conclude our journey through the decision process with a view of implementing the decision. We must try to experience the consequences of the decision before they occur by articulating some details of the specific sequence of steps we plan to follow on the path of action that will result from that decision. An examination of the demands placed upon the guide role will assure a successful implementation of the decision.

Visualizing the path for each alternative creates a sense of the dynamics involved in living out or implementing the decision. You will find that anticipating the experience of being on the path will give your decision a better grounding in reality.

Facing Procrastination and Impulsiveness

The premise in the previous skill is that each component is important to a decision. Conversely, a weakness in any one area is a potential source of procrastination or impulsiveness in a decision. Procrastination can occur when some block in one or more components causes a person to rationalize avoidance of the decision; impulsiveness can occur when a person is so captivated by one or more components that he or she is driven to a quick decision without giving appropriate consideration to the other components of the process.

As you work through the different components, you can judge if you are in an area where your approach tends to be impulsive: Perhaps you are too impatient to fully address the details of that part of the decision process. Impulsiveness can increase as the decision becomes simpler or lower risk. You can judge if the component identifies a source of your procrastination: Perhaps you are reluctant to take a stand on that component. Procrastination increases as the decision becomes more complex or higher risk.

Caution is the other side of the coin from procrastination. Perhaps an unwillingness to decide reveals serious issues that we want to resolve. Maybe we need more information, or maybe there are problems with alternatives or outcomes that require further thought or further investigation. If an issue is unresolvable, however, then we are back to facing our avoidance of decisions.

Similarly, intuition is the other side of the coin from impulsiveness. Perhaps our leaping into decision reveals a confidence in the correctness of our choice that will not be affected by more thoughtful or detailed analysis. If we are completely unable to articulate supportable reasons for our choice, however, then we are back to facing our wild leaping into decisions.

More impulsive people frequently view caution as a sign of procrastination, whereas procrastinating people frequently view use of intuition as a sign of impulsiveness. We can easily have groups of people responsible for decisions but pulled in both ways. Any individual can waver among procrastination, effective decision making, and impulsiveness as the situation changes. These twin problems for decision making are pervasive, and even the best decision makers can fall victim to them.

Clearly, careful attention to each of the components of the decision-making process is one way to face procrastination and impulsiveness. We must recognize, however, that these tendencies often have their origins in an emotional response to the decision. We do not like to talk about emotions in business, especially when we are dealing with decision making, when we tend to want people to address facts, information, and knowledge. By using the decision process, we would be trying to temper emotions by using a "rational" approach to decisions, even though the process embodies intuitive as well as analytic thinking, and this is not a fully satisfactory mechanism. It may be necessary to sort out the emotional roots of our procrastination and impulsiveness.

Whatever we choose, we need to recognize that facing procrastination and impulsiveness is an important skill for the sovereign. If you really want to empower others and give them decision responsibility, you must recognize that procrastination and impulsiveness are potential problems. The only way you can help someone face these problems is to have faced them yourself. If necessary, you may need to experiment by pushing yourself into decisions that will evoke your tendency toward procrastination or impulsiveness.

Learning Sovereign Role Skills

Empowering Others

- Determine the degree to which you are empowered by assessing your degree of decision authority.
- Identify decisions that people who report to you could make because they have sufficient access to appropriate information.
- Assess your own willingness to relinquish control of those decisions.
- Identify areas of your own accountability, and determine if you have decision authority sufficient to fully accept the limits of that accountability.
- Identify areas of possible accountability for people who report to you, and determine the decision authority they would need.
- Assess whether people are willing to be held responsible for the consequences of the decisions they currently make and could make.

Deciding

- As you read through the different components, you can treat the entire presentation as guidance for your own decisions.
- Use some examples that are important to you.
- Take the ideas and insights presented and apply them to your own decision.
- If a component does not seem important enough for your decision, trust your judgment and do not invest time in it.
- Determine if there is a pattern to which components are the most important for different types of decisions you face.
- Determine if you have some preference pattern for the components—emphasizing some and ignoring others.
- The purpose of this process is to give you guidelines for comprehensive decision making when there is a large stake in the decision. Using it several times will add to your capability and allow you to be more adept and rapid in its application.
- The detail in the components could lead you to become overly analytical in decisions. Intuition is a powerful and useful part of

decision making. If you have a strong intuitive sense about the entire decision or any component, trust it. Decide how much effort you want to invest in information gathering and analysis to test your intuition.

Facing Procrastination and Impulsiveness

- Determine which components seem to be your stumbling blocks, the ones that can lead to your own procrastination or impulsiveness.

- Procrastination can occur through lack of security and overanalyzing an issue.

- Impulsiveness can occur through overconfidence and insufficient attention to the component.

	Principal Leadership Process		
Principal Focus of Managing Effort	**Creating Order**	**Inspiring Action**	**Improving Performance**
Systems	**Sage** Designs Strategy	**Visionary** Innovates the Future	**Magician** Orchestrates Change
People	**Globalist** Bridges Cultural Differences	**Mentor** Motivates Development	**Ally** Builds Partnerships
Work	**Sovereign** Empowers Decisions	**Guide** Achieves Goals	**Artisan** Pursues Excellence

FOUNDATION OF ALL ROLES
CORE VALUES

CHAPTER TEN

Achieving Goals

Learning the Role of the Guide

Profile of a Guide

The role name *guide* is a perfect choice as it carries the image of people who aim at goal achievement, have a high level of expertise, make the process of achieving goals exciting, respond to the many diversions and challenges that occur on the path to the goal, and keep people highly involved.

If you were on a trip with a tour guide, what would be your expectations of that person? If you were about to go on a river rafting trip, what would you expect of the guide? If you were a pioneer family about to join a wagon train going west, what would you expect of the guide? If you were in a work group aimed at accomplishing a challenging task, what would you expect of a manager?

There is no way to escape the fact: When we are in a situation in which a guide is necessary, we are dependent upon that guide to consider our well-being while inspiring action to accomplish a task and reach a meaningful goal. The habits describe the guide role as quite active, whether performing the work, establishing and managing the work processes, or facilitating the work efforts of others.

A guide sets specific and challenging goals and then provides leadership to organize, schedule, and complete work to meet those goals. This is dynamic management, oriented toward action. The

Wells' Field Guide—How to Spot a Guide

Habitat

The guide can be found in the heat of the action. Dwelling will be well organized with everything in its place and ready to be used. Usually can be seen moving through obstacles.

Habits

Leads and inspires others to face challenges on the path of collective achievement.

Experiences deadlines and difficulty as inspirational.

Adjusts work processes to meet shifting conditions and respond to new opportunities.

Organizes work so that there is a clear identification of the value-adding role of each job in the accomplishment of goals.

Designs and implements well-organized, productive, and flexible work processes to bring work to completion in a timely fashion.

Sustains joint responsibility for managing work in relation to the needs, responsibilities, and goals of other work groups.

Elevates the participation of others to minimize or avoid the need to take control, give directions, and demand compliance.

Assures availability of necessary resources and information for task accomplishment.

Focuses on what is pertinent and critical to the task at hand and avoids or eliminates anything seen as wasteful, unproductive, or redundant.

---

guide directs effort toward whatever is happening in the present, confronting any problems that could inhibit the work. Firefighting certainly takes place in this role, but it comes from the unexpected, not the mismanaged.

Sometimes a manager in this role will take control, give directions, and demand compliance. These are often old patterns of behavior, and the stress of work may bring them out. Nevertheless the manager knows that increasing the level of involvement achieves the greatest success. Joint responsibility for managing the work has a high priority; otherwise the manager spends too much time solving every problem that arises.

In this chapter, we arrive at the point where "the rubber meets the road." The guide values action—doing the work, carrying out the mission, achieving specific goals, and moving toward the vision. All other leading-edge manager roles are preparation for this role—they are all necessary for providing context and different forms of cohesion and direction, but they do not get the actual work completed. The three system roles (sage, visionary, and magician) involve methods to gain a wider perspective on the context of the work. The three people roles (globalist, mentor, and ally) involve methods to sustain attention on cultures, individuals, and collaborative work relationships. Even the two other work roles concentrate on the context of work (the sovereign creating order through decisions and the artisan improving performance through attention to standards) rather than the work itself.

In some sense, the role of guide is a major test of manager competency and the value of the other roles. The guide is the leading-edge manager role with an unrelenting focus on getting the work done, implementing decisions made in the sovereign role and organizing work to meet the standards of excellence and quality set in the artisan role.

How the Guide Helps the Organization

This role reflects the combination of the leadership process of inspiring action and the work focus of managing effort. Whenever work is getting done but people see it as tedious, inspiring action is necessary leadership. Whenever people do not see the value or contribution of their work to the whole organization, or people seem to be losing energy, inspiring action is necessary leadership. When work is *not* getting done, we especially need the inspired action provided by a manager in this role.

This manager *achieves goals* that require a high level of achievement in order to contribute toward factors essential to the organization's success—those measurements or objectives that are most important for the ongoing viability and competitive effectiveness of the organization.

The guide manager must possess skills critical to accomplishing the task and achieving the goals. Sometimes difficulties occur because we expect and demand a guide manager to have substantial experience in the work and to view this work as the central focus of attention. We want them to show clear work leadership. Organizations frequently move managers around to gain insight into different parts of the company, and they bring this broader perspective to each assignment, but they inevitably have less work experience and task knowledge than the people they must lead.

On the other hand, we become quite critical if the manager does not delegate substantive responsibilities. In order to delegate, the manager does not need to possess high task-related skills. These opposing desires for high skills and delegation place an interesting challenge in the path of any guide. We all know that without the energy of the guide, the work could not get done. At the same time, the guide must place a high value on inclusion, on a collaborative approach to work, remembering that task accomplishment is not possible on his or her energy alone.

The more traditional, controlling, taking-charge manager is one extreme in the guide role. At the other extreme, the value for collaboration can override the focus on task accomplishment: The work gets sacrificed or the group bogs down in endless meetings or in trying to accommodate every whim and desire of each group member. When the group experiences lack of motivation, divisiveness, sharp disagreements, or some other crisis, the challenge is not to revert to either extreme but to bring in the necessary skills from the people-related roles (globalist, mentor, or ally) to solve the problem and retain the guide's strength of work focus.

This is obviously easy to say and difficult to do. Most managers experience a tradeoff between the people-level roles and the work-level roles. It seems impossible to do both at the same time, especially when there is a challenging situation. A strong guide recognizes and resolves issues involving people while ensuring that work continues. Although work is the central focus, the guide is keenly aware of the different things that can upset work progress and focuses on the goals and the actions most critical to succeed. Simultaneously, the guide uses peripheral vision to understand team members' needs and the nuances of changes in the environment that require adjustments to the path.

Success in the guide role requires the combined effort of all. Managers lose the guide role's power when they approach these situations with an attitude of taking over, putting their own imprint on the group, using the group to demonstrate their own competence, fixing the group, or thinking that people work *for* them rather than *with* them for the benefit of the whole organization.

The challenge to the manager is to find the right balance between providing a leading direction to the group and depending upon the group. The convergence of the broader perspective of the manager, who has some competency in the other leading-edge roles, with the work experience and task knowledge of others brings the full value of the guide role into the organization.

A guide manager provides overall direction to the work and inspires actions to complete the work by keeping tasks connected to the whole flow of work in the organization and to its major missions.

Tasks—These are simply specific work assignments. Tasks include work completed in an hour, continually repeated work (tasks with cycles), and larger projects that can take weeks or months. As the tasks grow in complexity, it is quite easy to divide larger tasks into smaller ones. Tasks are descriptions of the specific work assignments of anyone (team or work group) at any level within the organization hierarchy.

Missions—Missions define the major areas of work by which individuals and teams stay on track to move the organization toward its vision. The specific tasks become elements of fulfilling these missions.

Priorities—These are the items most important to manage for the success of the mission. In a strategic sense, they are the critical success factors that lead to a distinctive competitive presence in the marketplace. There is always a long list of things to do, but priorities focus the efforts of people toward the most important of those items. By establishing priorities, a guide manager creates a hierarchy of importance for task effort and is able to devote attention to the most critical tasks.

Goals—These are specific measures of achievement for work done on the priorities. It is possible to think of a hierarchy of goals that builds from individuals through teams and departments to the whole organization. The entire pyramid of goals exists on a time line and eventually culminates in the vision. An individual is responsible for a task with a specific goal; that task itself reflects the priorities. Teams achieve goals as members of the team accomplish their individual goals. Similarly, departments achieve goals as different teams within the department accomplish their goals. Thus achievement of organizational goals depends upon the accomplishment of departments acting separately and collectively. In setting and achieving goals, the guide manager is keeping tasks aligned with the overall direction of the organization.

Principles—These are specific guidelines for working on tasks. With a principle guiding a task, people can consider their options for doing work well. With a rule, on the other hand, people focus on behavior they must avoid to minimize problems. Successful guide managers use principles rather than rules, regulations, control, and compliance to guide task activity.

Enthusiasm—Enthusiasm is the energy that enlivens the workplace for everyone. Rather than draining each other's energy, people want to inspire each other to do well. They also want to avoid getting trapped by situations that they find unpleasant. They do not want to invest energy in complaining nor do they want to let things fester; instead, they seek to resolve problems that affect their task performance. The guide manager inspires action by sparking enthusiasm among people so they have the will to be responsible for the work they do.

How a Guide Is Value-Driven

Core values are critical to success in this role. What does it mean to have core values if they do not influence every action in the performance of a task? A guide understands the need for this guidance but often finds values to be too general or broad for specific tasks. Thus explicit guidance for the task at hand is preferable. The guide will translate values into principles clearly connected to specific tasks, thereby providing guidance for desired behavior in the performance of a task without needing to give the responsible person detailed directions for every activity. Rules, on the other hand, restrain undesired behavior without allowing room for choice.

For example, suppose a company has some broad value related to "valuing customers." A *principle* chosen by a guide could be,

Warning Signs of Excess

You know you have overdone the guide role if you

Always place work responsibilities above people's needs

Resist change that disrupts work efforts

Avoid thinking about the future

Ignore a broad perspective

Avoid most learning possibilities because they delay or risk achievement

See the purpose of motivation as a technique to get people to do the work

Believe effective teams can always be measured by results

Lack tolerance for cultural differences about the way to organize work

---

"Honor any customer request for a return." This principle guides the behavior of the person working with the customer as well as anyone else connected to processing information on returns. In contrast, a *rule* could state, "Only allow returns for a thirty-day period when the customer returns the merchandise with a receipt and unused." Although this rule may be useful, it may be difficult to see how it relates to the core value, as the main beneficiary is not the customer. With a rule in place, a guide is restraining behavior of employees, whereas with a principle in place, a guide is considering core values and giving employees leeway in their behavior to meet the goals that are important to the health of the organization.

Building Guide Skills

The three major guide skills developed in this chapter are the following:

- *Establishing Priorities*—getting tasks focused on those elements most important to the overall success of the organization

- *Setting and Achieving Goals*—choosing targets that measure progress on the priorities and are sufficiently challenging to achieve

- *Using Principles To Guide Activity*—making sure every action is consistent with core values

Establishing Priorities

Work must flow from the organization's vision, but we become so accustomed to our daily work responsibilities that we often forget that vision and think only about work defined by job titles or department names. The structure of the organization seems so fixed that it becomes the center of work focus, but the true purpose of the structure is to organize work to fulfill missions and reach the vision. Structure is the formal method of representing the different missions necessary for the vision.

For example, a vision for the city of San Jose, California, seems to be of a modern metropolis of suitable stature to match the growth and global significance of the region's high-technology industries. Specific missions to reach this vision focus on the many different things necessary for a healthy city, such as building a thriving cultural base (museums, a major library, an opera company, a ballet company, and a professional theater), creating a national identity through sports (a new arena with a major sports franchise), preserving historically significant buildings, restoring a major church, modernizing and increasing the value of mass transit, strengthening and diversifying a retail business base, attracting major new hotels and office complexes, and presenting seasonal events to draw families to the downtown area. The preceding statements define major arenas of work. They are useful as mission statements only if they convey a clear picture of the overall work activities and provide people with a "sense of mission" to inspire their action on task responsibilities. Each mission is a necessary piece of the vision. Coordination among missions is necessary simply for the reason that there is limited space in the downtown area. Construction for one project could easily disrupt construction or operation of another project. Funding is limited even though it comes from a diverse mixture of tax expenditures, bond issues, private investment, and donations. It would not make sense for managers of different missions to compete with each other.

Each of these missions requires guide work to implement and maintain them. Clearly, time requirements will vary for each mission, and managers will face different obstacles in completing their assignment. It is easy to see the numerous task assignments necessary for each mission; each task is a piece of a larger puzzle. However, people "lose themselves" in task assignments when all their attention is on the task and none of it is on priorities, principles, or goals. It is important to realize that each task's true significance derives from its contribution to fulfilling the mission. A successful guide manager keeps this relationship alive.

A prime guide responsibility is sustaining this mission focus so that any particular work advances the interest of the whole organization. For example, an accounting department task may be to audit and prepare accurate financial statements. This, however, is not the *mission* of the accounting department; a mission identifies the *use* of the financial statements. The mission may be to provide timely information for investment and cost management decisions. The wording is important in that it reveals the true nature of the work, not simply the definition of tasks, and provides people with a "sense of mission."

There are many ways of thinking about priorities in an organization. Priorities are those activities or issues that command the attention of the manager and form the focal point from which specific work flows. Missions shape the organization's direction and are important because they bring the manager's attention to the organization's environment. A guide tracks environmental conditions and determines those conditions most crucial to operating in that environment. Perhaps the guide thinks about the few things most important to maneuvering through the environment to achieve goals; this is survival mode thinking and aims at minimizing the negative effects of threats the environment may pose to completing the mission. There are times when a survival focus is necessary, but it will never sustain long-term competitive viability. Priorities that place the organization in a position to capitalize on opportunities rather than simply avoiding threats are critical success factors; they are the specific work items that must be present to ensure the organization's ongoing competitive effectiveness.

For example, many fast food restaurants have an organization-wide focus on uniformity of the product and on speed. These two factors are important to the organization's competitive position. With uniformity, the food always tastes the same regardless of where or when customers buy it. With speed, customers only wait a small amount of time before receiving food and experiencing instant gratification. Every job within the fast food facility must identify and manage specific work responsibilities or tasks using uniformity and speed as the priority base.

Ford Motor Company has an advertising slogan, "Quality is Job 1." A critical success factor permeating every job in production could be product reliability measured by the number of new car defects. With a specific goal of zero defects for this factor, a company commits to determining and eliminating the cause of any defect that shows up in a new car. Of course, it is possible that this standard is too costly to meet. Nevertheless it is possible to design each production job or task so that workers focus on potential defects as the vehicle is being produced; each task would have a specific priority that directs workers toward reduction of defects. It is for these reasons that some automobile companies have adopted the approach of allowing anyone to stop the production line upon seeing a problem with any vehicle on the line. With that type of principle in place, each person can act according to the priority or critical success factor of product reliability.

Federal Express advertises that it meets customers' needs for anything that absolutely, positively must be received overnight. Each job within that company must identify and manage specific details critical to meeting this guarantee for all customers. Each part (or mission) within the organization must have its own critical success factors that help the organization meet its overall critical success factor in the marketplace.

Critical success factors must be specific. Simple slogans such as customer service, quality, being the best, or being a technological leader are not sufficient. They may be useful in providing an overall context as part of vision or purpose statements, but when the focus is on the work, language must become quite specific to achieve missions leading to the vision. Critical success factors must provide a clear context for the organization of work.

Critical success factors reflect prevailing conditions in an industry, but the organization is also trying to find a way to establish a unique position in the industry by creating opportunities for a higher degree of competitive success. Therefore it can look at the industry in several different ways and identify critical success factors through considering the following:

- The factors that any organization must manage in order to be successful in its industry given current conditions
- The factors that respond to the opportunities and threats the environment is currently presenting to the organization
- The factors that reflect the current stage of product life cycle
- The factors that give the organization influence or control of the product life cycle
- The factors that seem to be important in the industry because of prevailing customs or usual ways of doing business rather than absolute necessity
- Factors that create possibilities for altering current patterns in the industry
- The factors that favor the capabilities or potential of the firm
- The factors that favor its competitors because of some lack in the organization's capability or potential
- The new factors that can alter the balance of competitive advantages
- The factors enabling the organization to open opportunities or reduce threats for its customers, suppliers, distributors, or partners in joint ventures and strategic alliances
- The factors enabling the organization to create threats or constraints for its competitors

Each of these methods provides a perspective for the whole organization and the context for missions and tasks. The guide looks at all of these things and determines the appropriate priorities.

Setting and Achieving Goals

Goals are quite simply ways of denoting some level of achievement or accomplishment. They are very often measurable. It is helpful when such measurements are precise and easily understood. Difficulties, however, can occur when goals are too precise and too easily understood. Such quantifiable goals capture people's attention and lead them to neglect other important aspects of work.

For example, it is difficult to set specific goals for the people-level managerial roles. If one is trying to bring more mentor skills into the organization and help people move to higher levels of motivation, we could call that a goal. It would not be meaningful, however, to have a quantified goal specifying the number of people at the highest stage of motivation within a certain time. This type of measurement takes the heart out of the work of the mentor because mentor work is not time related.

Here is another example. It is often important to increase capability in globalist skills to bridge cultural differences within the organization and to work in an international environment. But trying to measure this capability as a certain number of cultures understood within a certain time would not be helpful. Similarly, one cannot easily measure ally success by placing a time constraint on moving a work partnership to higher levels of trust, commitment, or conflict resolution.

Goals are most significant for the work itself. For example, the goal of zero defects is a significant one for the critical success factor of reliability of the product. When we buy a new car, we usually have little concern about failures in safety features such as brakes or tires because we expect high quality, reliable production of these critical components. Therefore, customers will judge the quality of the production and the vehicle by much smaller, non-safety-related items such as door handles. The goal of zero defects directs work efforts toward removing any problems in the fit and finish of the vehicle. Everyone can work toward the same goal; every job has a defect measurement.

There are instances where a hierarchy of goals is important. A goal hierarchy is similar to a pyramid: The major goals of the whole organization are at the top, and as one progresses downward through the pyramid to different levels within the organization, there are many more specific goals for each function and job that reflect the smaller number of broad organization goals.

A hierarchy exists whenever goals are arranged in such a time sequence that the accomplishment of some goals must happen before other goals are achievable. A hierarchy also occurs when goals of different work groups feed into larger goals spanning the work of many different groups or functions. Smaller goals must be achieved before one can have success with larger, more encompassing goals.

Goal hierarchies also exist when the organization's goal has a different measurement than goals for specific tasks. For example, Federal Express's critical success factor is the guarantee in the advertising. The goal is that any package picked up by a given time one day will be delivered by a given time the following day. To give this goal some real meaning, Federal Express must also be managing a relatively rapid response to request for pickup. People who are working in this part of the business—picking up parcels and bringing them to airports or key distribution points—cannot use the larger goal of the whole organization as an appropriate target. Their goal would be response time from request for a pickup. They would also organize to have a regular route of pickups to give some predictability to their customers.

In the fast food example, the critical success factors of uniformity and speed can have some measurable goals. However, the uniformity of taste goal is more difficult to measure. It tends to be a subjective measurement rather than an objective measurement. Objectivity can occur by having measurable goals at every stage of the food handling process that affects taste of the product. For McDonald's, that has meant careful management with specific goals for farmers growing potatoes used for french fries. The organization's speed goal is the time a customer waits for food. For the hamburger cook, however, a measurable goal of the number of hamburgers cooked within a given time affects the speed goal.

Using Principles To Guide Activity

Each act of the guide should reflect the core values. It is the ability of the guide to continuously remember the core values on a daily basis as part of the regular work routine that makes the core values a more living reality. If there is a value of ethics, a guide attuned to the value will be aware that each act and each direction given to the group has an ethical basis. People experience the guide's behavior as a reflection of the guide's and the organization's core values. Values are simply abstract statements of preferences unless specific principles translate them to each task of each mission.

By emphasizing principles in the guide role, we are reentering the field of values from a different perspective. Although values are the foundation of each role, principles are necessary to ensure that each role culminates in appropriate daily action. Each role has its importance to the organization. It is hard to imagine a successful organization where managers are lacking in some of these roles. The true test of the quality of leadership from these roles, however, is at the level of tasks and actions. All the good thinking of the system-level roles and the true concern exhibited in the people-level roles are meaningless if the essence of these roles remains on the sidelines when work is happening. Principles are necessary to help us remember what we hold important from the other roles when the immediate pressure of work forces us to maintain focus on the guide role.

Without principles, work becomes more mechanical, people become objects interchangeable with machinery, and people operate from a rule or procedure orientation. We could say that without principles, enthusiasm collapses and the work becomes less meaningful.

There is always some form of guidance for a task. Rules in organizations are quite similar to laws in society; they place limits on undesirable behavior. You create rules or laws by thinking about all the things that could go wrong or that could cause people to deviate from the desired path. An organization based upon rules is one of low trust that seeks control, conformity, and compliance to rules. Rules limit thinking; you simply obey.

Similarly, procedures describe a particular method of doing something, often detailing specific sequences of steps or operations. They keep action on a desired course and help people perform work in a predictable manner. Procedures also limit thinking. If conditions change, a strict following of procedures may be inappropriate.

Rules and procedures concentrate on action and limit thought. An organization with many rules and procedures and few principles quickly becomes a place with little enthusiasm. People may do their work well, but when any problem occurs they escape their responsibility by quoting rules and procedures. We have all heard statements such as "I am sorry, but this is company policy." Such an attitude is destructive when used to justify lack of flexibility in responding to customer requests. It is internally destructive as well when managers quote rules or procedures to people and avoid their individual concerns, needs, perspectives, and insights.

As a practical matter, however, any organization is going to have rules and procedures. In the fast food example, procedures do seem necessary to guarantee uniformity of taste. Specific activities for purchasing, storage, and cooking are necessary. People need to follow these procedures without deviation. We have our faults and are unwilling to risk the uncertainty of behavior entailed in a complete reliance on principles. There are some situations, safety issues for example, where we want narrow definitions of acceptable behavior. Even in these situations, though, we find that principles are still necessary as the rules needed to block all possible problems would be too numerous to remember.

The true challenge to the guide is moving increasing numbers of tasks to the level of principles. Principles are guidelines for value-based behavior in specific tasks. Behavior does not flow automatically from principles; it requires conscious thought. Principles allow for more flexibility; as conditions change, the principles remain, but behavior can shift. Principled action is the necessary fruition of core values in an organization and the final test of the true capability in all the other leading-edge roles.

Nordstrom is well known for its principle-based response to customer complaints, even in the face of unethical behavior by the customers. They prefer the principle and the possible extra expenses to a set of rules or procedures that would satisfy some customer complaints and limit their response to other customer complaints.

A friend of mine recently became president of a small company. He chose to move to a principle base by guaranteeing a rapid response to any employee complaint. His response was to take the requested action rather than to respond to the employee with a justification for inaction. For example, if someone did not like the color of paint on the plant building, he would have repainted it. He did not institute any rules requiring reasons for the request or procedures to gain approval for any expenditures. Did people make frivolous and wasteful requests? Yes, they did. Did that end his experiment with principles? No, it did not. People quickly realized he was serious and that in a very real sense they were wasting their own money. The significance of the principle is that people turned their attention to useful improvement suggestions because they knew there was an absolute commitment to trust their request and take rapid action.

Putting It All Together

The guide's perspective is to organize tasks—specific work assignments—to be consistent with mission, priorities, goals, principles, and enthusiasm. Table 11 provides tests to ensure you are maintaining consistency.

Table 11   Simple Tests for Organizing Tasks

Mission Test

Important task-organizing ideas related to mission are the following:

Design task to maximize facilitation and minimize interferences with other work on the mission.

Ensure task provides a unique contribution to the mission and doesn't replicate work done elsewhere.

Leverage task reliance upon other work for its mission contribution.

Priority Test

Important task-organizing ideas related to priorities are the following:

Explicitly connect task to a priority.

Identify things that divert attention from the priority to other issues.

Create latitude in the task to meet unexpected conditions and return to a priority focus.

Ensure priorities have motivational impact on task performance.

Goals Test

Important task-organizing ideas related to goals are the following:

Ensure specific goal measurements are relevant to task performance.

Determine the way less measurable but equally important results affect task performance.

Determine degree to which goal attainment is totally dependent upon the task or mutually dependent upon other tasks.

Identify effects of the task on other goals within the goal hierarchy.

Identify potential hazards, problems, or uncertainties in doing the task that will affect goal attainment.

Table 11   Simple Tests for Organizing Tasks (continued)

Principles Test

Important task-organizing ideas related to principles are the following:

Ensure principles provide sufficient guidance for appropriate task performance.

Ensure principles create freedom of action in the task and increase the likelihood of higher-level task performance.

Determine effects of unexpected conditions on the ability to operate the task according to the principles.

Determine degree to which the principles open different opportunities for action without delaying task performance.

Choose principles that affect actions to accelerate goal attainment.

Enthusiasm Test

Important task-organizing ideas related to enthusiasm are the following:

Determine how the task uses people's potential capability.

Determine how the task challenges people to improve their capability.

Identify the opportunities the task creates for people.

Determine if people are able to see the value of the work they do.

Determine if task performance depends upon a personal sense of mission.

Learning Guide Role Skills

Establishing Priorities—Using Missions

- Choose some personal or organizational vision.
- Identify the main arenas of work to move the whole organization toward that vision using the following possibilities:
  - Thinking about major issues required to sustain competitiveness
  - Thinking about the overall time frame described by the vision and a sequence of major activities to reach that vision
  - Thinking about major separable activities that define very different fields of operations
- Define a specific mission statement for each of these main arenas of work.
- Determine the value of thinking about missions to establish priorities and spark enthusiasm.

Establishing Priorities—Using Critical Success Factors

- Think of the work that you do or manage in your organization.
- Identify critical success factors for that organization. These are the things it does strategically to be competitively successful and relevant to its customers.
- Identify the factors most critical for you to manage to be successful in your work and help the organization on its critical success factors.
- Determine the value of thinking about critical success factors to establish priorities and spark enthusiasm.

Setting and Achieving Goals

- Identify specific goals that mark achievement or accomplishment in your work responsibility.
- Identify important aspects of your work responsibility not easily measured by specific goals.
- Determine how the achievement of your goals influences the achievement of goals of other work groups or the whole organization.

- Determine the degree to which you are dependent upon the goal achievement of others.
- Determine the extent to which there is a clearly articulated hierarchy of goals and the rationale for this hierarchy.
- Analyze the extent to which your goals and those in the hierarchy adequately reflect the priorities.
- Determine how understanding the relationship of a goal to a priority sparks enthusiasm.
- Determine how you will balance attention between easily measured specific goals and more qualitative goals.

Using Principles To Guide Tasks

- List different tasks that you or others have within your organization.
- Determine the nature of guidance for these tasks—rules, procedures, or principles.
- Determine the relative effectiveness of the guidance in terms of productivity of results and personal commitment to the work.
- Analyze where there are possibilities to shift rules or procedures to principles.
- Articulate principles that reflect core values and the particular requirements of the task.
- Identify the specific risks and possible negative consequences of these changes.
- Identify the longer-term benefits of these changes.
- Determine how increasing the use of principles to guide tasks sparks enthusiasm.

Principal Focus of Managing Effort	Principal Leadership Process		
	Creating Order	Inspiring Action	Improving Performance
Systems	**Sage** Designs Strategy	**Visionary** Innovates the Future	**Magician** Orchestrates Change
People	**Globalist** Bridges Cultural Differences	**Mentor** Motivates Development	**Ally** Builds Partnerships
Work	**Sovereign** Empowers Decisions	**Guide** Achieves Goals	**Artisan** Pursues Excellence

FOUNDATION OF ALL ROLES
CORE VALUES

CHAPTER ELEVEN

Pursuing Excellence
Learning the Role of the Artisan

Profile of an Artisan

The role name *artisan* depicts someone who has old-fashioned pride in work and excellence. The artisan is always looking for ways to create and redesign the product. If we remember that we often have customers within the company—for example, the accounting group provides support service to other departments—then we realize that artisans can be in any management position.

Artisans value anything that induces higher standards. Customer pressure for better products and services is an important incentive, as are competitor innovations, product changes, and price reductions.

Quality may be subjective, but nevertheless the artisan is quite able to judge quality. Practicality and aesthetics guide the artisan to improve everything on a piece-by-piece basis. Artisans have an ongoing willingness to challenge the status quo; long before problems occur, they ask, "How can we do things better?" They perceive that a lax attitude toward standards results in reactions to problems after they happen.

If you do not truly care about the work you do, you can never be good in the artisan role; there is no technique that will compensate for your lack of interest. No buzz words, no clever programs,

Wells' Field Guide—How to Spot an Artisan

Habitat

The artisan can be found in the fine-tool section of stores. Dwelling will be artistically pleasing. Usually can be seen taking something apart.

Habits

Treats work as a craft by seeking higher standards and levels of mastery.

Thrives on customer and competitive pressures to design and create product or service improvements that raise the level of practical and aesthetic appeal.

Involves each individual in the ongoing search for refinements in quality standards for products and processes that anticipate and respond to changing market conditions and competitor capability.

Instills pride in identifying and creating quality that reflects the stated and unstated needs of customers.

Challenges the status quo by examining work to seek ways of improving and reaching higher standards of excellence and quality.

Maintains complete attention to detail in every job, task, and work process.

Possesses little tolerance for errors or mistakes derived from lack of attention but has great patience for actions reaching toward higher standards even if problems occur.

---

no exhortations can substitute for the attitude of someone who cares. If you want a passion for excellence you better have a passion for your job. You do not need to love everything about your work, nor do you need to love your organization, but you cannot claim that the organization or external structures have suppressed your interest.

Your job must provide a powerful hook of some sort. Maybe it is some essential quality of your work in which you truly believe or that creates a nearly unexplainable level of excitement. Maybe the work connects with your personal vision, your core values, or what you see as your role or purpose in life; maybe it provides an avenue for the expression of your talents.

On the other hand, your work need not become an obsession or constitute the whole of your life. You do not need to work unending hours always pursuing ever-rising standards. Finding that hook and avoiding obsession are challenges you must pursue outside the guidance provided in this book. Clarity about those is a precondition to success in the artisan role and your ability to manage others and inspire them to have a similar commitment to improving work performance.

In your own organization, you can sponsor or participate in any variety of quality programs, but you will never achieve true success if you do not have the artisan love and pride in work. You cannot admonish others to seek high standards if it is not a part of your own life. One important premise of the leading-edge model is that you can never properly manage others until you are able to manage yourself; this is the true meaning of "Practice what you preach."

Core values bring integrity to management. The artisan has a different influence on a person's integrity. When an individual seeks changes or higher-quality work from others without being an artisan, people notice the lack of sincerity. You must live the role if you expect others to follow. On the other hand, whenever we are in the presence of true artisans, we are willing to forgive some of their errors because we know this enthusiasm will eliminate many of the negative effects of the other roles.

How the Artisan Helps the Organization

This role reflects the combination of the leadership process of improving performance and the work focus of managing effort. Attention to detail in every job, every task, and every work process leads to success in any program of reengineering, continuous improvement, or total quality management. Each performance of a job may reveal a way to raise standards. Advancing quality levels is always possible; room for improvement always exists.

A manager in this role *pursues excellence* by involving each individual in the ongoing search for refinements in quality standards of products (or services) and processes that anticipate and respond to changing market conditions and competitor capability. There is a continuing push to improve performance to enhance the customers' experience of the value they derive from the product and ensure that each operation within the organization adds distinctive value to the product or to the process of its creation.

The artisan role has received significant attention in many popular business books and recent organization change efforts. Many corporate programs include terms such as *total quality, continuous improvement, learning organizations,* and *high performing systems.* Phil Crosby, Edward Deming, and J. M. Juran are well known in the areas of quality, and it has become hard to think of excellence without thinking of Tom Peters and Robert Waterman. The most recent approach capturing attention in business is reengineering or total process redesign, spearheaded by of Michael Hammer and James Champy, among many others. The annual competition for the Malcolm Baldridge Award has spurred improvement efforts in many organizations with many feeling that the efforts devoted to completing the application have been beneficial, whether or not they win the award.

All these books, consultants, and corporate programs are trying to create a whole organization in which being an artisan is the norm. Creating widespread artisanship is a major challenge for the manager. Each person feels pride in his or her own work because he or she is working to high standards and knows how that work adds value to the products of the organization.

All these approaches restructure the organization and its operations to improve competitive effectiveness. To some extent, however, the various program words have been so overused as to seem trivial. After all, very few people go to their job determined to do mediocre work that adds no value to anyone, just as no organizations have a purpose, vision, or mission that declare an intention to ignore the customer by doing passable work of low quality. Organizations simply do not survive with the core value of "Let's see what we can get away with today."

Do we really believe that people want to leave work each day having no pride in anything they did that day? Such a condition would be unnatural. On the other hand, it is unreasonable to expect people who feel themselves to be poorly treated, ignored, excluded from decisions, or threatened by layoffs to fully contribute to organizational efforts to increase the standards of work and competitiveness, even though they would experience more satisfaction from working that way.

The challenge in working with others, especially in a hierarchical arrangement with rewards and punishments, is that people will not be objective in their own self-assessment or possible improvements in work standards. They will resent work standard assessments by others because they fear ideas about improvements will lead to work reductions, task responsibility redesigns, or layoffs. When it is possible to get an honest self-assessment from individuals, regardless of their level in the organization, we find that people can indeed articulate changes to improve the quality of their work.

The people-level managerial roles are necessary to change the atmosphere at work and the experience of employees. If quality of work is an important issue, then it is inextricably tied to quality of work life. The mentor and ally roles are necessary to develop individuals and build true work partnerships so that people support the value of revealing areas for improvement in their own work responsibilities. The globalist helps by forming an organizational culture that values capability to raise work standards rather than mete out punishment for less acceptable performance.

Do a survey in your organization; the number of people who feel that they have a higher concern for standards than their co-workers will amaze you. We may have people with an unrealistic assessment of their ability rather than artisan qualities. This sense of standards, however, does reveal importance of the artisan role.

Although an artisan is not a perfectionist, there is never a true end point to improving performance. Like the search for the Holy Grail, we have a good idea about what we want but never fully expect to find it. In fact, the journey has as much significance as the result. Markets are dynamic—there is always something new desired by customers. Other products change, and that affects the way people live; the people, in turn, demand changes in a wider field of products. Competitors are always looking for ways to improve their products, change their technology, or reduce costs in their production. Some organizations are serious about "valuing people" because they need to compete for employees and do not want to lose people to better jobs elsewhere. There is no way to survive in a dynamic, competitive environment without artisan management. Organizations talk about creating a learning environment with continuous improvement, because they know there is always something new to learn to improve operations for the organization, the employees, the suppliers, and the customers. Being an artisan means constantly upgrading standards of performance, seeking perfection by focusing on the details.

Some of the preceding discussion may lead to confusion between the artisan and guide roles. The guide inspires action toward achieving goals, operating from principles in organizing and bringing the work to completion. The guide remains flexible to alter work responsibilities as conditions change. The artisan is the source of many of these changed conditions, because he or she is sufficiently knowledgeable about the work to recognize whenever there is a possibility of raising standards of performance. The artisan constantly thinks, How can I do this better?

A guide does not think about raising the standards but rather wants to find the best way to organize work to meet existing standards and deals with difficulties as they arise. An artisan, however, will continually learn through work experience to find new ways to operate that exceed existing standards in work processes and products. Artisans balance quality standards for practicality or function with quality standards for aesthetics or form.

How an Artisan Is Value-Driven

Craft is an expression of values in the creation of a product. Pursuing excellence is living from a core value, which provides foundational guidance for behavior. We also use the word *value* for products when we talk about the benefits derived from the product. Artisans operate from core values trying to improve this second form of "value" in the product. In their work, they create an interesting connection between these two concepts of value. Think about when you bought a product or received a service that displayed clear attention to detail. Organizations reach for this experience when they sincerely try to "delight the customer" rather than simply "satisfy the customer." As consumers in this situation, our experience often goes beyond the benefit we

Warning Signs of Excess

You know you have overdone the artisan role if you

Cannot leave well enough alone

Are never satisfied with the way things are done

Always choose quality over cost

Believe the only way to do something right is to do it yourself

Have no patience with any compromise of standards

Believe focus on quality improvement is sufficient for vision

Believe the only purpose of learning is to improve quality

Have a low level of trust for the quality standards of others

Only value knowledge that aids insight into raising quality

See what went wrong or could be improved rather than what went right

---

receive; it inspires us to think about our own core values. The artisan's use of core values indirectly influences others through the fruits of their efforts at improvement.

People in the organization directly experience the influence of the artisan in this attention to detail to improve performance. Artisans must influence others around them to commit to ever higher standards. This is impossible with core values absent; core values provide a sense of appropriate standards and elevate the drive to change standards. This need becomes even more prevalent when things are going well and it is necessary to alter the currently successful process or product to move to higher standards.

Building Artisan Skills

The three major artisan skills developed in this chapter are the following:

- *Pursuing excellence*—managing work to find improvement possibilities in all dimensions of excellence

- *Balancing practical and aesthetic quality standards*—recognizing the significance of balancing function with form in the eyes of the customer

- *Maintaining attention to detail*—focusing on every element of a product or process as a possibility for improvement

Pursuing Excellence

Excellence and *quality* must be two of the most overused and misused buzzwords circulating the corridors of organizations. What do we really mean when we use these terms? No one pursues mediocrity; it comes naturally. No customer wants low quality; they just want low prices. Thus excellence and quality are important pursuits for the artisan manager. First we address the skill of excellence; then we focus upon quality standards.

The four basic dimensions of excellence pursued by an artisan are the following:

- *Efficiency*—the least expensive way to achieve the result by eliminating waste, redundancies, repetitions, or unnecessary steps

- *Effectiveness*—the critical means to achieve the desired results

- *Fairness*—the necessary conditions for people to experience fair treatment in all organizational actions and results

- *Future Possibilities*—balancing improvement in the other three dimensions to enhance the organization's reputation and expand productive possibilities for it

Disaster results when organizations allow only one of the first three dimensions to dominate attention. In challenging economic times, it is usually improvements in efficiency that dominate thinking at the expense of the other dimensions of excellence. We wind up with efficiency-driven cost cutting and layoffs as the main mechanism to improve competitive effectiveness. This approach will not succeed over the long run. The artisan must work with all four dimensions to drive improvement to greater levels rather than focusing only on one of them; it is the only path to sustaining competitive effectiveness.

Efficiency

Efficiency is improving performance when things get smaller, faster, and/or use less energy. How can the work become more efficient? Where can we reduce costs without jeopardizing the output? In a truly efficient organization, any cost-reduction program would cut some crucial value-adding activity and damage the quality of the organization's processes and products. Most organizations are not completely efficient; they have slack and therefore can identify cost reductions that do not have a noticeable effect on outputs. For each function, efficiency means finding a way to add value while minimizing the use of inputs.

The focus on shrinkage—less space, time, or energy—affects the producing process and the product. The computer is an obvious example of a product that exhibits all of these efficiency shrinkage characteristics. Over the years, the price for computing power has declined because computers have become smaller with more rapid processing time. People use computers because they increase their own efficiency in their processes and products. It is a simple example of artisan product improvements leading to customer improvements in their endeavors.

Artisan efficiency improvement questions.
1. Where do waste or redundant efforts exist?
2. If budgets were cut by 10 percent (20 percent, 30 percent, etc.), what would we cut and how would that affect outputs?
3. What can we change about our products that would improve the efficiency of our customers in their operations?
4. How do our own attempts at further efficiency affect the efficiency needs of our customers?
5. Where can we reduce space requirements, time, or energy usage in our own processes?
6. Where can we reduce that for our customers?
7. How does the efficiency of our suppliers affect us?
8. What demands do we place on our suppliers that help or hinder their ability to be efficient?

Effectiveness

Effectiveness is the ability to achieve the right results, those that most closely correspond to what the market needs. Product changes aimed at changing features to match new customer needs or innovations by competitors are effectiveness improvements rather than efficiency improvements. Each function's effect on adding value derives from understanding the customer's perspective on desired results.

When something is effective, that means it does exactly what it is supposed to do. An effective information systems function, for example, would be accumulating, storing, and distributing the information needed by the other functions for their effective performance.

Conflicts can occur with efficiency. A dominant focus on effectiveness reduces attention on tight cost controls or keeping the whole operation efficient. Effectiveness tends to be an expansive perspective that seeks improvements to achieve something better. Its aim is to do *the right things.* Efficiency is a more concentrating perspective that seeks improvements that limit waste. Its aim is to do *things well.*

Artisan effectiveness improvement questions
1. What are the most significant things to our customers?
2. What are they required to do in order to make the best use of our products?
3. Do they need other products, services, or training?
4. How could we enhance our product to improve our customers' ability to be more effective in their own products and more competitive in their own markets?
5. What is happening in our environment and the environment of our customers that will change the requirements for effective products?
6. What do we communicate to our suppliers to help them become more effective in meeting our needs?

Fairness

Fairness can mean different things. For example, in our judicial system we tend to hold fairness as ensuring that everybody has the same opportunity or treatment. This concept of fairness relates to abstract principles. Another concept of fairness is treating people differently based upon their needs and the particular situation. Regardless of the definition of fairness, people will regard fairness as being treated the way they want to be. The golden rule is useful here.

For example, Nordstrom places a high value on customer satisfaction and will go to extraordinary lengths to assume the customer is always right, even when the customer is acting in an unreasonable fashion. They respond to the needs of the particular customer, but they do not treat each person in exactly the same way because the needs of people vary. They only infrequently contradict the customer. Their approach may not work for every organization. However, customers may experience fairness if they know that people in the organization took the time to understand their need and try to help even if they were not able to resolve the issue in the way the customer preferred.

Fairness also applies within the organization over a wide range of issues such as the treatment of different functions when cost reductions or other cutbacks are necessary, the determination of promotions and salary increases, the assignment of responsibility and authority, or the effects on people of improvements in efficiency and effectiveness.

Artisan fairness improvement questions
1. Would your customers say they are being treated fairly?
2. What are their needs for fairness? How are complaints treated?
3. Do they feel that people within your organization or work group listen to and fully comprehend their needs?
4. Would your suppliers say they are being treated fairly?
5. What demands does your organization place on them?
6. How are improvements in efficiency and effectiveness managed for fairness to people within the organization?
7. What opportunities exist for improving the experience of fairness?
8. How will fairness improvements affect efficiency and effectiveness?

Future Possibilities

The fourth dimension of excellence builds potential for future success. Artisans balancing efficiency, effectiveness, and fairness always consider long-term possibilities or opportunities. The artisan seeks excellence by finding ways to improve the organization's reputation and integrity.

Within the organization, the artisan can only build potential for the future by having a highly charged, creative atmosphere. People need to find their work personally rewarding and challenging with a clear sense that their views on improvements are important. The artisan manager must help others experience their own artisan qualities.

Artisan improvement questions for future possibilities
1. What is being done within the organization to keep open to new possibilities in the future?
2. How do current demands for efficiency, effectiveness, and fairness increase and decrease receptivity to new possibilities?
3. What potential does your organization possess?
4. How would you respond to a sudden crisis, for example, a major shift by one of your competitors?
5. How would you respond to a sudden opportunity, for example, a dramatic increase in demand for your product?
6. Where have you missed opportunities by not being in a state of readiness?
7. How does the focus on creating future possibilities influence your current attempts at efficiency, effectiveness, and fairness?
8. How do customers, suppliers, and employees assess the organization's reputation and integrity?

Balancing Practical and Aesthetic Quality Standards

There is much talk in this country about the need to improve quality; businesses claim that quality is an important focus for them. But despite the claims and all the well-designed programs for statistical quality control, precise definitions or measurements of quality are often difficult to come by. Some forms of quality may be measurable and more easily controlled, but customers often think of quality the same way many people think about art: "I can't describe it, but I know it when I see it." That statement may seem simple or unfocused, but it contains a fundamental truth.

We notice quality in many different things. There is a difference between being on a team that sticks to a work responsibility and a team that also has some spirit in working together and getting the job done well. There is a certain excitement or enhancement in receiving a service from a person you experience as having some spirit about work, in contrast to a person who may perform the service adequately or well but conveys a feeling of dissatisfaction or boredom. We experience quality in physical products when they absolutely perform as expected with consistency and reliability.

In all of these cases, we can say that when we experience something material being infused with spirit, we feel an attraction to that thing. We feel elevated by being in contact with something or someone with that heightened state of awareness. An interesting effect of quality in a product or service is our feelings of enhanced or greater opportunity for ourselves in other endeavors. High quality has a major uplifting effect; we transfer the spirit we feel in one product or service to our own responsibilities. Seeing someone with true concern and pride in work makes us question our own relationship with work and often aspire to their level.

Quality is a dimension that goes beyond excellence. The absence of quality may be the reason people often reject products or leave jobs that achieve the dimensions of excellence but do not contain the full feeling of life experienced when quality is present. Thus the Japanese automobile industry has begun to shift from one form of quality—*atarimae hinshitsu* (defect free) to *miryokuteki hinshitsu* (that which fascinates, delights, or bewitches). The first form of quality has specific measurements—reliability, conformance to standards, rejection rates in the factory, predictability, and return rates. One could say that regardless of the price of a product, customers expect this form of quality. Customers do not search for poor quality; they expect reliability, that the product will do what it was designed to do. After all, the dictionary defines quality only as an inherent or distinguishing characteristic, attribute, or trait that can make something good or bad, commendable or reprehensible.

This quantifiable or objective quality can be built into the products and is easily observable. This is the realm of practical quality standards.

However, the second form of quality is purely qualitative and based entirely on the experience of the customer. It cannot be as easily controlled as the first form of quality. Even the first form, of course, is a challenging pursuit for many companies. For example, when Ford says "Quality is Job 1," they are probably referring to the first form of quality. But Mazda tells customers that its cars "just feel right." If they succeed, they are achieving the second form of quality. For products and services, it is difficult, if not impossible, to attain this type of quality without first attaining the first form. The artisan's attention to detail must maintain high levels of practical quality—the quantifiable type—to create a base where the second form—purely qualitative or subjective—is possible. This is the realm of aesthetic quality standards.

We could say that the first form of quality appeals to the rational processes of the left side of the brain, whereas the second form of quality appeals to the processes of the right side of the brain. We can read tests and publications to verify the first form of quality, but we need to experience the product to have a true sense of the second form of quality.

Nevertheless, quality does remain an elusive target. So many companies claim to be building the highest-quality products that it tends to become meaningless. Besides, do we all really want the highest quality available? For example, I was recently looking for a new front door for my house. The prices range from $150 to $1,500. All of the doors are the same size and thickness with the same ability to keep out burglars. For the door's functional purpose, there is not much variation in quality. So they must be selling a different form of quality. This is not an easily settled issue for any product, but we can say that there is some combination of built-in quality and experienced quality that appeals to customers.

Highest quality should mean appropriate or relevant quality. In the final analysis, it is the customers' perceptions of quality that will determine which product will be successful. Artisans have faith that the spirit they bring through their concern and pride in work combined with their ability to manage others to do the same will lead to a customer experience of practical and aesthetic quality.

Either practical or aesthetic quality standards has the possibility of meeting existing customer expectations or delighting customers by exceeding expectations. Practicality means that some product feature has a clear functional use to the customer; it is not practical to the customer if the feature is not used. Think of all the calculators with complex capabilities that people use only to balance their checkbooks. The extra features may seem intriguing to the engineering design team, but they are not practical for the customers. In the artisan role, it is necessary to have an absolutely thorough knowledge of customer use of the product or service.

Any feature is practical if it fits the customers' conditions and the value they are trying to create for themselves in the use of the product. It is practical if it is easy to use and does not require extra effort from the customer. I have a telephone answering machine that requires pressing only one button once to play messages and reset the machine. An older model required three buttons to play messages and three more to erase the messages and reset the machine. Thus the new one is more practical: They both reliably receive messages, but the new one is easier to use.

Minivans are now designed with cupholders. Should people drink in a moving vehicle? They do; therefore, it is practical to accommodate their use of the vehicle. Minivans have fold-down seats, removable seats, enough floor space for plywood, twelve-volt power sockets in the rear of the vehicle, etc. Each feature reveals attention to customer use of the vehicle. They have features a customer may not think of but when it exists can easily see its practical use.

It takes effort to consider different market segments and different possible uses for your product or service so that it possesses the practical features that will satisfy and delight customers. If you excel in this, why devote resources to aesthetic standards? Aesthetics are matters of artistic beauty, taste, appearance, or style. Would any customer sacrifice practicality for aesthetics? It is unlikely. Do aesthetics influence customer impression and purchase of products? Absolutely. People care about the color and shape of the vehicle they buy, the color and texture of the fabric on the seats, the feel of the steering wheel.

Aesthetics are obvious when we look at products in the marketplace. The fact is, every task you face has both aesthetic and practical sides. If you are making a presentation to others in the company, both content and form are important. Therefore your challenge in the artisan role is to balance the effort placed into practical and aesthetic standards. Remember that aesthetics are not ephemeral, mystical, or idealistic notions. It is always practical to enhance the aesthetic appeal of your efforts, and to enhance the aesthetic appeal of the physical work environment if it has a substantive impact on employee impressions of the organization.

Maintaining Attention to Detail

Artisans attend to details that others may easily ignore. An artisan managing a restaurant covers every detail of the dining experience: each element of the physical environment; waiting time in seating people, taking orders, bringing food, bringing the check, bringing change; the menu's visual impact; placement of tables; etc. This attention to detail is part of an ability to focus completely on an item and see it as part of the total experience. Next time you walk into a room, store, restaurant, or office, take your time to really look around for improvement possibilities. You will notice that you need to think not only about specific items but also about the purpose of the place itself. You will be concerned not only with neatness but with how well each detail fulfills an overall goal, purpose, or mission.

When Lexus talks about the relentless pursuit of perfection, they are talking about an attention to detail that must permeate every job, every part of the automobile, every possible interaction between customer and company. When you see things this way, there are thousands of opportunities for small, often low-cost improvements that have incremental but additive effects on employees and customers alike.

When organizations speak of sustaining continuous improvement, they mean this attention to detail. An artisan does this by balancing personal characteristics of dedication, discipline, and joy. As with practical and aesthetic standards, the balancing effort does not involve trade-off; this is not a zero-sum game. Balance means the right mix for the purpose and ensuring the presence of each. It is easy to see these characteristics in musicians: In a symphony orchestra, the violinist in the last row attends to detail through dedication to classical music, discipline to excel, and joy in playing and listening to others, even if he or she has no possibility of ever being first violinist.

Earlier I said you cannot be an artisan if you do not care about what you are doing. These three characteristics—dedication, discipline, and joy—define what it means to care. *Dedication* is commitment and devotion to the task—you must believe in what you are doing. It does not matter what kind of products or services you create; most things we do and buy are not that important in the overall scheme of things, and in a global sense, our efforts may not matter. So these considerations are not important. What does matter is that we can see our effort making a worthwhile contribution to some endeavor, whether that endeavor is playful or serious, short lived or long lasting. The role of the artisan is to ensure that dedication is possible for each employee by gaining clarity about the significance of that employee's contribution to the overall effort.

Discipline is the characteristic of sustaining effort to seek improvement regardless of the pressure to relax and leave things at their current level. Nonartisans will be satisfied with the status quo: "Don't rock the boat." "If it ain't broke, don't fix it." But when others feel things are good enough, it is the artisan who has the discipline to make things better. The artisan is not a critic, seeing what's wrong but having no responsibility to do anything about it; rather, the artisan will apply the most severe judgment to his or her own efforts in task responsibilities. An artisan will often have difficulty working with people who do not have the same level of discipline.

Joy is the characteristic of seeing work as a source of happiness, pleasure, or satisfaction. If there is no enjoyment, work drains energy, and it is very hard to gather momentum for improvement. An artisan will also seek improvements that can increase the possibilities for others to have more joy in their work.

Learning Artisan Role Skills

Pursuing Excellence

Use the artisan improvement questions from the skill section for your work responsibilities and for your organization's products.

Balancing Practical and Aesthetic Quality Standards

- Identify the quality you are trying to build into your products.
- Identify the quality your customers experience when they use your products.
- Analyze the dimensions where you would say that your quality is excessive.
- Analyze the dimensions where you would say that your quality is insufficient.

Maintaining Attention to Detail

- Experiment with simple situations as well as with your job responsibilities, your department, and your company.
- In each case, try to list as many details as you can.
- Define the relationship between each detail and the overall purpose of the focus of your example.
- Identify improvement possibilities for each detail—better achievement of the current purpose, ability to shift to a higher purpose, or effects on excellence and quality.
- Get a sense of the dedication and discipline you would need to maintain this attention to detail.
- Test your affinity for the artisan role by seeing the extent to which you find this attention to detail painful or joyful.

CHAPTER TWELVE

The Leading-Edge Manager Roles in Action

At this point, we return to statements from the book's preface on objectives for the model of leading-edge roles. Choose the use most suited to your need:

- Assessing your strengths and weaknesses
- Guiding your chosen focus on further learning
- Gaining greater effectiveness in a wider range of circumstances
- Developing an appropriate career path
- Understanding and appreciating the strengths of others
- Evaluating the effectiveness of a work group
- Balancing capabilities within a work group

Assessing Your Strengths and Weaknesses

In the different suggestions for assessments that follow, remember the distinction and connection between strengths (or weaknesses) and preferences. My personal experience and that of many people with whom I have worked on the leading-edge manager roles is that preferences seem to appear at a young age. Certain things draw our attention that seem less important to others. We notice that we have a way of viewing things that may be different from our friends who have other preferences. At that time in our lives, we are not thinking about these roles, but some of the significant personal traits embedded within the roles often appear. It would only be natural to seek out experiences that match these preferences. Over time, we are likely to develop strengths where our preferences lie and weaknesses where we had low preferences. At the same time, we are exposed to a wide variety of learning experiences. As we do well in some and less well in others, it is likely that we begin to increase our preferences where our strengths lie. For most of us, therefore, it is reasonable to assume a close relationship between strengths and high preferences (and weaknesses and low preferences). So you can choose to assess strengths and weaknesses or preference patterns for the roles.

The simplest approach is to use the grid diagram that displays all the roles along with the roles summaries in Chapter One. Number the roles from 1 to 9 based on your own belief about your strengths and weaknesses (or preferences). When you do this assessment, try to avoid getting stymied by the thought, Well, it depends upon the situation. We know that each role is appropriate to a different situation. So think about different situations, if it helps you, and decide where you are more effective or which ones are more attractive to you in order to rank the roles.

A more detailed approach to self-assessment comes from the role chapters, each of which has a table labeled "Wells's Field Guide—How to Spot a _____." These describe what are usually major activities of someone who is effective in each role. Give yourself a score of 1 to 10 to represent the level of your capability for each activity (these statements are less amenable to thinking about preferences). Get an average number for each role by adding the scores and dividing by the number of statements. The average is necessary as there are different numbers of statements for each role. The distribution of averages should reveal a pattern of strengths and weaknesses.

The final method focuses upon preference patterns. In Appendix B, you will find a self-scoring form. In Appendix C, you will find a mail-in assessment form; you are welcome to use the form at the back of the book to receive results for this assessment. This form is usually more accurate than the self-assessment as it requires different types of forced choices. By forcing choices among positive statements that represent the different roles, you will wind up with an accurate depiction of your distribution of preferences for the roles.

Guiding Your Chosen Focus on Further Learning

With one or more of the assessment methods, you will gain a better understanding of your strengths. Use the learning cycle from Chapter Seven on the mentor role.

Conceptual Understanding

- Reread the brief summary of the role in Chapter One or the role chapter to get a full picture.
- Check the references in Appendix A for lists of different books associated with each role.
- You may also find company-sponsored or outside workshops or seminars related to these roles. There are plenty of options for the key content of each role.

Low-Risk Practice

Start working on the skills in low risk circumstances—perhaps outside the workplace if that is a helpful way to reduce risk. This approach is especially useful and even fun for the personal qualities associated with some of the roles. As you guide yourself through the thinking skills in that role, you should experience these as very low risk and be able to devote effort to them.

Hands-On Experience

- Seek out assignments or challenges at work that require skills associated with that role.
- Choose risk levels that are sufficiently high to challenge you to use the role but do not cause you to back away from it.

Reflective Analysis

- Pay attention to your "normal" work activities—those in which learning is not the central concern. Try to observe your relative effectiveness in different situations. Determine if the times you sense a lower level of effectiveness occur when you use your strength to dominate or compensate for a weakness. This is especially important if that role weakness, developed into a strength, would have been more appropriate for the situation. These can then become additional learning possibilities.

- Increase effectiveness by working to keep core values intact in situations that increasingly challenge that role. With this foundation more firmly in place, it may then be easier to effectively use the specific characteristics of a given role.

Gaining Greater Effectiveness in a Wider Range of Circumstances

Although this book is devoted to aiding development, I want to reemphasize that your objective should not be to master every single role. I think it likely that preferences will remain and we will always tend to have greater strengths and effectiveness in situations that match those preferences. Although it is desirable to have increased competency in more roles, it is equally important not to get blind-sided in situations where we should be using one role but our strengths or preferences lead us to choose a different role. Therefore a useful step in gaining greater effectiveness is an ability to analyze a situation, determining which role is preferable and which role reflects your personal inclination. The leading-edge manager roles help the situation analysis through their overall structure. Use the leadership processes and focus of managing effort from the grid diagram.

First, determine the primary focus of managing effort in the situation:

- *Systems*—a longer-term situation involving a well-defined system within the whole organization, the whole organization, the organization and its environment, or coordination among parts of the organization

- *People*—a situation directly involving people, individually or collectively, in relation to development, collaborative processes, or diversity

- *Work*—a shorter-term situation involving day-to-day task responsibilities, making and carrying out decisions regarding tasks, and attention to product (or service) quality standards

Then determine the primary leadership process need in the situation:

- *Creating Order*—The situation is complex, involves divergent perspectives and information, and requires some unifying or integrating choice that identifies a path to follow or distinguishes the important from the peripheral.

- *Inspiring Action*—The situation requires the identification of a clear direction with some form of challenging achievement that energizes people to become actively involved and work toward their potential, thus expanding the possibilities for people and the whole organization.

- *Improving Performance*—The situation requires committed effort and necessary changes to raise standards for the structure, systems, and processes of the whole organization, the effectiveness of teams, or any outputs (products or services delivered to customers or other groups within the organization).

Finally, combine the diagnostics from the first two steps to identify the role. You will then be aware if this is a role of less strength and preference for you and alert to the hazards if you are trying to use a different role that is not a perfect fit. There is no doubt that given equivalent levels of competency in two different roles, the role most suited to the situation is more effective. When competency varies among two roles, you are making a choice between two unattractive alternatives: high competency in a role mismatched to the situation or low competency in a well-matched role. You are much better off making a deliberate choice, as you can anticipate the different problems that may arise for you from either of these choices. You will have a greater chance for learning and improving your effectiveness in the future if you choose the role with lower competency.

Developing an Appropriate Career Path

All the roles are appropriate to different levels of an organization, but it would be nearly impossible to be effective in the top levels of management without one or more of the system roles. People move up organization ladders and advance their careers for a variety of reasons, but at the top it is hard to avoid strategy, vision, or change; one or more of these will be necessary. Given the way business is evolving, it will also become increasingly difficult to be at top levels of organizations without the globalist role. Although people at these levels may have or need other strengths, these roles seem to be the most important for managing on the leading edge.

One thing to do if you are trying to move up in the organization is to determine if my brief assessment in this chapter is accurate for your organization. Are the primary roles of success in the top of your organization those of sage, visionary, magician, globalist, or a combination of those roles? If not, think about that organization and about what their needs will be as they move into the future. Think of how the industry and the organization are evolving and the kinds of situations that will arise. Use the situation analysis described in the previous section to identify the significant roles. This approach will be valuable to any manager regardless of career aspiration. If you have desire for advancement to high levels, you must develop those roles most crucial to success in that organization.

Many people want successful careers but do not define success as position in the organization's hierarchy. You may prefer to use your knowledge about yourself to seek out positions or assignments that best play to your strong preferences or strengths; you will be more effective in those situations. No matter how strong a preference or a strength, there is always challenge in pushing that role to further limits. It is possible that this approach will not lead to the greatest possibility of unending advancement, but it may lead to the greatest job satisfaction. If you have any belief in personal purpose, it may also be that your preferences do indicate the way in which you can make your greatest contribution. In relation to managing and leading, maybe this contribution is what you were born to do.

Understanding and Appreciating the Strengths of Others

Once you are familiar with the leading-edge manager roles, there is a great temptation to evaluate your co-workers and friends. "Bob is a strong sage and mentor; Sally is a strong magician and guide." I hope you do that in the spirit of understanding and appreciating them rather than seeing their faults or trying to type-cast them. No matter what someone seems to be, our own assessments may be inaccurate, and we need to give each other the room to grow and develop.

By calling for understanding and appreciation, I am perhaps being idealistic to believe that people will use the leading-edge manager roles to increase the tolerance and value for individual diversity within an organization. There are many different approaches to situations. Although I have said that you should analyze a situation to determine the best role, we all know that most situations faced in business are quite complex, and even in analyzing the situations we find that they require more than one role. This is an excellent time to be open to more than one way of approaching a problem—let people use their strengths where they are appropriate.

I also hope that in assessing other people, you will have greater ability to understand their perspectives at meetings when many issues are on the table. It should be true for most of us that fair use of this framework in viewing others will improve our skills as ally—understanding how others are thinking, what they find important, why they say what they say, why they make certain choices, and why they act the way they do. These characteristics are part of their role preferences.

Evaluating the Effectiveness of a Work Group

This approach to leading-edge manager roles is quite effective for evaluating a work group. I have used it with several groups who have only seen the grid and then been given a brief explanation of each role. They are able to very quickly look at their entire team and determine its collective strengths and weaknesses. The team members are not assessing individuals at this point, and they are not talking about preferences; they are trying to determine what they do well and what they do less well as a group. They can then look at the roles and determine if they face a sufficient number of situations that require development of team weaknesses. They may, for example, collectively work on the mentor role because development is an important issue. Or they may use the visionary role to create a joint vision.

What is interesting for a team is that while the members are working on any role, they are also engaged, perhaps indirectly, in a team-building exercise. One way to build strength in a team is collectively choosing a skill important for their further effectiveness and working on it together. These sessions usually are less charged than typical "work" sessions connected to their normal responsibilities, where old patterns, including conflict, often reemerge. Having the group work together on team strength in a leading-edge manager role is a way of avoiding parts of the past and focusing on something that is worthwhile for the future.

There is an important but subtle point: We do not always solve problems by working directly on them. Sometimes the solution emerges by working on a different issue that creates experience to counter the negative knowledge of the past. Typically, when managers want to improve teamwork, they approach it directly, often bringing in a consultant on team building or sending the group to a workshop. A weak team lacks ally skills. To build ally skills, it is often necessary to work on issues related to other roles so that people have an experience of being allies on something else that is important.

Balancing Capabilities Within a Work Group

This final use of the framework addresses the possible need for balance across roles within the group. In this case, in comparison with the previous section, it is necessary to have each team member engage in some form of self-assessment. This is a good time to do peer evaluations. Forms are available for self-assessment and peer assessments if you want us to do scoring for a more consistent methodology. Alternatively, you can use an approach similar to any of the self-assessment methods, but this time have people rate each other. You must choose if the ratings need to be anonymous or open. Whichever you choose, it is often better to have examples of instances or reasons for the ratings accompany the assessments you do of each other. You can then see how balanced the group is in the different roles. You do need to have a reasonable trust level to allow peer assessments and sharing of results within the group. If you do not have a high trust level, use a common approach and form for self-evaluation. Keep names off the results, and share them with each other. In this way, you may be able to guess the subject of the assessment, but at least each person will have a picture of the distribution of capability within the group.

Once again, you need to think about the situations you face and the degree to which a balance among the roles is necessary for your group. This balance is a little different from the last section. Here you are thinking about individual capability, so you may need to change the composition of the group. The other alternative is to ensure that there are development opportunities for people, an approach that naturally leads to a mutual mentoring within the group. You may want to alter work assignments within the group so that people have a chance to build their skills and add to the balance of the group.

Balance comes in a variety of forms: It can occur through ensuring that at least one person in the group is strong in each role. It can also happen where you need more widespread strength in some roles because of the responsibilities of your group. The work situation may demand that everyone has strength in the same role in addition to the other strengths they possess.

Epilogue

Can We Talk or Do We Have a Failure to Communicate?

Communication is a skill of great importance for all leading-edge roles. Even when the focus of managing effort is on systems or work, there is still ongoing interaction with others. No manager lives in a vacuum; effectiveness only occurs through work with others. People are present in the efforts of a manager focusing on systems or work, but they are not the central area of concern. Yet at the system level, a manager cannot design a strategy, innovate a vision, or manage change by sitting in an office in solitary confinement. Similarly, at the work level, decisions, goal achievement, and quality are meaningless topics without communication to others. Even if the manager does some work in isolation, he or she must communicate the results of that work to others. When the manager acts in concert to reach conclusions (a method represented by the overused and misused phrase *participative management*), communication skills are important. It is impossible to have true success in the people roles—globalist, mentor, ally—without communication skills.

Unfortunately, we frequently place too much emphasis on techniques to become a better communicator—written and verbal clarity in communicating one's own thoughts, understanding body language, etcetera. I want to emphasize three aspects of communication skills that are more consistent with the approach of this book:

- People want to be informed
- Listening is as important as being articulate
- Integrity with values creates credibility for communication

Frequently, when people list communication as a necessary skill for effective leadership, they are thinking of all the times they have been kept in the dark. They are not interested in *how well* things are being said; they are interested in the *content*. They feel that the manager has access to important information from other parts of the organization. When they do not receive this information, they are often suspicious of the reasons for excluding them. They may be overreacting, but their feelings undermine the other efforts of the manager. It is probably better to inform people that you cannot disperse information rather than simply trying to avoid the subject. Even when you need to work on your own for any of the system or work roles (the people roles imply interaction with others), people want to be informed about your conclusions and your reasoning for them.

Communication is a two-way street. At meetings, too many people patiently wait their turn to articulately express their views and often to challenge the views of others. Too infrequently do people really hear the views of others, not just their words but the meaning and intention behind them. The future of any organization lies with its people; therefore communication is necessary to tap into the intelligence of the whole organization. I am not advocating an empty form of participative management. If the knowledge and thinking capability of people are unimportant to you, then you do not need two-way communication. But remember that when people feel they are not being heard or there is no interest in their perspectives, they begin to lose interest in what they are being told. Good articulation skills will not compensate for this phenomenon.

In the final analysis, good communication is not really about technique. Certainly a good technique can win over an audience in a presentation or a sales pitch, but the roles discussed in this book relate to managing on an ongoing basis, not one-time interactions. When you are working with people over a longer period of time, you realize that a significant part of the value placed on communication concerns credibility, not technique; people allow leeway regarding communication skills when the speaker is credible. Credibility can clearly come from knowledge about a subject, but the only way to sustain your credibility as a manager is through your own core values. For important subjects, if people experience you as unwavering in your commitment to core values, you will have greater credibility and skill at communicating than if they suspect that your values are inconsistent. Such insincerity cannot be continually camouflaged by good communication techniques. Therefore in this book I have addressed the skill of communication only through a discussion of the foundation of core values.

In this book I have described a model of nine leading roles. Each one identifies a specific significant contribution to the health and success of an organization. As you have read through this book and deepened your sense of each role, you should also have better insight into your own preference and capability patterns. I hope you have found the skill building sections useful. I would like you to emerge from this reading experience with renewed appreciation for diverse individual styles in managing, leading, and learning.

However you choose to use the leading-edge manager roles, I wish you well in the ongoing growth of your skills, your effectiveness in your organization, and your support of the development needs of others.

How Similar Are the Roles?

As you read through the chapters, you were able to see the distinctiveness of each role, but I am sure you also saw overlap among the roles. This is natural for the simple reason that the situations you face at work often call on a multitude of skills, and you find that you need more than one role to effectively handle complex situations. In addition, you have your own preference pattern among the roles, and when you are naturally operating from your strengths, you use a combination of qualities that could represent more than one role. For these two reasons, the roles may seem to have similarities.

The most typical experience of role similarities is among the leading-edge roles for each focus of managing effort—systems, people, and work. It is easy to see the differences among focuses on systems, people, and work; these are quite distinctive categories, and we are accustomed to thinking about business in these categories. Within any focus, however, the distinctiveness of the roles is dependent upon an ability to see the uniqueness of each leadership process. I also said earlier that these three processes constitute a complete cycle of leadership. Therefore experiencing a relationship among them would be quite common.

Let's start with the systems roles. Is it rational to expect an organization to have a vision without a strategy to achieve it? No. Is it rational to orchestrate a change effort without a clear vision or a well-formed strategy? No. The organization requires coordination among the results of these roles. For individual managers, however, the talent to *create order* by choosing a strategy in the face of a complex, ambiguous, changing, and often contradictory environment (sage) differs quite dramatically from the talent to *inspire action* by articulating a vision that sufficiently innovates an exciting, possible future causing other people to devote the highest level of energy to its achievement (visionary). Both of these talents are very different from the talent required to *improve performance* by orchestrating the multiple levels of change, competing needs, dislocations, uncertainties, lack of stability, and turbulence that exist when an organization shifts from the status quo to a desired state or has to more or less maintain itself in a state of constant change (magician).

We can see a similar flow of organization requirements and management talents among the people roles. Is it rational to expect successful partnerships or collaboration among people without recognizing and responding to diverse cultural perspectives or the needs of individuals for growth? No. The talent, however, to *create order* in the face of diversity of cultures (within the organization and in its global operations) by building strong bridges among differences to pull people together (globalist) differs quite dramatically from the talent to *inspire action* by completely focusing on the motivation and development of a single individual, one person at a time (mentor). Both of these talents are very different from the talent required to *improve performance* by accelerating the effectiveness of all collaborative efforts—every instance of two or more people working together—and reducing the tremendous waste of energy that frequently occurs through collective effort (ally).

We can see analogous ideas among the work roles. Is it rational to separate the need for decisions in the face of complex, competing alternatives from the actions needed to achieve important organizational goals? No. Is it rational to seek higher levels of product quality or excellence without any connection to actions taken to achieve existing goals? No. The talent to *create order* by the responsible exercise of power to decide and the empowerment of others to decide (sovereign) is quite different from the talent to *inspire action* by providing the appropriate level of guidance and support to achieve goals that are meaningful and challenging (guide). Both of these talents differ from the talent required to *improve performance* by continually finding ways to push the boundaries of standards and achieve higher levels of market-relevant product quality and excellence (artisan).

One pattern that should clearly emerge from the discussions of the focus of managing effort—systems, people, and work—is that the leadership process of *improving performance* is dependent upon clear efforts in the other two leadership processes. On the other hand, effective work in this portion of the leadership cycle creates a need to review the efforts in the other roles. Improving performance changes the situation—a new reality emerges—and the need arises to create order and inspire action under a new set of circumstances.

From the beginning of this book, I have been emphasizing that effective management requires matching the role with the situation in the organization. One of the main reasons for improving your strength is to allow you to break away from instinctive use of your strengths in situations where a different role is more appropriate. With greater knowledge of the roles, you are able to analyze the situations that you commonly face at work.

You have probably noticed that sometimes there is conflict between roles. Suppose you are organizing work on a new project. Do you use the guide role and help people take on tasks to achieve well-formulated goals? Alternatively, do you use the mentor role and give people responsibilities that will challenge them to learn and accept the risk of less efficiency or lower performance compared with people who are already capable? How do you choose?

I would not be so presumptuous as to tell you what to do, but I can tell you the most typical pattern when faced with a choice among roles: The work roles dominate. They are the roles connected to day-to-day management and endless deadlines. It is very hard to think of vision when you have weekly, monthly, or quarterly results that you must achieve; to take the time to think about strategy (after all, nothing appears to be happening) when you have immediate problems requiring a decision; to elevate the quality of collaboration when groups have work needing completion; or to justify funds for training and development when cost cutting in work processes becomes a priority.

Should the work roles dominate? You need to answer that question for your own situation; deliberate choice is necessary. It is quite easy to rationalize the choice of a work role, but in the long run, balanced use of all roles sustains the organization's viability. Balance does not mean equal time for each role; it does mean making choices to devote time to roles that invest in the organization's future as well as those that create immediate results. Balance requires that you take the risk to engage in situations that challenge your capabilities in addition to easily excelling in those situations that access your strengths. The organization's future depends upon your willingness to learn.

Reading List for Further Learning of the Roles

This reading list is organized according to the chapters of the book. It is a selective list of some of the better and more relevant current books on the market. I am sure that I have excluded many excellent books, but I chose to only list a few books that seem to have some bearing on the roles. Please recognize when you connect the books with the roles that the authors were not thinking of these roles, so their books will probably contain overlaps among various roles. These books will also give you an opportunity to get a different perspective on qualities and skills associated with each role.

Chapter 1—Management Models and Books on Leadership

The books listed for this chapter provide general approaches to management and leadership using simple models or lists of traits, qualities, or skills. I organized them in three different categories to try to convey some sense of their orientation.

Traditional Management

Barnard, Chester I., *The Functions of the Executive,* 1968, Harvard University Press (30th Anniversary ed.), Cambridge, MA 02163.

Mainstream Management Thinking

Bennis, Warren, *On Becoming a Leader,* 1989, Addison-Wesley, One Jacob Way, Reading, MA 01867.

Koestenbaum, Peter, *Leadership: The Inner Side of Greatness,* 1991, Jossey-Bass, 350 Sansome St., San Francisco, CA 94104.

Kouzes, James and Barry Posner, *The Leadership Challenge,* 1987, Jossey-Bass, 350 Sansome St., San Francisco, CA 94104.

Senge, Peter, *The Fifth Discipline: The Art and Practice of the Learning Organization,* 1990, Doubleday, 666 Fifth Ave., New York, NY 10103.

Management Thinking on the Boundary

Adams, John D., *Transforming Leadership,* 1986, Miles River Press, 1009 Duke St., Alexandria, VA 22314.

Ray, Michael and Alan Rinzler (Eds.), *The New Paradigm in Business: Emerging Strategies for Leadership and Organizational Change,* 1993, Tarcher/Perigree, 200 Madison Ave., New York, NY 10016.

Renesch, John (Ed.), *New Traditions in Business: Spirit and Leadership in the 21st Century,* 1992, Berrett-Koehler, 155 Montgomery St., San Francisco, CA 94104.

Wheatley, Margaret J., *Leadership and the New Science: Learning About Organizations From an Orderly Universe,* 1992, Berrett-Koehler, 155 Montgomery St., San Francisco, CA 94104.

Chapter 2—Core Values

Bennett, William J., *The Book of Virtues,* 1993, Simon and Schuster, 1230 Avenue of the Americas, New York, NY 10020.

Covey, Stephen R., *Principle-Centered Leadership,* 1990, Simon and Schuster, 1230 Avenue of the Americas, New York, NY 10020.

Lappe, Francis Moore, *Rediscovering America's Values,* 1989, Ballantine Books, New York, NY 10022.

Chapter 3—Designing Strategy

Hamel, Gary and C. K. Prahalad, *Competing for the Future: Breakthrough Strategies for Seizing Control of Your Industry and Creating the Markets of Tomorrow,* 1994, Harvard Business School Press, 60 Harvard Way, Boston, MA 02163.

McWhinney, Will, *Paths of Change: Strategic Choices for Organizations and Society,* 1992, Sage, P.O. Box 5084, Newbury Park, CA 91359-9924.

Ohmae, Kenichi, *The Mind of the Strategist: Business Planning for Competitive Advantage,* 1982, Penguin Books, 40 West 23rd St., New York, NY 10010.

Porter, Michael, *Competitive Advantage: Creating and Sustaining Superior Performance,* 1985, Free Press, 866 Third Ave., New York, NY 10022.

Porter, Michael, *Competitive Strategy: Techniques for Analyzing Industries and Competitors,* 1980, Free Press, 866 Third Ave., New York, NY 10022.

Treacy, Michael and Fred Wiersema, *The Discipline of Market Leaders: Choose Your Customers, Narrow Your Focus, Dominate Your Market,* 1995, Addison-Wesley, One Jacob Way, Reading, MA 01867.

Chapter 4—Innovating the Future

Campbell, Andrew and Laura L. Nash, *A Sense of Mission: Defining Direction for the Large Corporation,* 1992, Addison-Wesley, One Jacob Way, Reading, MA 01867.

Collins, James C. and Jerry I. Porras, *Built to Last: Successful Habits of Visionary Companies,* 1994, Harper Business, 10 East 53rd St., New York, NY 10022.

Liebig, James E., *Merchants of Vision: People Bringing New Purpose and Values to Business,* 1994, Berrett-Koehler, 155 Montgomery St., San Francisco, CA 94104.

Nanus, Bert, *Visionary Leadership: Creating a Compelling Sense of Direction for Your Organization,* 1992, Jossey-Bass, 350 Sansome St., San Francisco, CA 94104.

Pascarella, Perry and Marl Frohman, *The Purpose-Driven Organization,* 1989, Jossey-Bass, 350 Sansome St., San Francisco, CA 94104.

Chapter 5—Orchestrating Change

Argyris, Chris, *Knowledge for Action: A Guide to Overcoming Barriers to Organizational Change,* 1993, Jossey-Bass, 350 Sansome St., San Francisco, CA 94104.

Beckhard, Richard and Wendy Pritchard, *Changing the Essence: The Art of Creating and Leading Fundamental Change in Organizations,* 1992, Jossey-Bass, 350 Sansome St., San Francisco, CA 94104.

Berquist, William, *The Postmodern Organization: Mastering the Art of Irreversible Change*, 1993, Jossey-Bass, 350 Sansome St., San Francisco, CA 94104.

Bridges, William, *Managing Transitions: Making the Most of Change*, 1991, Addison-Wesley, One Jacob Way, Reading, MA 01867.

Gouillart, Francis J. and James N. Kelly, *Transforming the Organization: Reframing Corporate Direction, Restructuring the Company, Revitalizing the Enterprise, Renewing People*, 1995, McGraw-Hill, 11 West 19th St., New York, NY 10011.

Hammer, Michael and James Champy, *Reengineering the Corporation: A Manifesto for Business Revolution*, 1993, Harper Business, 10 East 53rd St., New York, NY 10022. Followup books in 1995 with Harper Business: James Champy, *Reengineering Management: The Mandate for New Leadership*. Michael Hammer (with Steven A. Stanton), *The Reengineering Revolution: A Handbook*.

Heifetz, Michael L., *Leading Change, Overcoming Chaos: A Seven-Stage Process for Making Change Succeed in Your Organization*, 1993, Ten Speed Press, P.O. Box 7123, Berkeley, CA 94707.

Kanter, Rosabeth Moss, Barry A. Stein, and Todd Jick, *The Challenge of Organizational Change: How Companies Experience It and Leaders Guide It*, 1992, Free Press, 866 Third Ave., New York, NY 10022.

Morgan, Gareth, *Riding the Waves of Change: Developing Managerial Competencies for a Turbulent World*, 1988, Jossey-Bass, 350 Sansome St., San Francisco, CA 94104.

Smith, Douglas K., *Taking Charge of Change: 10 Principles for Managing People and Performance*, 1996, Addison-Wesley, One Jacob Way, Reading, MA 01867.

Chapter 6—Bridging Cultural Differences

Frost, Peter J., et al. (Eds.), *Reframing Organizational Culture*, 1991, Sage, P.O. Box 5084, Newbury Park, CA 91359-9924.

Gannon, Martin J. *Understanding Global Cultures: Metaphorical Journeys Through 17 Countries*, 1994, Sage, P.O. Box 5084, Newbury Park, CA 91359-9924.

Gray, John, *Men Are From Mars, Women Are From Venus*, 1992, Harper & Row, 10 East 53rd St., New York, NY 10022.

Helgesen, Sally, *The Female Advantage: Women's Ways of Leadership*, 1990, Currency, 666 Fifth Ave., New York, NY 10103.

Jamieson, David and Julie O'Mara, *Managing Workforce 2000: Gaining the Diversity Advantage*, 1991, Jossey-Bass, 350 Sansome St., San Francisco, CA 94104.

Kotter, John P. and James L. Heskett, *Corporate Culture and Performance*, 1992, Free Press, 866 Third Ave., New York, NY 10022.

Schein, Edgar, *Organizational Culture and Leadership: A Dynamic View* (2nd ed.), 1992, Jossey-Bass, 350 Sansome St., San Francisco, CA 94104.

Tannen, Deborah, *You Just Don't Understand: Women and Men in Conversation*, 1990, Morrow, 105 Madison Ave., New York, NY 10016.

Chapter 7—Motivating Development

Benfari, Robert, *Understanding Your Management Style: Beyond the Myers-Briggs Type Indicator*, 1991, Lexington Books, 866 Third Ave., New York, NY 10022.

Jaffee, Cabot L., et al., *The Art of Managing: How to Assess and Perfect Your Management Style*, 1991, Addison-Wesley, One Jacob Way, Reading, MA 01867.

Kolb, David A. and Donna M. Smith, *Learning Style Inventory: User's Guide*, 1986, Hay-McBer & Company, 137 Newbury St., Boston, MA 02116.

Murray, Margo with Marna A. Owen, *Beyond the Myths and Magic of Mentoring: How To Facilitate an Effective Mentoring Program*, 1991, Jossey-Bass, 350 Sansome St., San Francisco, CA 94104.

Quinn, Robert, et al., *Becoming a Master Manager: A Competency Framework*, 1989, Wiley, 605 Third Ave., New York, NY 10158.

Chapter 8—Building Partnerships

Hackman, Richard J. (Ed.), *Groups That Work (and Those That Don't): Creating Conditions for Effective Teamwork*, 1989, Jossey-Bass, 350 Sansome St., San Francisco, CA 94104.

Katzenbach, Jon R. and Douglas K. Smith, *The Wisdom of Teams: Creating the High-Performance Organization*, 1992, Harvard Business School Press, Boston, MA 02163.

Ketchum, Lyman D. and Eric Trist, *All Teams Are Not Created Equal: How Employee Empowerment Really Works*, 1992, Sage, P.O. Box 5084, Newbury Park, CA 91359-9924.

Larson, Carl E. and Frank M. J. Lafasto, *Teamwork: What Must Go Right/What Can Go Wrong*, 1989, Sage, P.O. Box 5084, Newbury Park, CA 91359-9924.

Nirenberg, John, *The Living Organization: Transforming Teams into Workplace Communities*, 1993, Pfeiffer/Business One Irwin, Homewood, IL 60430.

Parker, Glenn, *Team Players and Teamwork,* 1990, Jossey-Bass, 350 Sansome St., San Francisco, CA 94104.

Tjosvold, Dean T. and Mary M. Tjosvold, *Leading the Team Organization: How To Create an Enduring Competitive Advantage,* 1992, Lexington Books, 866 Third Ave., New York, NY 10022.

Zenger, John H., Ed Musselwhite, Kathleen Hurson, and Craig Perrin, *Leading Teams: Mastering the New Role,* 1993, Business One Irwin, Homewood, IL 60430.

Chapter 9—Empowering Decisions

Driver, Michael, J., Kenneth R. Brousseau, and Phillip L. Hunsaker, *The Dynamic Decision Maker: Five Decision Styles for Executive and Business Success,* 1993, Jossey-Bass, 350 Sansome St., San Francisco, CA 94104.

Herman, Stanley M., *A Force of Ones: Reclaiming Individual Power in a Time of Teams, Work Groups, and Other Crowds,* 1994, Jossey-Bass, 350 Sansome St., San Francisco, CA 94104.

Kaye, Harvey, *Decision Power: How to Make Successful Decisions with Confidence,* 1992, Prentice Hall, Englewood Cliffs, NJ 07632.

Russo, J. Edward and Paul J. H. Schoemaker, *Decision Traps: The Ten Barriers to Brilliant Decision-Making and How to Overcome Them,* 1989, Doubleday, 666 Fifth Ave., New York, NY 10103.

Chapter 10—Achieving Goals

Sayles, Leonard R. *The Working Leader: The Triumph of High Performance Over Conventional Management Principles,* 1993, Free Press, 866 Third Ave., New York, NY 10022.

Schaffer, Robert H., *The Breakthrough Strategy: Using Short-Term Successes to Build the High Performance Organization,* 1989, Harper Business, 10 East 53rd St., New York, NY 10022.

Chapter 11—Pursuing Excellence

Juran, J. M., *Juran's New Quality Road Map: Planning, Setting, and Reaching Quality Goals,* 1991, Free Press, 866 Third Ave., New York, NY 10022.

Sashkin, Marshall and Kenneth J. Kiser, *Putting Total Quality Management to Work: What TQM Means, How to Use It, & How to Sustain It Over the Long Run,* 1992, Berrett-Koehler, 155 Montgomery St., San Francisco, CA 94104.

Schmidt, Warren H. and Jerome P. Finnigan, *TQManager: A Practical Guide For Managing In a Total Quality Organization,* 1993, Jossey-Bass, 350 Sansome St., San Francisco, CA 94104.

Walton, Mary, *The Deming Management Method,* 1986, Putnam, 200 Madison Ave., New York, NY 10016.

Leading-Edge Portrait

Self-Scoring Role Assessment

Using This Portrait

There are two versions of the Leading-Edge Portrait provided in this book. Both have the important feature of containing statements about managers that describe desirable, positive behavior. There is nothing in either portrait designed to make you feel wrong or incorrect. This self-scoring version is used to give you a quick view of your own assessment of your strengths in each of the roles by asking you to rank your capability in thirty-six different behaviors (four for each of the nine roles). This form is designed for ease of self-scoring. This portrait version is less accurate than the mail-in version as most people find it difficult to give themselves a full range of rankings given the desirable nature of the behaviors described. Therefore, the results for each of the nine roles tend to cluster, reducing one's ability to see a pattern of relative strengths among the roles. Nevertheless, the form is easy to use and will give you some insight about yourself.

Guidance for Completing the Portrait

- The statements in this portrait are designed to describe highly desirable managerial behavior. There are no right or wrong answers.
- The value of this portrait will increase with your own degree of objectivity and thoughtfulness.
- Remembering a variety of situations, events, or circumstances when you observed the behavior or noticed its absence will be helpful.
- Respond on the basis of what you *observe* now in your behavior, not on the basis of what you *desire* to be true.

Scoring Instructions

1. Read each of the statements and determine your typical level of behavior:

   Rarely—The behavior is seldom expressed and only under very favorable circumstances.

   Occasionally—The behavior is likely to be expressed when conditions are relatively favorable.

   Frequently—The behavior will be expressed even when there are some challenging or difficult circumstances.

   Consistently—The behavior is absolutely reliable, and ways will be found to make the behavior relevant to any existing circumstance.

2. Respond to the statements in the space provided below each statement.

3. When all thirty-six responses are complete, transfer them to the one-page scoring sheet on page 263.

4. Total the number of responses in each column for each managerial role.

5. Multiply that number of responses by 1 for R—Rarely, 2 for O—Occasionally, 3 for F—Frequently, and 4 for C—Consistently.

6. Total the scores across the four columns for each of the nine roles and determine the current level of capability:
   4–6 Novice Level, 7–10 Apprentice Level,
   11–14 Practitioner Level, and 15–16 Mastery Level

Example:	Sage			
	R	O	F	C
1	☐	☐	☑	☐
10	☐	☐	☐	☑
19	☐	☑	☐	☐
28	☐	☑	☐	☐
Total responses	0	2	1	1
Multiply by	x1	x2	x3	x4
Subtotal	0	4	3	4
Total score		11		

Behaviors that describe your predominant and critical ways of acting in typical situations

1. Monitor current state, changes, and trends to discern what is pertinent to the continuing success of the organization.
   ❑ *Rarely*   ❑ *Occasionally*   ❑ *Frequently*   ❑ *Consistently*

2. Identify specific domains of responsibility that will move the organization toward its vision.
   ❑ *Rarely*   ❑ *Occasionally*   ❑ *Frequently*   ❑ *Consistently*

3. Implement each phase of the change effort at a rate corresponding to the capability of people and the organization to bring about the change.
   ❑ *Rarely*   ❑ *Occasionally*   ❑ *Frequently*   ❑ *Consistently*

4. Judge the situational value of cultural and individual diversity without using bias from your own background and capabilities.
   ❑ *Rarely*   ❑ *Occasionally*   ❑ *Frequently*   ❑ *Consistently*

5. Use a variety of practical methods to support individual learning needs.
   ❑ *Rarely*   ❑ *Occasionally*   ❑ *Frequently*   ❑ *Consistently*

6. Build individual capability to increase the effectiveness of all forms of collaborative work.
   ❑ *Rarely*   ❑ *Occasionally*   ❑ *Frequently*   ❑ *Consistently*

7. Exercise power to minimize delay of decision and delay between decision and action.
   ❑ *Rarely*   ❑ *Occasionally*   ❑ *Frequently*   ❑ *Consistently*

8. Assure necessary resources and information for task accomplishment while avoiding methods of control and compliance.
   ❑ *Rarely*   ❑ *Occasionally*   ❑ *Frequently*   ❑ *Consistently*

9. Challenge the status quo by examining work to seek ways of improving and reaching higher standards of excellence and quality.
   ❑ *Rarely*   ❑ *Occasionally*   ❑ *Frequently*   ❑ *Consistently*

Behaviors that describe your interactions with others

10. Encourage an open flow of ideas and information among people within the organization and with people in its environment.
    ❏ *Rarely* ❏ *Occasionally* ❏ *Frequently* ❏ *Consistently*

11. Inspire committed participation by all stakeholders in the formation, understanding, and/or implementation of the vision.
    ❏ *Rarely* ❏ *Occasionally* ❏ *Frequently* ❏ *Consistently*

12. Understand and manage the causes of resistance to change and fear of change while acknowledging the reality of change in organizational life.
    ❏ *Rarely* ❏ *Occasionally* ❏ *Frequently* ❏ *Consistently*

13. Seek to understand the perspective and thinking of others to create a climate of inclusion.
    ❏ *Rarely* ❏ *Occasionally* ❏ *Frequently* ❏ *Consistently*

14. Motivate individuals by recognizing their individual development needs and helping them use their unique potential to contribute to the organization.
    ❏ *Rarely* ❏ *Occasionally* ❏ *Frequently* ❏ *Consistently*

15. Develop team spirit, trust, and commitment and enable resolution of conflicts that challenge these.
    ❏ *Rarely* ❏ *Occasionally* ❏ *Frequently* ❏ *Consistently*

16. Manage participation by addressing individual differences on decisions and tolerance for uncertainty and risk.
    ❏ *Rarely* ❏ *Occasionally* ❏ *Frequently* ❏ *Consistently*

17. Sustain joint responsibility for managing work in relation to the needs, responsibilities, and goals of other work groups.
    ❏ *Rarely* ❏ *Occasionally* ❏ *Frequently* ❏ *Consistently*

18. Instill pride in identifying and creating quality that reflects the stated and unstated needs of customers.
    ❏ *Rarely* ❏ *Occasionally* ❏ *Frequently* ❏ *Consistently*

Behaviors that describe your thought processes or development of ideas

19. Use systems thinking to see patterns in often contradictory information and relate it to ongoing organizational needs.
    ❏ *Rarely* ❏ *Occasionally* ❏ *Frequently* ❏ *Consistently*

20. Articulate a worthwhile future that capitalizes on the unique potential of the organization in its markets and community.
    ❏ *Rarely* ❏ *Occasionally* ❏ *Frequently* ❏ *Consistently*

21. Orchestrate the relationships among things that must be changed, things that accelerate change, and things that inhibit change.
    ❏ *Rarely* ❏ *Occasionally* ❏ *Frequently* ❏ *Consistently*

22. Develop a unifying corporate culture to access the strength and manage the conflicts of diversity within the organization.
    ❏ *Rarely* ❏ *Occasionally* ❏ *Frequently* ❏ *Consistently*

23. Match needs of organization with development, learning strategies, and capabilities of specific individuals.
    ❏ *Rarely* ❏ *Occasionally* ❏ *Frequently* ❏ *Consistently*

24. Delineate a wide range of collaborative internal and external relationships necessary for the organization's ongoing success.
    ❏ *Rarely* ❏ *Occasionally* ❏ *Frequently* ❏ *Consistently*

25. Utilize comprehensive and consistent decision-making methods in a wide variety of decisions.
    ❏ *Rarely* ❏ *Occasionally* ❏ *Frequently* ❏ *Consistently*

26. Organize work so that there is a clear identification of the value-adding role of each job in the accomplishment of goals.
    ❏ *Rarely* ❏ *Occasionally* ❏ *Frequently* ❏ *Consistently*

27. Design processes and products based upon clear principles of efficiency, effectiveness, fairness, and future possibilities.
    ❏ *Rarely* ❏ *Occasionally* ❏ *Frequently* ❏ *Consistently*

Behaviors that are energizing, enlivening, or inspiring and show you at your best

28. Discover opportunities by using multiple approaches to understand increasingly complex situations.
❏ *Rarely* ❏ *Occasionally* ❏ *Frequently* ❏ *Consistently*

29. Speculate about the future, fantasize, create scenarios, and pursue the seemingly impossible.
❏ *Rarely* ❏ *Occasionally* ❏ *Frequently* ❏ *Consistently*

30. Sustain momentum in the turbulence of the transition from the current state to the desired state.
❏ *Rarely* ❏ *Occasionally* ❏ *Frequently* ❏ *Consistently*

31. Savor the cacophony of cultural and individual diversity while bringing focus to a common ground.
❏ *Rarely* ❏ *Occasionally* ❏ *Frequently* ❏ *Consistently*

32. Champion ongoing individual development as a cornerstone of the organization's competitive effectiveness.
❏ *Rarely* ❏ *Occasionally* ❏ *Frequently* ❏ *Consistently*

33. Create and join interdependent work partnerships where members must rely upon the capability and responsibility of each other.
❏ *Rarely* ❏ *Occasionally* ❏ *Frequently* ❏ *Consistently*

34. Welcome accountability in situations with attractive and complex alternatives even when there are high stakes and risk.
❏ *Rarely* ❏ *Occasionally* ❏ *Frequently* ❏ *Consistently*

35. Overcome the challenges experienced on the path to the collective achievement of significant goals.
❏ *Rarely* ❏ *Occasionally* ❏ *Frequently* ❏ *Consistently*

36. Thrive on competitive and customer pressures to create product changes that have improved practical and aesthetic appeal.
❏ *Rarely* ❏ *Occasionally* ❏ *Frequently* ❏ *Consistently*

R – Rarely **O** – Occasionally **F** – Frequently **C** – Consistently

	Sage	Visionary	Magician
	R O F C	R O F C	R O F C
	1 ☐☐☐☐	2 ☐☐☐☐	3 ☐☐☐☐
	10 ☐☐☐☐	11 ☐☐☐☐	12 ☐☐☐☐
	19 ☐☐☐☐	20 ☐☐☐☐	21 ☐☐☐☐
	28 ☐☐☐☐	29 ☐☐☐☐	30 ☐☐☐☐
Total responses	☐☐☐☐	☐☐☐☐	☐☐☐☐
Multiply by	x1 x2 x3 x4	x1 x2 x3 x4	x1 x2 x3 x4
Subtotal	☐☐☐☐	☐☐☐☐	☐☐☐☐
Total score	☐	☐	☐

	Globalist	Mentor	Ally
	R O F C	R O F C	R O F C
	4 ☐☐☐☐	5 ☐☐☐☐	6 ☐☐☐☐
	13 ☐☐☐☐	14 ☐☐☐☐	15 ☐☐☐☐
	22 ☐☐☐☐	23 ☐☐☐☐	24 ☐☐☐☐
	31 ☐☐☐☐	32 ☐☐☐☐	33 ☐☐☐☐
Total responses	☐☐☐☐	☐☐☐☐	☐☐☐☐
Multiply by	x1 x2 x3 x4	x1 x2 x3 x4	x1 x2 x3 x4
Subtotal	☐☐☐☐	☐☐☐☐	☐☐☐☐
Total score	☐	☐	☐

	Sovereign	Guide	Artisan
	R O F C	R O F C	R O F C
	7 ☐☐☐☐	8 ☐☐☐☐	9 ☐☐☐☐
	16 ☐☐☐☐	17 ☐☐☐☐	18 ☐☐☐☐
	25 ☐☐☐☐	26 ☐☐☐☐	27 ☐☐☐☐
	34 ☐☐☐☐	35 ☐☐☐☐	36 ☐☐☐☐
Total responses	☐☐☐☐	☐☐☐☐	☐☐☐☐
Multiply by	x1 x2 x3 x4	x1 x2 x3 x4	x1 x2 x3 x4
Subtotal	☐☐☐☐	☐☐☐☐	☐☐☐☐
Total score	☐	☐	☐

Score Code:
4–6 Novice, 7–10 Apprentice, 11–14 Practitioner, and 15–16 Master

Leading-Edge Portrait
Role Assessment With Mail-In Scoring

Using This Portrait

There are two versions of the Leading-Edge Portrait provided in this book. Both have the important feature of containing statements about managers that describe desirable, positive behavior. There is nothing in either portrait designed to make you feel wrong or incorrect. This mail-in scoring is used to give you a significantly more accurate assessment of your pattern of preferences for the nine roles. Many people see that they have significantly different levels of preference for different roles—high preferences for using some roles and low preferences for using other roles. The accuracy of this form in reflecting an individual's true role preferences occurs because each section contains forced choice questions. You choose between desirable behaviors rather than ranking yourself or desirable behaviors as in the self-scoring version. The larger number of questions is necessary in this form to increase the accuracy of the results by forcing you to choose among statements of behavior. I encourage you to use this version, mail in the completed form from the back of the book, and receive your free scoring. Although, you will not have instantaneous results, as with the self-scoring version, you will have a more useful depiction of your preferences and guidance for your development. There are also versions of the mail-in form, available for purchase, that will give an individual a 360-degree assessment, with evaluation by peers, direct reports, and boss.

Guidance for Completing the Portrait

- The statements in this portrait are designed to describe highly desirable managerial behavior. There are no right or wrong answers.

- The value of this portrait will increase with your own degree of objectivity and thoughtfulness.

- Remembering a variety of situations, events, or circumstances when you observed the behavior or noticed its absence will be helpful.

- Respond on the basis of what you *observe* now in your behavior, not on the basis of what you *desire* to be true.

- Mark your answers on the form on page 281 (after the Index, at the end of the book).

- Make sure you have one response for each question number.

- Make sure you have followed the specific instructions for the six sets of questions (questions 50 to 103).

- Make sure you have completed the information on the other side of the answer sheet.

- Remove the answer page from the back of the book, make sure both sides are completed, put it in an envelope, and mail it to the address on the form.

- You must use this form in the book to receive a free scoring of your assessment.

- Expect to receive results within one week of our receipt of your completed questionnnaire.

Choose the one answer that best represents your behavior

1. In managing your responsibilities, you emphasize:
    a. Figuring out what can be changed or improved
    b. Making the best use of available resources
    c. Structuring complex issues to identify key areas
2. To ensure success in a work group, you think most about:
    a. Strategy and vision
    b. The way people are working with each other
    c. The tasks that need to be accomplished
3. When faced with a new situation, the first thing you do is:
    a. Get concrete facts and set objectives
    b. Try to understand it in a larger context
    c. Determine the roles of people and the impacts upon them
4. You feel at your best when you:
    a. Create order in a chaotic situation
    b. Seek improvements to reach higher quality
    c. Provide focused direction for work efforts

Choose the one answer that best represents your typical approach

5. a. Choose a few basic issues to focus information gathering
   b. Keep casting a wide net to track a broad range of issues
6. a. Establish comprehensive, well-organized work procedures
   b. Use a few basic principles to allow flexibility in work processes
7. a. Have a vision that stretches the imagination and may be very challenging to achieve
   b. Have a vision that has a high chance of success in a reasonable time frame
8. a. Have the best people doing the jobs to which they are most suited
   b. Ensure that people are given challenges where they may have some risk of failure but will also learn
9. a. Stress the value of people effectively using relatively similar and agreed upon methods
   b. Give support to different perspectives and styles in methods
10. a. Drive for higher standards regardless of how well something is working
    b. Devote energy to maintain stability and focus energy on specific problem areas when they arise
11. a. Keep things relatively smooth through small incremental changes
    b. Tolerate the turbulence caused by major change
12. a. Try to maximize independent action and individual responsibility
    b. Try to maximize mutually dependent action and responsibility
13. a. Understand the risks and make decisions in a relatively quick manner
    b. Take the time to study things in a relatively thorough manner before deciding

For each word pair below, choose the word that best describes you, your attitude, or your inclination. Always choose one word regardless of how difficult you find the choice.

	A	B		A	B
14.	Question	Harmonize	32.	Inclusive	Focused
15.	Create	Navigate	33.	Foresight	Insight
16.	Capability	Quality	34.	Relationship	Restructure
17.	Encourage	Challenge	35.	Revolution	Evolution
18.	Alternatives	Beliefs	36.	Participate	Empower
19.	Ideal	Flexible	37.	Future	Present
20.	Support	Responsibility	38.	Augment	Risk
21.	Discuss	Implement	39.	Organized	Changeable
22.	Action	Ideas	40.	Universal	Personal
23.	Complexity	Turbulence	41.	Group	Individual
24.	Differences	Agreement	42.	Detailed	Broad
25.	Improve	Achieve	43.	Delegate	Decide
26.	Enable	Imagine	44.	Unite	Conceive
27.	Counsel	Coordinate	45.	Transition	Tradition
28.	Intuitive	Analytical	46.	Determined	Cooperative
29.	Enhance	Appreciate	47.	Development	Knowledge
30.	Impermanence	Resolution	48.	Learning	Doing
31.	Contemplate	Collaborate	49.	Thinking	Choosing

Carefully consider the nine numbered responses in each of the following six situations and rank your behavioral responses for each situation by

- Choosing exactly *three behaviors* that you are *most likely* to use (mark the box in the "A" column on page 281).
- Choosing exactly *three behaviors* you are *moderately likely* to use (mark the box in the "B" column on page 281).
- Choosing exactly *three behaviors* you are *least likely* to use (mark the box in the "C" column on page 281).
- Make sure that each set of nine responses for each of the six situations has three responses in each column or your results will not be accurately calculated.

SITUATION 1 – In ongoing work responsibilities, you will tend to

50. Seek input and accept criticism that lead to higher quality
51. Enjoy difference but seek and hold to a common ground
52. Willingly face risks and uncertainties
53. Direct efforts toward immediate, significant needs
54. Help people face challenges that aid their learning
55. Let things stay unsettled until a change is completed
56. Resolve conflicts in a way that builds trust
57. Think about the relationship of your work to the work of others and the needs of the organization and its customers
58. Use enthusiasm about a vision to guide work

SITUATION 2 – In working with others, you

59. Create a climate that values different perspectives and thinking
60. Develop team spirit, trust, and commitment
61. Encourage an open flow of ideas and information
62. Inspire committed participation in working toward a vision
63. Instill pride in creating quality that meets customer needs
64. Manage the tensions and stress caused by change
65. Motivate people by helping them contribute to the organization
66. Balance accountability with individual and collective power to decide
67. Target task responsibility toward mutually desired goals

SITUATION 3 – To get some structure in a new situation your approach is to determine how to

68. Achieve more immediate goals
69. Alter things to reach even higher standards
70. Find opportunities to improve work relationships among people
71. Make the decisions that are possible given the current state of information
72. Manage the situation so that it fits in with long-term plans
73. Operate so that learning is maximized
74. Understand the connection of different things to this situation and the various factors that influence those things
75. Coordinate this situation with other changes being made
76. Work with differences among people

SITUATION 4 – Given a normal amount of stress and pressure, you will continue to

77. Break comfortable patterns to reach new, more effective patterns
78. Identify differences in what people need to learn and the way they learn
79. Look at a wide range of issues including those not having an immediate impact
80. Keep a focus on the desired future
81. Remain patient with different views
82. Keep specific tasks aligned with the organization's direction
83. Search for possibilities for doing things better
84. Sustain relationships regardless of current work benefits
85. Work on complex decisions that have high levels of uncertainty

SITUATION 5 – You will take a stand when it is necessary to

86. Allow a new perspective when others are not receptive
87. Keep the work on track when pressure exists to cut costs
88. Gain better understanding before acting
89. Hold a team together when the members are pulling it apart
90. Incur costs or sacrifice gains for longer-term benefits
91. Make radical changes
92. Promote people when their talents are not appreciated by others
93. Reject work when the standards are not high enough
94. Take responsibility for unpopular or risky decisions

SITUATION 6 – In the most difficult and trying circumstances, you are able to

95. Ensure individuals continue to have the opportunity to learn
96. Continue to find ways to raise quality standards
97. Keep team spirit at a high level
98. Make necessary decisions despite the degree of uncertainty
99. Overcome roadblocks to important goals
100. Remain flexible and able to face instability
101. Remain open to different perspectives
102. Stay connected to larger, more complex issues
103. Sustain active commitment to the long-term vision

Index

Mail-In Scoring Form

To ensure proper scoring, you *must* answer each question and fill in the appropriate box with black pen or pencil. In *each* of the *six* sets of questions from 50 to 103, be sure to choose *exactly* three in the "A" column—most likely, *exactly* three in the "B" column—moderately likely, and exactly three in the "C" column—least likely.

	A	B	C			A	B			A	B	C			A	B	C
1.	☐	☐	☐		14.	☐	☐		50.	☐	☐	☐		77.	☐	☐	☐
2.	☐	☐	☐		15.	☐	☐		51.	☐	☐	☐		78.	☐	☐	☐
3.	☐	☐	☐		16.	☐	☐		52.	☐	☐	☐		79.	☐	☐	☐
4.	☐	☐	☐		17.	☐	☐		53.	☐	☐	☐		80.	☐	☐	☐
					18.	☐	☐		54.	☐	☐	☐		81.	☐	☐	☐
	A	B			19.	☐	☐		55.	☐	☐	☐		82.	☐	☐	☐
5.	☐	☐			20.	☐	☐		56.	☐	☐	☐		83.	☐	☐	☐
6.	☐	☐			21.	☐	☐		57.	☐	☐	☐		84.	☐	☐	☐
7.	☐	☐			22.	☐	☐		58.	☐	☐	☐		85.	☐	☐	☐
8.	☐	☐			23.	☐	☐										
9.	☐	☐			24.	☐	☐			A	B	C		86.	☐	☐	☐
10.	☐	☐			25.	☐	☐		59.	☐	☐	☐		87.	☐	☐	☐
11.	☐	☐			26.	☐	☐		60.	☐	☐	☐		88.	☐	☐	☐
12.	☐	☐			27.	☐	☐		61.	☐	☐	☐		89.	☐	☐	☐
13.	☐	☐			28.	☐	☐		62.	☐	☐	☐		90.	☐	☐	☐
					29.	☐	☐		63.	☐	☐	☐		91.	☐	☐	☐
					30.	☐	☐		64.	☐	☐	☐		92.	☐	☐	☐
					31.	☐	☐		65.	☐	☐	☐		93.	☐	☐	☐
					32.	☐	☐		66.	☐	☐	☐		94.	☐	☐	☐
					33.	☐	☐		67.	☐	☐	☐					
					34.	☐	☐								A	B	C
					35.	☐	☐			A	B	C		95.	☐	☐	☐
					36.	☐	☐		68.	☐	☐	☐		96.	☐	☐	☐
					37.	☐	☐		69.	☐	☐	☐		97.	☐	☐	☐
					38.	☐	☐		70.	☐	☐	☐		98.	☐	☐	☐
					39.	☐	☐		71.	☐	☐	☐		99.	☐	☐	☐
					40.	☐	☐		72.	☐	☐	☐		100.	☐	☐	☐
					41.	☐	☐		73.	☐	☐	☐		101.	☐	☐	☐
					42.	☐	☐		74.	☐	☐	☐		102.	☐	☐	☐
					43.	☐	☐		75.	☐	☐	☐		103.	☐	☐	☐
					44.	☐	☐		76.	☐	☐	☐					
					45.	☐	☐										
					46.	☐	☐										
					47.	☐	☐										
					48.	☐	☐										
					49.	☐	☐										

Please complete the other side of the page before mailing in your scoring form.

To receive free scoring of your Leading-Edge Portrait, please remove this completed form from the book, put it in an envelope, and mail it to the address below.

_____

Name

_____

Job title

_____

Company

_____

Address

_____

Phone #

Please give us these additional alternatives to return your results.

_____

Fax

_____

E-mail

Mail responses to:

Leading Edge Consulting Group
P. O. Box 67
Saratoga, CA 95071-0067

❑ Please check here if you would like additional information from the Leading Edge Consulting Group.